Galaxy S4

the missing manual®

The book that should have been in the box·

Preston Gralla

O'REILLY®

Beijing | Cambridge | Farnham | Köln | Sebastopol | Tokyo

Galaxy S4: The Missing Manual
By Preston Gralla

Published by O'Reilly Media, Inc., 1005 Gravenstein Highway North,
Sebastopol, CA 95472.

O'Reilly books may be purchased for educational, business, or sales promotional
use. Online editions are also available for most titles (safari.oreilly.com). For more
information, contact our corporate/institutional sales department: 800.998.9938 or
corporate@oreilly.com.

Executive Editor: Brian Sawyer

Editor: Nan Barber

Production Editor: Melanie Yarbrough

Proofreader: Nan Reinhardt

Illustrations: Rebecca Demarest

Indexer: Julie Hawks

Cover Designers: Monica Kamsvaag

Interior Designer: Monica Kamsvaag,
Ron Bilodeau, & J.D. Biersdorfer

August 2013:   First Edition.

Revision History for the First Edition:

  2013-08-15   First release

See *http://oreilly.com/catalog/errata.csp?isbn=9781449316303* for release details.

ISBN: 978-1-449-31630-3
[LSI]

Contents

PART IV   **Advanced Features**

The Missing Credits

About the Author

Preston Gralla is the author of more than 40 books that have been translated into 20 languages, including *Galaxy S II: The Missing Manual, Windows 8 Hacks, NOOK HD: The Missing Manual, Galaxy Tab: The Missing Manual, The Big Book of Windows Hacks, How the Internet Works*, and *How Wireless Works*. He is a contributing editor to *Computerworld*, a founder and editor-in-chief of Case Study Forum, and was a founding editor and then editorial director of *PC/Computing*, executive editor for CNet/ZDNet, and the founding managing editor of *PC Week*.

He has written about technology for many national newspapers and magazines, including *USA Today*, Los Angeles *Times*, Dallas *Morning News* (for whom he wrote a technology column), *PC World*, and numerous others. As a widely recognized technology expert, he has made many television and radio appearances, including on the CBS *Early Show*, MSNBC, ABC *World News* Now, and National Public Radio. Under his editorship, *PC/Computing* was a finalist for General Excellence in the National Magazine Awards. He has also won the "Best Feature in a Computing Publication" award from the Computer Press Association.

Gralla is also the recipient of a Fiction Fellowship from the Massachusetts Cultural Council. He lives in Cambridge, Massachusetts, with his wife (his two children have flown the coop). He welcomes feedback about his books by email at *preston@gralla.com*.

About the Creative Team

Nan Barber (editor) has worked with the Missing Manual series since its inception—long enough to remember booting up her computer from a floppy disk. Email: *nanbarber@oreilly.com*.

Melanie Yarbrough (production editor) lives in Cambridge, MA. When not ushering books through production, she's baking and writing up whatever she can imagine. Email: *myarbrough@oreilly.com*.

Yvonne Mills (technical reviewer) Writer, blogger and gadget addicted she-geek. Equally comfortable in the corporate world as she is blogging from within a fort made out of her extensive tablet collection. Follow her musings at *www. acerbicblonde.com*.

Nan Reinhardt (proofreader) is a freelance copyeditor and proofreader, as well as a writer of romantic fiction. She has published one novel and is releasing two more in the fall of 2013. In between editing gigs, she is busy working on her fourth book. She blogs regularly at *www.nanreinhardt.com*. Email: *reinhardt8@ comcast.net*.

Julie Hawks (indexer) is an indexer for the Missing Manual series. She is currently pursuing a master's degree in religious studies while discovering the joys of warm winters in the Carolinas. Email: *juliehawks@gmail.com*.

Acknowledgements

Many thanks go to my editor, Nan Barber, who not only patiently shepherded this book through the lengthy writing and publishing process, but provided valuable feedback and sharpened my prose. Thanks also go to Brian Sawyer, for making the introduction that ultimately led to this book. And thanks to Yvonne Mills, technical reviewer extraordinaire, for trying out everything in this book on her own Galaxy S4.

I'd also like to thank all the other folks at O'Reilly who worked on this book, especially Melanie Yarbrough and Rebecca Demarest for bringing the beautiful finished product to fruition, Nan Reinhardt for excising errors, and Julie Hawks for writing the index.

—Preston Gralla

The Missing Manual Series

MISSING MANUALS ARE WITTY, superbly written guides to computer products that don't come with printed manuals (which is just about all of them). Each book features a handcrafted index and cross-references to specific pages (not just chapters). Recent and upcoming titles include:

Access 2010: The Missing Manual by Matthew MacDonald

Access 2013: The Missing Manual by Matthew MacDonald

Adobe Edge Animate: The Missing Manual by Chris Grover

Buying a Home: The Missing Manual by Nancy Conner

Creating a Website: The Missing Manual, Third Edition by Matthew MacDonald

CSS3: The Missing Manual, Third Edition by David Sawyer McFarland

David Pogue's Digital Photography: The Missing Manual by David Pogue

Dreamweaver CS6: The Missing Manual by David Sawyer McFarland

Dreamweaver CC: The Missing Manual by David Sawyer McFarland and Chris Grover

Excel 2010: The Missing Manual by Matthew MacDonald

Excel 2013: The Missing Manual by Matthew MacDonald

FileMaker Pro 12: The Missing Manual by Susan Prosser and Stuart Gripman

Flash CS6: The Missing Manual by Chris Grover

Galaxy Tab: The Missing Manual by Preston Gralla

Google+: The Missing Manual by Kevin Purdy

HTML5: The Missing Manual by Matthew MacDonald

iMovie '11 & iDVD: The Missing Manual by David Pogue and Aaron Miller

iPad: The Missing Manual, Fifth Edition by J.D. Biersdorfer

iPhone: The Missing Manual, Sixth Edition by David Pogue

iPhone App Development: The Missing Manual by Craig Hockenberry

iPhoto '11: The Missing Manual by David Pogue and Lesa Snider

iPod: The Missing Manual, Tenth Edition by J.D. Biersdorfer and David Pogue

JavaScript & jQuery: The Missing Manual, Second Edition by David Sawyer McFarland

Kindle Fire HD: The Missing Manual by Peter Meyers

Living Green: The Missing Manual by Nancy Conner

Mac OS X Lion: The Missing Manual by David Pogue

Microsoft Project 2010: The Missing Manual by Bonnie Biafore

Microsoft Project 2013: The Missing Manual by Bonnie Biafore

Motorola Xoom: The Missing Manual by Preston Gralla

NOOK HD: The Missing Manual by Preston Gralla

Office 2010: The Missing Manual by Nancy Conner and Matthew MacDonald

Office 2011 for Macintosh: The Missing Manual by Chris Grover

Office 2013: The Missing Manual by Nancy Conner and Matthew MacDonald

OS X Mountain Lion: The Missing Manual by David Pogue

OS X Mavericks: The Missing Manual by David Pogue

Personal Investing: The Missing Manual by Bonnie Biafore

Photoshop CS6: The Missing Manual by Lesa Snider

Photoshop CC: The Missing Manual by Lesa Snider

Photoshop Elements 11: The Missing Manual by Barbara Brundage

PHP & MySQL: The Missing Manual, Second Edition by Brett McLaughlin

QuickBooks 2012: The Missing Manual by Bonnie Biafore

QuickBooks 2013: The Missing Manual by Bonnie Biafore

Switching to the Mac: The Missing Manual, Mountain Lion Edition by David Pogue

Switching to the Mac: The Missing Manual, Mavericks Edition by David Pogue

Windows 7: The Missing Manual by David Pogue

Windows 8: The Missing Manual by David Pogue

WordPress: The Missing Manual by Matthew MacDonald

Your Body: The Missing Manual by Matthew MacDonald

Your Brain: The Missing Manual by Matthew MacDonald

Your Money: The Missing Manual by J.D. Roth

For a full list of all Missing Manuals in print, go to *www.missingmanuals.com/library.html*.

Introduction

WHAT GIVES YOU HIGH speed Internet access, runs the hottest games and apps, lets you take high-resolution photos and HD videos, gives you immediate access to your favorite social networks, handles any email you can throw at it, and keeps you in touch by phone, text, and video chat?

It's the Samsung Galaxy S4—the smartphone with a big 5-inch screen that you can control with a wave of your hand.

The Galaxy S4 brings together superb hardware from Samsung with Google's powerful, flexible Android operating system. Many people consider the Galaxy S4 to be the best smartphone on the planet. If you're holding this book in your hand, you're probably among them—or soon will be.

This book will help you get the most out of your Galaxy S4, and there's a lot you can get out of it. Whether you're just looking to get started, or want to dig deep into the phone's capabilities, this book has got you covered.

About the Samsung Galaxy S4

WHAT MAKES THE GALAXY S4 so great starts with its hardware. Samsung gave it a 5-inch, high-resolution screen; a 13-megapixel camera for high-res photos and video; and a front-facing 2-megapixel camera for video calling and video chat. Its brain is a superfast 1.9 GHz dual-core processor. For keeping you connected, the Galaxy S4 has antennas for Bluetooth, WiFi, and GPS.

NOTE This book was written based on the T-Mobile version of the Samsung Galaxy S4. Versions from other carriers may have minor variations in what you see onscreen.

It has access to speedy 3G and 4G networks, which let you talk, text, and surf the Web almost anywhere in the U.S. (Anywhere important, anyway.)

Google contributed its Android operating system, with seamless access to YouTube, Google Talk, and other Google services. The worldwide developer community has created hundreds of thousands of apps in the Google Play Store (with more coming every day).

Put it all together, and you can do just about anything. You can get turn-by-turn directions, check weather and traffic, and identify landmarks. You can work with word processing and spreadsheet files and manage your email and calendar. You can take pictures and share them on Facebook, or shoot videos and upload them to YouTube. You can even turn the Galaxy S4 into a WiFi hotspot for getting up to five computers online.

Oh, and it's also a darn good phone with great sound quality and all the calling features you could ask for.

You could figure out how to make the most of all these features on your own, but by that time there'd be a whole other generation of smartphones to learn. This book will put you on the fast track to all the Galaxy S4's magic.

The Samsung Galaxy S4 Family

The Galaxy S4 has become such a successful phone—one of the most popular in the world—that it's no longer merely a single device, but an entire smartphone family. In addition to the flagship big-screen Galaxy S4, there's a Mini version with a smaller screen than the original (4.3 inches for the Mini compared to 5 inches for the full S4), and a less-powerful processor (1.7GHz dual-core processor, compared to a 1.9 GHz quad-cord for the full S4). But the Mini is still packed with power—more than many other phones that call themselves full sized.

The software on the Galaxy S4 Mini is the same as the software on the big-brother version, so you can use this book to learn about the Mini as well.

There's also a Samsung Galaxy S4 Google Play Edition, which has the exact same hardware as the original S4, but somewhat different software.

The Google Play Edition has a pure version of Google's Android operating system on it—the Jelly Bean version (Android version 4.2.2, for those of you who are keeping track). As you'll learn later in Chapter 1, the original S4 also has Jelly Bean under the hood, but layered on top of it is Samsung's TouchWiz interface, which contributes many additional features.

There's even a waterproof version of the S4 called the Samsung Galaxy S4 Active, so you can take it underwater with you—just in case you want to make phone calls or send text messages while snorkeling. But the S4 is so successful, don't be surprised if there are more new family members introduced as well.

This book will help you learn about all the TouchWiz Galaxy S4 models, but doesn't cover the pure-Jelly-Bean Google Play Edition.

What's New in the S4

Its predecessor the Samsung Galaxy S3 was a very popular and powerful smartphone. But the Samsung Galaxy S4 is nothing short of remarkable. It introduces countless new features, all of which are useful, and some of which seem more akin to magic than anything else. Here are some of the highlights:

- **Group play.** Using this, a group of people can view and interact with music, pictures, games, and more simultaneously. That means playing games against one another, listening to music together, sharing pictures and more. Find out about it in Chapter 13, "Transferring Files and Using Group Play."

- **Smart Scroll.** Using this amazing new feature, you can scroll through web pages and other screens just by moving your eyes. Go to Chapter 1, "The Guided Tour" to find out how.

- **Air Gestures.** This feature was introduced in an earlier Galaxy model, but the S4 brings it to a whole new level. Move your hands to browse the Web, scroll through email, and do plenty more as well. (Again, see Chapter 1.)

- **S Beam.** Beam me up, Scotty! This lets you share files by beaming them directly between your S4 and another device. Find out about it on page 347.

- **Easy Mode.** Don't like a complex interface filled with small icons and too many features? Turn on Easy Mode, which makes using the S4 much easier, including big, easy-to-read icons. For more details about Easy Mode, see Chapter 1.

- **Dual Shot and Drama Shot.** These are two new, nifty ways to use the S4's cameras. In Dual Shot, you combine pictures or video from the front camera with pictures or video from the back camera in one frame. With Drama Shot, you take photos of a series of a subject moving, and then combine them into one photo, so you can perform the action. Head to Chapter 5, "Camera, Photos, and Video," for details.

- **S Health.** Want to get healthier? Use S Health. It's an app that tracks your health, fitness, and diet by using sensors built into the S4 to turn it into a pedometer to track how many steps you take, and more. For details, go to Chapter 12, "Downloading and Using Apps."

- **S Travel.** Find out everything you want to know about travel destinations, book travel, and so on. More details in Chapter 1.

- **New sensors.** The S4 bristles with sensors that do things such as track the humidity, air pressure, and temperature. Check out Chapter 1 to see the amazing things they can do.

About This Book

THERE'S AN ENTIRE WORLD to explore in the Samsung Galaxy S4, and the little leaflet that comes in the box doesn't begin to give you all the help, advice, and guidance you need. So this book is the manual that should have accompanied the Galaxy S4.

The brain running the Galaxy S4 is a piece of software from Google called Android. Samsung then tweaked Android to operate seamlessly with Samsung's TouchWiz interface. Both Google and Samsung regularly issue updates that improve the way the Galaxy S4 works. So there's a chance that since this book was written, there have been some changes to the Galaxy S4. To help keep yourself up-to-date about them, head to this book's Errata/Changes page, at *http://tinyurl.com/gs4-mm*.

About the Outline

GALAXY S4: THE MISSING Manual is divided into six parts, each of which has several chapters:

- **Part One: The Basics.** Covers everything you need to know about using the Galaxy S4 as a phone, as well as how to type on it, send text messages, and use all the phone features. So you'll get a guided tour of the S4, learn how to dial calls, manage your contacts, use caller ID and similar features, make conference calls, and more, including fancy phone tricks like Visual Voice Mail. You'll even learn how to control your phone without using your hands.

- **Part Two: The Built-In Features.** Gives you the rundown on using the Galaxy S4 for taking pictures, recording videos, viewing pictures, playing videos, and playing and managing your music. You'll also learn all the new Google Maps features, how to navigate using GPS, and find any location in the world. There's also the Calendar app, which you can synchronize with your Google or Outlook calendar.

- **Part Three: The Galaxy S4 Online.** Tells you everything you need to know about the Galaxy S4's remarkable online talents. You'll find out how to get online, either over your service provider's network or a WiFi hotspot, see how you can turn your Galaxy S4 into a portable WiFi hotspot, master email, browse the Web, and download and use countless apps from Google Play Store.

- **Part Four: Advanced Features.** Covers a wide variety of advanced subjects, including how to sync and transfer files between the Galaxy S4 and your PC or Mac, how to use the Galaxy S4 at your workplace, and how to control the Galaxy S4 by talking to it. You'll also find a comprehensive listing of the Galaxy S4's settings.

- **Part Five: Appendixes.** Has three reference chapters. Appendix A shows you how to activate your Galaxy S4. Appendix B shows what kind of accessories you can get for your Samsung Galaxy S4, such as cases, chargers, and screen protectors. Appendix C offers plenty of help troubleshooting issues with the phone's operation.

About→These→Arrows

IN THIS BOOK AND in the entire Missing Manual series, you'll find instructions like this one: Tap Settings→Call Settings→"Voicemail settings." That's a shorthand way of giving longer instructions like this: "Tap the Settings button. From the screen that opens, tap Call Settings. And from the screen that opens after that, tap 'Voicemail settings'."

It's also used to to simplify instructions you'll need to follow on your PC or Mac, like File→Print.

About the Online Resources

AS THE OWNER OF a Missing Manual, you've got more than just a book to read. Online, you'll find example files so you can get some hands-on experience, as well as tips, articles, and maybe even a video or two. You can also communicate with the Missing Manual team and tell us what you love (or hate) about the book. Head over to *www.missingmanuals.com*, or go directly to one of the following sections.

Missing CD

So you don't wear down your fingers typing long web addresses, the Missing CD page offers a list of clickable links to the websites mentioned in this book. Go to *www.missingmanuals.com/cds/gs4tmm* to see them all neatly listed in one place.

Registration

If you register this book at *www.oreilly.com*, you'll be eligible for special offers—like discounts on future editions of *Galaxy S4: The Missing Manual*. Registering takes only a few clicks. To get started, type *http://oreilly.com/register* into your browser to hop directly to the Registration page.

Feedback

Got questions? Need more information? Fancy yourself a book reviewer? On our Feedback page, you can get expert answers to questions that come to you while reading, share your thoughts on this Missing Manual, and find groups for folks who share your interest in the Samsung Galaxy S4. To have your say, go to *www.missingmanuals.com/feedback*.

Errata

In an effort to keep this book as up-to-date and accurate as possible, each time we print more copies, we'll make any confirmed corrections you've suggested. We also note such changes on the book's website, so you can mark important corrections into your own copy of the book, if you like. Go to *http://tinyurl.com/gs4-mm* to report an error and to view existing corrections.

Safari® Books Online

SAFARI® BOOKS ONLINE IS an on-demand digital library that lets you easily search over 7,500 technology and creative reference books and videos to find the answers you need quickly.

With a subscription, you can read any page and watch any video from our library online. Read books on your cellphone and mobile devices. Access new titles before they're available for print, and get exclusive access to manuscripts in development and post feedback for the authors. Copy and paste code samples, organize your favorites, download chapters, bookmark key sections, create notes, print out pages, and benefit from tons of other time-saving features.

O'Reilly Media has uploaded this book to the Safari Books Online service. To have full digital access to this book and others on similar topics from O'Reilly and other publishers, sign up for free at *http://my.safaribooksonline.com*.

The Basics

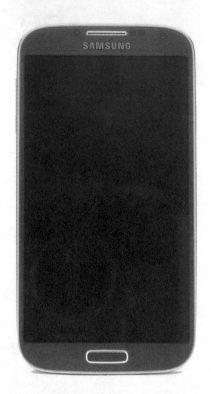

You'll learn to:

- Lock and unlock the screen

- Add apps and widgets and change wallpaper

- Use easy mode

- Replace the battery

- Control the S4 by touch and with the magic of gestures

CHAPTER 1

The Guided Tour

THE SAMSUNG GALAXY S4—a svelte, elegant phone—is an enticing gadget, and the first time you hold it in your hands, you'll immediately want to put it through its paces: calling friends, browsing the Web, checking your email, and more. As you'll see in the rest of this book, it can do some remarkable things that make you feel as if the phone has superpowers.

To help you unlock all those powers, though, you need a solid understanding of how the Galaxy S4 works and familiarity with all its different parts. You'll want to know where all its buttons, keys, and ports are located, for example—not to mention how to get to your Home screen and panes, and use some of the device's amazing new features, like its ability to let you navigate by merely moving your eyes.

Power/Lock Button

THREE-QUARTERS OF THE WAY up on the right side of the Galaxy S4, you'll find a small, rectangular silver button. It may be only a single button, but it's a hardworking one, and it performs multiple functions. Press it with your S4 turned off, and your S4 springs to life. Press and release it when your S4 is turned on and active, and it puts the phone into Standby mode. If your S4 is turned on, press and hold it and a screen appears that lets you do the following:

- **Power off.** Turns off the S4's power.

- **Airplane mode.** In Airplane mode, all wireless communications are switched off, but you can still use the phone's apps and other features. Tap this option to enter Airplane mode. If you're already in Airplane mode, tap again to get out. As the name suggests, Airplane mode is what the cabin crew wants you to turn on while in the air.

- **Restart.** Turns off your S4 and restarts it.

- **Mute.** Turns off all sounds.

- **Vibrate.** Turns off vibration. If vibration is turned off, you can turn it back on here.

- **Sound.** If your phone is muted, tap here to turn the sound back on.

TIP The Power/Lock button also performs a useful trick that people near you will appreciate—it shuts off your ringer when you receive a call. Press it once when you get a call, and your ringer turns off. You'll be able to see who's calling, without the ring, and decide whether to answer the call or ignore it. If you ignore the call, it gets sent to voicemail.

Locking the Screen

When you put the Galaxy S4 on Standby using the Power/Lock button, the screen stops responding to touch. It blacks out, indicating that the screen is *locked*. Always lock the screen before putting the Galaxy S4 in your pocket or bag to avoid accidental screen taps and potentially embarrassing unintended phone calls. In fact, every time you leave the phone untouched for a certain amount of time—as little as 15 seconds to as much as 10 minutes (page 397)— the screen automatically locks itself.

While the screen is locked, the Galaxy S4 still operates behind the scenes, checking email and Facebook on schedule. You can still get phone calls and text messages, and even listen to music while the screen is locked.

When you again want to use the Galaxy S4, you'll need to unlock it. Press the Power button or the Home key. Then put your fingertip on the screen and slide it to the right or left. Your Galaxy S4 is now ready to do your bidding. You'll get notifications about missed calls, text messages, and so on. If you've set up a PIN on your phone so that only someone with a password can use it, you'll have to type in the PIN before you can use your phone. (See page 394 for details on how to set up a PIN.)

TIP You can adjust the amount of time it takes for the Galaxy S4 to lock itself. You can also turn off Locked mode entirely. And for added security, you can also require that a password be used to unlock your S4, or even that a specific finger swiping motion be performed on the keyboard before it can be unlocked. For details, see page 394.

Headset Jack

AT THE TOP OF the Galaxy S4, you'll find a 3.5-millimeter headset jack. Notice that it's a head *set* jack, not just a garden-variety head *phone* jack. It doesn't just let you listen; it accepts incoming sound as well. That's so you can plug a headset (like an earbud headset) into it and use it for making phone calls.

Of course, it's also a headphone jack, so you can plug in headphones or even external speakers and enjoy the phone as a music machine, since it also offers full stereo.

About the Screen

THE SCREEN IS WHERE you and the Galaxy S4 do most of your communicating with each other. Compare the Galaxy S4's screen to that of almost any other phone, and you'll immediately notice how roomy it is—5 inches, measured diagonally (technically, that's 1920 x 1080 pixels). It's got extremely high resolution (443 pixels per inch, for the techie crowd). When you turn it sideways, it switches to a widescreen TV and movie format.

But there's a lot going on behind that pretty display.

TIP Because you're going to be touching the display with your fingers, it's going to get dirty and streaky. Simply wipe it clean with a soft, lint-free cloth or tissue. The screen is scratch-resistant, but if you're worried about scratches, get a case or screen protector. See Appendix B for ideas.

Built-in Sensors

Underneath its flat black screen, the Galaxy S4 has a whole bunch of sensors that perform a lot of its magic:

- **Proximity sensor.** Have you ever noticed that when you're talking on your S4, the screen often goes blank? That's thanks to the proximity sensor. It senses when your face is close to it during a phone call and automatically turns off and blanks the touch screen as you keep talking. It does this to save power, and so you don't accidentally touch the screen while talking and perform some unwanted task.

- **Ambient light sensor.** Senses the light level and adjusts your screen's brightness as a way to save battery power. So in bright light, it makes the screen brighter and easier to see: in dim light, it makes the screen dimmer, since bright light is not needed.

- **Accelerometer.** As its name implies, this sensor measures acceleration and motion. The Galaxy S4 uses the accelerometer to sense the orientation of the screen and turn it to either landscape or portrait mode. But clever app makers use it for other things as well, such as automatic collision notification, which detects when you're in an accident and then automatically makes a call for assistance for you. There's even an app that works with the phone's magnetometer to detect potholes as you drive, and create a log about their locations, which you can then email to your local department of public works. (It's called Pothole Agent. Search for it on Google Play, as described on page 301.)

- **Magnetometer.** Measures the strength and direction of the Earth's magnetic field. It's used for compass apps and can also work with the accelerometer.

- **Gyroscope.** This measures motion and is used for a host of features. For example, the S4 uses the gyroscope in concert with the accelerometer to interpret motion gestures you make and let you operate the phone by waving your hands.

- **Humidity, pressure, temperature.** The obvious use of these sensors is for weather and related apps. But that's not necessarily their most important uses. In combination with WiFi and GPS, they can also be used for indoor navigation and location apps, for example, mapping out shopping malls, museums, and more. These kinds of location apps aren't available yet, but likely will be soon.

- **Infrared gesture.** This sensor uses infrared light to sense your gestures so that you can control the S4 without touching it. Yes, you read that right. You can control it by waving and other gestures thanks to this sensor. And as you'll see later in this chapter, you can even control scrolling by moving your eyes. (You'll learn all about these tricks later in this chapter on page 38.)

Status Bar Icons

THE GALAXY S4 MAKES sure to keep you updated with information about its current status and any news, updates, and information it thinks is important. It does so by displaying a variety of icons in the status bar at the top of the screen. The status bar is divided into two parts. On the right side, you'll find icons that inform you about the current state of the Galaxy S4, such as signal strength, 3G or 4G connection status, the time of day, and so on. At left is the Notification area, which alerts you when you have email or voice messages waiting, an event on your calendar is about to occur, and more.

Notifications

Many applications have their own icons that notify you about news, informa-tion, and updates. These always appear on the left side of the status bar. You'll see alert icons from Gmail, Facebook, and others.

Here are the most common icons you'll come across:

- **Cell signal.** The more bars you see, the stronger the signal. The stronger the signal, the clearer the call and the lower the likelihood that you'll lose a connection. If you have no connection at all, instead of this signal, you'll see the much-hated warning: (No service).

NOTE When you see a notification on the left side of the status bar, drag down the Notification panel to see more details. You can also act upon the notification by tapping its icon after you drag it down—like checking your email or running an app that you've just downloaded. There's also a Clear button that makes all notifications go away.

- **Roaming.** If you're outside your carrier's service area and connected via another network, you'll see the Roaming icon. Keep in mind that typically you're charged for making calls or using data when you're roaming, so when you see this icon, be careful what you do on your Galaxy S4—maybe it's not the time to download 30 songs and a half-hour TV show.

- **3G/4G.** This one appears when you're connected via 3G or 4G high-speed broadband service, which should be most of the time. It means that download and upload speeds are fast. The little arrows underneath the symbol show when data is being sent and received. You'll notice that the arrows may turn black even when you think you're not sending or receiving data. That's because the Galaxy S4 may be checking for email, updates, and so on.

- **Bluetooth connection.** This icon indicates that you've turned on Bluetooth, for making a connection to a headset or some other device.

- **Mobile hotspot.** Your Galaxy S4 can serve as a mobile hotspot, providing Internet service to up to five computers, smartphones, or other devices and gadgets via WiFi. See page 198 for details. When you turn the phone into a mobile hotspot, this icon appears.

- **Airplane mode.** When you use Airplane mode, you turn off WiFi and cellular communications, so you can still keep using your phone's apps, but it doesn't interfere with navigation equipment.

- **Downloading.** When you're downloading an app or media file, you'll see this icon.

- **New email message.** You've got mail! See page 255 for more about reading new email.

- **GPS.** Your GPS radio is turned on.

- **Upcoming event.** Now you'll never forget your anniversary—or your dentist appointment. The Galaxy S4 alerts you via this icon when you've got an event about to happen.

- **Voicemail message.** You've got mail—voicemail, that is. (See page 90 to learn how to check your voicemail.)

- **Missed call.** Someone called you, and you didn't answer. You see this icon appear even if the person left no voicemail.

- **Vibrate.** 📳 This symbol indicates that you've set your Galaxy S4 to vibrate when you get a call.

- **TTY symbol.** 📺 You've turned on Teletypewriter mode, a special mode that lets the Galaxy S4 communicate with a teletypewriter. That's a machine that deaf people use to conduct phone calls by reading and typing text.

- **Alarm.** ⏰ Who needs an alarm clock when you've got your Galaxy S4? This icon indicates that the alarm is on. You can even set multiple alarms.

- **Time.** 11:03 AM Shows you what time it is. Say goodbye to your watch.

> **TIP** Want to see today's date? Hold your finger on the right end of the status bar, and the date appears. Remove your finger and it goes away.

- **Battery.** 🔋 Get to know this icon—it shows you how much battery life you've got left. When the battery is charging, you see a battery-filling animation and a tiny lightning bolt.

- **Connected to VPN.** 🔲 If you use your Galaxy S4 to connect to your company network via virtual private networking (VPN), this icon shows when your connection is active. You can check your work email and do anything else your company lets VPNers do. (If you're interested in getting VPN access, you'll need your IT department's help, as described in Chapter 14.)

- **Disconnected from VPN.** You were on the VPN, and now you're off.

- **USB connection.** 🔌 You'll connect your phone to your computer via a USB cable for a variety of reasons, including copying and syncing files (Chapter 13). Here's the icon you'll see when you make the connection.

- **SD card is full.** 📇 This icon appears when your SD card (page 21) has run out of space. It's time to get a bigger or newer one, or start deleting files.

- **Smart Scroll.** 👁 This icon appears when you're using the S4's amazing Smart Scroll feature, which lets you scroll through pages by moving your eyes (page 38).

The Three Keys

Most of the time you use your Galaxy S4, you'll be tapping on virtual buttons on the keyboard. But down at the bottom of the Galaxy S4, there are three keys, one fat, black physical one and two virtual ones that light up only when you touch them. From left to right, here's what they do.

Menu Key

This key opens up a menu that lets you perform some kind of task or customization related to what you're currently doing. In geek-speak, it's *context sensitive*, which is a fancy way of saying that the menu that appears changes according to what you're doing at the time. So if you're looking at your contacts, for example, the menu shows you options like deleting a contact or displaying only a certain group of contacts. If you're looking at your calendar, you can quickly create a new event, change the time period that your calendar displays, or similar options.

When you're at the Home screen and you press the Menu key, here's the menu that appears and what each command does:

- **Add apps and widgets.** Lets you add a shortcut to your Home screen or a pane that when tapped launches an app or widget. A widget does things like set an alarm or show you how many apps are running. For details on shortcuts, see the note on page 34.

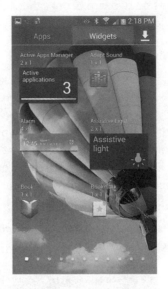

- **Create folder.** As the name says, this option creates a folder that lets you store files.

- **Set wallpaper**. Tap this option, and you can change your Home and Lock screen wallpaper. Some of the choicest choices here are the *live* wallpapers that display changing information, like a windmill that reflects how windy it is at your current location. For more details, see page 31.

- **Edit page.** This lets you delete any one of your five (yes, that's right, count 'em, five!) home screens, also called *panes*. You can even create a new pane. See page 36 for details.

- **Search.** Tap here to search the Internet and your phone by using Google. See page 68 for details.

- **Settings.** Lets you change all your Galaxy S4 settings. For details, see Chapter 16.

Home Key

Repeat after me, Dorothy: There's no place like home, there's no place like home.... Wherever you are on the Galaxy S4, press the Home key and you'll come back to the familiar Home screen. You won't even need to tap your ruby slippers together.

The key does more than just bring you home, though. Holding it down brings up a list of all your currently running apps. Tap any to jump right to it.

Ah, but that's just the beginning of what you can do. Look down at the bottom of the screen. Tap the icon of a chart on the left, and you come to an app manager. Most of the screen shows you which apps are running, along with details about them, such as how much RAM each takes up. Tap End, and you kill the app (and free up that RAM).

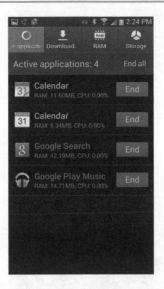

If you tap the Downloaded button at the top of the screen, you see all the apps on your system, along with details, such as how much space they take up. Tap Uninstall to uninstall any.

Tap RAM at the top of the screen, and you come to a simple RAM manager. It shows you how much RAM is currently being used. Sometimes apps are sloppy, and even after you close them down, they continue to use RAM. So tap "Clear memory," and it clears up some of that left-behind RAM so you get more to use.

NOTE RAM stands for *random access memory*, and it's the memory that your S4 uses to do things like run its operating system and apps.

Tap Storage at the top of the screen, and you see how much storage you have on your S4, how much you've used up, and how much remains.

Now, take a look back to the screen you get to when you hold down the Home key. Tap the Google icon at center bottom and you enter the world of Google Cards—a series of compact panels that give you any information important to you. Google Cards can keep you apprised of the weather, any trips you have coming up, what the traffic is like on the way to work, and more. See page 372 for details.

Finally, tap the icon of the X superimposed over three straight lines (it's the rightmost icon), and you close down the list of apps.

Back Key

Wherever you are, tap this key, and you go to where you just were. The Back key works in apps as well as in menus. So when you're browsing the Web, for example, it acts as your Back button. Pressing the Back key also makes a displayed keyboard or menu disappear.

Micro USB Port and Charger

FOR TRANSFERRING FILES AND syncing music and movies between your computer and the Galaxy S4, there's a micro USB port at the bottom of the phone. A micro USB port is much smaller than the normal one on devices like printers. To connect the S4 to your computer, you'll need a micro USB cable, one of which comes in the Galaxy S4 box. The S4 can connect to both Macs and PCs. When you connect your S4 to a computer by USB cable, your phone gets power and charge from the computer. But it charges at a much slower rate than when you use the normal charger.

The Micro USB port is also a charger port. Connect the charger attachment to one end of the USB cable and the other end to your phone to start the charging process. If you use power-hungry features like video and GPS, you may have to charge the S4 every night. If you stick to mostly phone calls and text messages, you may be able to get by with charging only two or three times a week.

TIP You can use the Galaxy S4 while it's charging, unless the battery has run down completely. In that case, it'll need to build up a charge before you can turn it on.

This port does one more thing as well. The S4 may be small enough to fit in the palm of your hand, but it's still a big-time entertainment machine. That's because it's HDMI (High-Definition Multimedia Interface) capable. With it, you can view videos and photos taken on your Galaxy S4 right on your computer or TV screen—as long as they also have HDMI ports. Plug one end of the cable into your Galaxy S4, the other into your PC or TV, and you're ready to go. What does that have to do with the USB port? Plenty: You can buy a special attachment to connect your phone to an HDMI device. See page 145 for details.

When you connect your Galaxy S4 to a PC for the first time, your PC may not recognize it. That's because your PC may need special drivers (small pieces of software) to communicate with the Galaxy S4. Windows will try its mightiest to find the drivers, but there's a chance it won't be able to locate them. If it doesn't, you can go over to the Samsung help website (*www.samsung.com/us/support/*) and search for *Samsung Galaxy S4 drivers*. Then download the drivers and follow the instructions for installing them.

Ringer Volume

IS YOUR RINGER TOO loud? Too soft? Get it just right by using this long silver key on the S4's upper left. Press the top part to make the volume louder, and the bottom one to make it softer. When you press, a ringer volume app pops up on your screen, showing you how much louder or softer you're making the ring.

Microphone

THAT TINY LITTLE HOLE at the bottom of the Galaxy S4 is the microphone. Yes, it's small, but it does the job very nicely.

Battery

THE GALAXY S4 HAS a battery cover. Yes, that's right, an actual battery cover—you can remove the battery and replace it with a new one, unlike some other cellphones. To remove the battery, flip the S4 over, put your finger underneath the small plastic slot on the upper left and pull off the battery cover. You'll see the battery, which you can easily remove by putting your finger into the slot at the bottom and gently pulling up. Don't pull it hard or yank it.

Before removing the battery, make sure to turn the Galaxy S4's power off via the Power/Lock key.

To replace the battery, simply put it back into place. After you've put the battery back in place, replace the battery cover. Now turn the phone back on.

MicroSD Slot

SIM Card

Battery

Maximizing Your Battery Charge

The Galaxy S4, despite its large screen and considerable capabilities, can go a reasonably long time on one battery charge. But if you use a lot of power-sucking features, you may not even be able to get through one whole day without having to recharge. In addition to turning off the screen or putting it into Standby mode when you're not using it, there's a lot you can do to make your battery last:

- **Be smart about email fetching**. The more often the Galaxy S4 checks email, the faster the battery runs down. Either check email manually only when you need to, or increase the interval at which the phone checks. Launch the Email app, press the Menu key, and then select Settings and tap the name of your email account. Tap "Sync schedule"→"Set sync schedule." You can choose from intervals between 15 minutes and 12 hours, or manually.

- **Use "Power saving mode."** Power saving mode turns your Galaxy S4 into a power-sipper. To do it, from the Home screen, tap the Settings button, select Settings→"My device" and then turn on "Power saving mode."

- **Turn off antennas you're not using**. If you're not using a Bluetooth headset, and don't need WiFi or GPS services at the moment, by all means turn them off. They use up tons of power. Pull down the Notification panel, and you'll find widgets for turning off (and back on) WiFi, GPS, and Bluetooth. Putting the Galaxy S4 into Airplane mode turns off all these settings at once, as well as turning off the radio that connects you to the cellular network. Find the Airplane mode widget by sliding the widgets to the left.

- **Watch out for power-sapping apps**. Some, such as 3D games, can use serious amounts of juice. If, after installing an app, you notice your battery running low quickly, consider deleting it, or running it only when necessary.

SIM Card

DEPENDING ON YOUR CARRIER, you may need a SIM card to use your phone. If so, you'll get the SIM card when you buy the phone. The carrier may put it in for you, or you may need to do it yourself. It's located above the battery. When you insert it, make sure the gold-colored contacts face down.

MicroSD Card

JUST ABOVE THE BATTERY, you'll also find a small slot for the MicroSD card, which is about the size of a fingernail—and much smaller than the normal SD memory cards used in cameras. Your Galaxy S4 may not have come with an SD card, so you may have to buy one. The S4 can use one that stores up to 64 GB of data. Place the card in the slot with the arrow facing in. You'll hear a click when it's in place. After that, replace the battery cover.

After you install the card, and you turn on the phone, you'll see a notification that the S4 is preparing the microSD card for your use. Then, go to the Home screen and press the Menu key. Select Settings→Storage. Scroll down, and you'll find a new group of settings under "SD card," listing information like how much total space is on the SD card and how much space remains. (If that information doesn't appear, it means that your SD card hasn't been formatted properly. There's a simple solution: tap, "Mount SD card." If your phone doesn't recognize it after that, tap "Format SD card." That should do the trick.)

WARNING If you've got a MicroSD card in your phone and you've stored files on it, make sure not to tap "Format SD card." When you do that, you erase all the data stored on it.

If you want to replace the SD card—for example, if you have a 16 GB card and want to replace it with one that has more capacity—it's easy. From the Home screen, press the Menu key, and then select Storage Settings. Then tap "Unmount SD card" in the SD card section.

When you've done that, turn off the phone's power and remove the battery cover. You can then slide out the MicroSD card. Then insert a new MicroSD card and follow the instructions in this section for telling your Galaxy S4 to recognize it.

Camera

YOUR SAMSUNG GALAXY S4 includes not one, but two cameras, both capable of taking videos as well as photos. The camera on the back, which is the one you'll normally use for taking photos and videos, has a whopping 13-megapixel resolution. The camera that faces you is primarily designed for video calling and video chat, although you can also take photos with it (self-portraits mostly). It's got a 2-megapixel resolution. Don't look for a physical camera button for taking photos; instead, you tap an onscreen button (page 137).

Samsung and Google Accounts

TO ENJOY ALL THE services your Galaxy S4 is capable of delivering, you need to have a Google account, and possibly a Samsung account as well. On your smartphone, an *account* is a central location for managing all the services you can get. The Google one is absolutely necessary, but you may want to set up a Samsung one as well. This section tells you what you need to know about each.

Google Account

In order to use your S4, you need a Google account. That's because the S4's underlying software is made by Google, and uses many Google services, such as Maps, Gmail, and more. If you already have a Google account—if you've ever used Gmail, for example—great! You can use that account and all the information and settings you've stored in it. Or, you can create a new Google account when you sign in to your S4 for the first time and start fresh.

When you first start your phone, it prompts you to walk through logging into your account or setting up a new one. After that, if you want to make changes, you can head to one central location. At the Home screen, press the Menu key, and then choose Settings→Accounts→Google.

Samsung Account

If you like to use additional Samsung services you can also set up a Samsung account. Otherwise, you don't need it. Depending on your carrier, you may be prompted to create a Samsung account or log into an existing one when you first set up your phone, right after you log into or create a Google account.

But if not, you can create one afterwards. At the Home screen, press the Menu key, and then choose Settings→Accounts→Add Account, and follow the prompts. To change settings, press the Menu key, and then choose Settings→Accounts→Samsung Account.

Home Screen

WELCOME TO YOUR NEW home, the Galaxy S4 Home screen. Get to it by pressing the Home key no matter where you are.

NOTE What you see on the Home screen and panes may differ somewhat from what you see here. Cell phone carriers often customize them, put their own apps on them, and sometimes even change them over time.

The screen is chockful of useful stuff, populated by the following:

- **Status bar.** As detailed on page 8, this bar displays the status of many phone features and a variety of notifications, like when you've got email waiting for you.

- **App icons.** Typically, the Home screen has four icons—one for checking email (right on the icon, you see how many new messages you've got), one for checking your calendar, one for using the camera, and one, called Play Store, to let you search for and download new apps—tens of thousands of them, many of them free. As you'll see later in this section, you can add or delete icons from the Home screen.

- **Dock.** Just below the app icons is a row of five icons. They sit in an area called the *Dock*, and they're different from the app icons. Unlike the app icons, you can't delete them. As you'll see in a little bit, there are other screens you can move to, called *panes* or *panels*, but the icons in the Dock stay in place no matter which pane you visit. (The app icons change according to what pane you're on.) The Phone icon launches the Phone app; the Contacts icon shows you your contacts; the Messaging icon lets you send and receive text messages (it shows how many messages you've got waiting); the Internet icon launches your web browser; and the Apps icon reveals a whole new screen called the App Drawer, filled with apps, apps, and more apps.

- **Pane indicator.** Just above the Dock you'll see four small circles, two on either side of an icon of a house—the Home screen. They each represent a different pane. The brightest circle shows you which pane you're currently viewing. To jump to any pane, tap its button (or slide your finger across the screen).

Above the icons you'll find widgets—a text input box for searching Google, a weather widget that shows you the current weather, and above that, the date and the time.

App Drawer

Press the Launcher icon, and up pops the App Drawer, which includes all the Galaxy S4's preinstalled applications, plus any apps that you've downloaded and installed. There's more than can fit on one screen, so swipe your finger to the right to get to another screen filled with them. Tap any icon to run the app.

Look up at the top of the App Drawer. There are three tabs: Apps, Widgets, and Downloads (represented by a down-arrow icon). The Apps tab, naturally, shows all your apps. Tap Widgets, and you'll see all the widgets on your S4—these are handy little gadgets that accomplish tasks for you, like displaying weather or traffic information.

Tap the Download icon, and you'll see just the apps that you've downloaded to your S4. Those apps also show up in the Apps tab, which lists every app on your S4, whether built in or downloaded.

The Panes

What you see on the four panes, two to either side of the Home screen, may vary according to your carrier, and what Samsung put there before you bought the phone. You may well see things onscreen that aren't covered in this section.

In general, though, you'll find apps and widgets that perform plenty of common and not-so-common things, like checking your calendar and weather, seeing what your friends are up to on Facebook and other social networking sites, playing music and videos, and more.

To get to another pane, slide your finger to the left or right on the Home screen, and you move from the Home screen to one of the panes. What's on the pane changes—you'll generally see a mix of app icons and widgets. If you don't like what you see on any pane, don't worry; as you'll see on page 30, you can fiddle with it to your heart's content. (The Dock, however, remains the same no matter where you go.) The pane indicator has changed—a different button now shines brighter, to show you which pane you're on.

The Software Behind the Galaxy S4

I hear a lot of names for the Galaxy S4's software—TouchWiz, Jelly Bean, Android. Well, which is it?

The short answer: All the above.

Here's the long answer:

The Galaxy S4 is powered by an operating system from Google called Android, as are many other phones, such as the HTC EVO 4G and HTC One. The Android operating system is constantly getting updated, and those updates are automatically sent to your phone when they're available. So what you see on your S4 may vary slightly from what you see onscreen here, depending on the version of Android you have on your phone. At this writing, the Galaxy S4 comes with Android version 4.3, nicknamed Jelly Bean.

Also, it's common for the manufacturer to tweak the phone's interface, sometimes in significant ways. Samsung adds its own TouchWiz interface, which makes many changes to Android. So when you compare the Galaxy S4 to other Android phones, you'll notice differences.

There's still another reason why your Galaxy S4 may differ slightly from what you see in this book. This book happens to be written based on the Samsung Galaxy S4 sold for T-Mobile phones, so it may slightly differ from what you see on phones from other carriers.

S Travel

Among the various apps and widgets on your panes, one will almost certainly be S Travel, Samsung's travel app. It's free and worthwhile to check out. Samsung didn't build S Travel from the ground up by itself. Instead, it partnered with the TripAdvisor to provide the content and power the app. TripAdvisor is an extensive website for travelers, and S Travel puts the whole thing in the palm of your hand.

It's hard to miss S Travel—you'll see a big widget for it on one of the panes, taking up about a third of the screen. Tap it to get started.

The first screen you come to asks to select a city to which you want to travel, or else to view popular destinations. To select a city, tap "Select city," search for the city, and S Travel takes you straight to where you want to go.

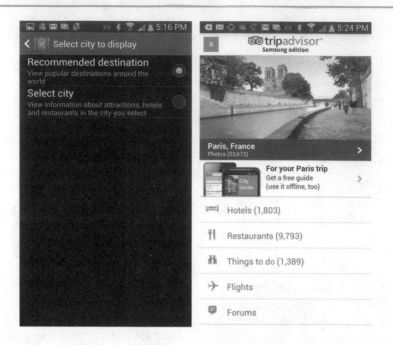

If you instead want to choose from popular destinations, life gets a bit more confusing. Start by tapping "Recommended destination." But when you do that, nothing happens. You must tap the Back button—the one at the top left of your screen in the app, not the normal one at lower right. When you do that, the app sends you straight to a destination of its choosing—you get no say in the matter. But this method might be just the thing when you're looking for new travel ideas.

NOTE Depending on your cell service provider, the S Travel app may instead be called TripAdvisor.

Whichever way you get there, you'll soon get to a city. The information you see is all taken from the TripAdvisor site. It's a tip-top place to start researching your trip.

If you're looking for hotels, tap the Hotels link, and you can get the lowdown on places to stay, complete with ratings, reviews, price, and category information (romantic, family, business, and so on). Tap any to get more details about it, including reviews from people who have visited, photographs, its location on a map, and plenty more.

NOTE
When you tap, you may be asked whether you want to download a free city guide app and use that to browse hotels instead. Or you can decline the city guide and continue using S Travel. Either way, you get the same information.

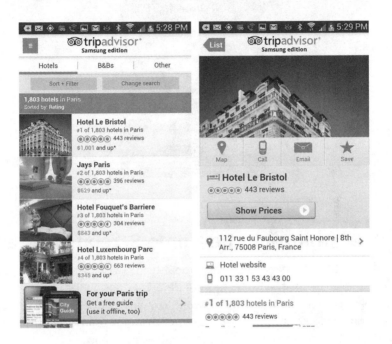

Back on your destination's main screen, you can get similar information about restaurants and things to do. You can also book flights and visit travel forums. The forums offer a wealth of detailed information—if you want to find out whether it's better to travel between Florence and Sienna by train, bus, or car, for example, they're the place to go.

Easy Mode and Standard Mode

WHEN IT COMES TO the basic layout of your Home screen, you've got two choices: Standard Mode and Easy Mode. In Standard mode, you see the normal home screen layout described so far in this chapter, with all its widgets and apps. But maybe you don't want to see all those widgets and apps. Maybe you want something simpler, with big, easy-to-see icons. In that case, you want Easy Mode. On the Home screen, simply tap the Settings button, and then tap "Home screen mode." On the screen that appears, choose Standard or Easy mode.

Customizing the Home Screen and Panes

HERE'S ONE OF THE many nice things about the Galaxy S4—it's easy to put your personal mark on it. Wish there were different apps on the Home screen? No problem; you can easily add them. Want to change the location of apps, or move around widgets and add new ones to each of your panes and the Home screen? It's a breeze. The rest of this section shows you how.

Adding Widgets, Folders, Shortcuts, and Wallpaper

The Home screen and all its panes are much like a prepared canvas, waiting for your Picasso-like touches. Instead of paint, you can add widgets, shortcuts, and folders, and new, original wallpaper.

To do any of the above, the first step is the same: Press and hold your finger anywhere on the Home screen or a pane. A "Home screen" menu appears, with the following options.

NOTE The Home screen and panes have limited real estate—there's only so much you can put on them. In fact, when the phone is factory fresh, the Home screen and panes may already be full. If you try to put something new on them, like an app or a widget, the S4 won't let you do it. Nothing happens when you hold your finger on the screen or pane. In that case, you have two options: delete apps or widgets (page 35) or create a new pane (page 36).

Set wallpaper

Here's where the Picasso part comes in. You can add a wallpaper image to the background of your Home screen, just like adding wallpaper to your computer desktop. When you select this option, you're first asked whether you want to set wallpaper for your Home screen, Lock screen, or both.

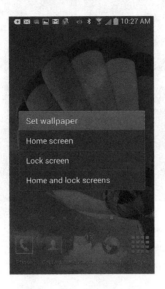

Make your selection. When you do, you have three choices—Gallery, Live wallpapers, or Wallpapers.

If you choose Gallery, you can take any of your own photos (page 119) and use it as wallpaper. The Wallpaper choice lets you simply use a static wallpaper. No matter which you choose, you get to preview the wallpaper first. Live wallpapers are backgrounds that change, either because they're animated or because they grab information from somewhere and then display it as part of the wallpaper background. So the Bubbles wallpaper, for example, displays bubbles rising, falling, growing, and moving across your screen. After you preview it, tap "Set wallpaper," and you're set.

NOTE When you add wallpaper to your Home screen, it also shows up as the background on all your panes. And when you add it to a pane, it shows up on your Home screen.

If you select a picture from the Gallery, you can crop the photo to fit the screen. The S4 suggests a crop for you. You can change it by moving any of the squares that define the crop. Make your selection, tap Done, and you'll see only the cropped area fill your screen.

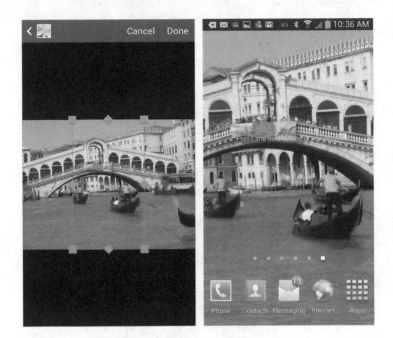

Apps and widgets

This option lets you add apps or widgets to your Home screen or any pane. A *widget* is an applet that performs a small, specific task, often grabbing and displaying information from the Galaxy S4 or the Internet. When you select this option, you get sent to the App Drawer, with the Home screen or a pane in the background. You'll see the familiar tabs along the top—Apps, Widgets, and the download icon. Tap either Apps or Widgets, depending on which you want to add. Swipe to see more apps or widgets if there are more than can fit on one screen. If you want to add an app, hold your finger on it. Then drag it up into the brighter portion of the screen above it and let it go.

NOTE When you add an app to your Home screen or a pane, you're not actually moving that app to the screen or pane. Instead, you're adding a *shortcut* to the app, and that's a good thing. When you tap the shortcut, you run the app, just as if you had tapped it in the App Drawer. But there's a difference: If you delete the shortcuts on the Home screen or pane, you don't delete the app itself. It still lives on. But, if you delete the app *from the App Drawer*, it disappears from your S4.

The same holds true for widgets. Tap the Widgets tab, hold your finger on the widget you want to add, and drag and drop it where you want it to be.

You can't customize the App Menu (also called the App Drawer) the same way that you can the Home screen. If you hold your finger on it, nothing happens.

Folders

Folders hold information and files, the same way they do on computers. You've already got lots of folders on your Galaxy S4, like your folder full of contacts, and bookmarks from your browsers. When you install apps, they may create their own folders as well—the Pandora Internet radio app, for example, creates a folder of your radio stations. You type in a name before placing the folder.

Page

This adds a new pane. So why is it called a page rather than a pane? That's anybody's guess.

OK, time to go crazy. You can now trick out your Home screen or pane in countless ways.

TIP Some widgets can be resized or customized after you add them to your Home screen or pane. Press and hold your finger on a widget and then release it. An outline appears around the widget, with four circles, which are sizing indicators. Move those to resize the widget.

Deleting and Moving

Once you've added widgets, folders, and shortcuts to your Home screen, you're not stuck with them, or with where you've placed them:

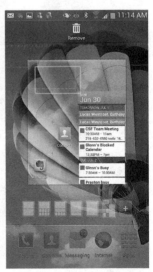

- To move a widget, folder, or shortcut, hold your finger on it for a second or two. The pane or Home screen gets outlined, and a small highlight box appears around the widget, folder, or shortcut. Drag it to its new location and take your finger off. That's where it'll stay. You can even drag it to another pane—just move toward that edge of the screen.

- To delete a widget, folder, or shortcut, also hold your finger on it for a second or two until the highlight box appears. You'll notice a Delete icon in the shape of a Trash can at the top of the screen. Drag the doomed item to the Trash can. When you see it turn red, release it—it's gone.

Deleting and Adding Panes

LET'S SAY YOU'VE GOT a pane tricked out with widgets, shortcuts, and folders. You decide that you'd like it all to go—every widget, every shortcut, every folder. Rather than deleting them one by one, you want to delete them in one fell swoop. Just delete the entire pane. So for example, if you had the Home screen and six panes, you'd end up with the Home screen and just five panes. Fear not—you can also add a new pane back.

To delete a pane, when you're on the Home screen or a pane, tap the Menu key and select "Edit page." Thumbnails of the Home screen and all the panes appear, including even smaller thumbnails of the widgets, shortcuts, and folders on each. At the top of the screen, you see a trash icon.

Drag the pane whose content you want to delete onto the trash can. Release your finger when the can turns red. When asked if you're sure want to delete it, answer yes, and the pane, including all its content, is gone. The thumbnails appear again, but this time there's a big + sign instead of the former pane. Tap it to add a new blank pane. You'll see it as a new thumbnail. Tap that thumbnail and you'll be sent to the new pane. It's blank, awaiting your Picasso-like touches.

Controlling the Galaxy S4 with Your Fingers

WITH THE GALAXY S4, your fingers do the walking. They do all the work that you do on a computer with a mouse or keyboard. Here are the eight finger strokes you can use on the phone's screen.

Tap

Tapping is as basic to the S4 as clicking is to a mouse. This simple gesture is how you press onscreen buttons, place the cursor for text entry, and choose from menus. Note that's a *finger* tap; the screen is designed to detect a fleshy fingertip, not a stylus.

Touch and Hold

Touch an object and hold it for several seconds, and depending on what you're holding, an option menu may appear. For example, when you touch and hold the Home screen, a menu appears that lets you add an object such as a widget, change your wallpaper, and so on. You also touch and hold an object as a way to grab onto it if you then want to drag the object somewhere.

Drag

After you've grabbed something, you can drag it with your finger—like dragging an icon to the Trash.

Slide

Slide your finger across the screen to perform some specific tasks, like unlocking your phone after it's been put into Standby mode, or answering a call if the phone is locked. You'll also use the sliding motion to move through all five panes.

Flick

Think of the flick as a faster slide, done vertically when scrolling through a list, like your contacts list. The faster you make the flicking motion, the faster your screen scrolls—sometimes too fast. You can stop the motion, though, by touching the screen again.

NOTE Flicks seem to actually obey the laws of physics, or at least as much as virtual movement can. When you flick a list, it starts off scrolling very quickly, and then gradually slows down, as if it were a ball set in motion that gradually loses momentum.

To scroll through large lists quickly, you can flick multiple times.

Pinch and Spread

In many apps, such as Google Maps, Mail, Browser, and the Gallery, you can zoom in by spreading your fingers—placing your thumb and forefinger on the screen and spreading them apart. The amount you spread your fingers will determine the amount you zoom in.

To zoom out, put your thumb and forefinger on the screen and pinch them together. The more you pinch, the more you zoom out.

Double-Tap

When you're viewing a map, a picture, or a web page, you can zoom in by double-tapping. In some instances, once you've reached the limit of zooming in, double-tapping again restores the zoom to its original size.

The Magic of Air Gesture, Smart Scroll, Smart Screen, and Air View

LOOK MOM, NO HANDS! No longer is that only the cry of a child showing off riding a bicycle without touching the handlebars. You can do the same thing with your S4. Amazingly enough, you can control it by just moving your hands without touching the screen, or more remarkably, simply moving your eyes.

Here's how to make each of them do their magic.

Smart Scroll and Smart Screen

These are probably the most mind-boggling new features added to the S4. All you need to do is move your eyes to control the screen. And it's so easy, that you don't really need to do anything except what comes naturally, because they follow the way you normally move your eyes when you read.

Smart Screen is made up of four related technologies, one of which is Smart Screen:

- **Smart Scroll.** When this is turned on, the S4 uses its camera and software magic to let you scroll through screens and web pages by merely tilting your head. Tilt your head down to scroll down, and up to scroll up. You'll know Smart Scroll is turned on when you see an eye icon in the status bar. If you prefer, you can instead tilt the S4 forward or back to scroll. But what fun is that?

NOTE Smart Scroll doesn't respond instantaneously. It may take a few seconds for it to notice that you've tilted your head.

Smart Stay. This fixes one of the most common annoyances with a smartphone. You're doing something on the phone, but you haven't touched the screen for a while, so the screen turns off. Smart Stay fixes that. As long as you're looking at the phone, it stays on. (Smart Stay is the only feature that's not brand-new with the S4. It's been around since the S3, but it works better now.)

- **Smart Pause.** Here's another very cool feature. While you're watching a video, if you look away from the screen, the S4 pauses the video. Look back and the video starts playing again.

- **Smart Rotation.** This feature adjusts the screen to the angle at which you're looking at it.

NOTE Some people have had problems getting some or all of these features working. Samsung is working on a fix.

You can turn these features on and off. To do it, from the Home screen or pane tap the Menu key and select Settings→My device→Smart screen.

Air Gesture

Here's another way to control the S4 without touching the screen. You just make gestures above it, like a magician on stage. Air gestures don't work everywhere on the S4, since apps have to be built to recognize them. So you may need to do some experimentation before you find the ones that do. At this writing, that includes email and the browser.

To use air gestures, you make specific hand movements across a sensor that's built into the upper-right of the screen. Here's what you can do:

- **Air browse.** Move a hand to the right or the left across the sensor, and you can browse through things like photos, web pages, and songs.

- **Air jump.** Scroll through the body of your emails and web pages by moving your hand up and down above the sensor.

- **Quick glance.** If your S4 is on a flat surface, facing up, with its screen turned off move your hand to above the sensor and you'll be able to see various pieces of status information, like missed calls, unread messages, your battery power, and others.

- **Air move.** Move icons to other panes and screens by holding down the icon with the finger of one hand, then moving your other hand to the right or left across the sensor.

- **Air call-accept.** To take an incoming call, move your hand across the sensor. This also puts the call on speakerphone. (You can disable the automatic speakerphone, as you'll see next.)

You can turn Air gesture on and off and customize how it works. On any pane, tap the Menu key and select Settings→My device→"Motion and gestures." Slide the "Air gesture" button to turn the feature on or Off. When it's turned on, tap the "Air gesture" setting itself, not the button, and you'll come to a menu that lets you customize how it works. You can turn individual gestures on and off and customize them individually, like setting which notifications you want to receive using Quick glance and turning off the speakerphone in Air call-accept.

Air View

This feature, which originated on the Samsung Galaxy Note II, lets you hover your finger over the S4 to get information from it. For example, hovering over a web page magnifies it, hovering over a picture in the Gallery opens it, hovering over a Calendar event reveals more details about it, hovering over a truncated text message reveals the full message, and so on.

To turn on Air view, see the full list of what you can do, and customize it, go to the Home screen or pane, tap the Menu key and select Settings→My device→"Air view." Slide the "Air view" button to On to turn it on, and Off to turn it off. Tap the words "Air view" when it's turned on to select which actions you want to be able to take by hovering your finger and then customize them.

Using Multi Window

Multi Window is an S4 feature you could easily miss—but don't. It lets you do more than one thing on the phone at the same time. For example, watch a video while your also checking your email. What could be handier?

Right out of the box, Multi Window is turned on. To use it, when you're doing something, like browsing the Gallery or viewing a photo, press and hold the Back key. A menu appears down the right-hand side of the screen, with icons for a variety of apps: web browser, email, text messaging, and so on.

Drag the icon of the app you want to use (in addition to the one you're currently using) to a portion of the screen, and then drop it there. The second app opens, so you have two apps open on your screen simultaneously.

Drag the separator between the two windows to change the relative size of each app on screen. Hold down the separator and then release your finger, and you'll display a set of Multi Window controls. They let you switch the relative position of the windows, make one of the windows full-screen, or close down either of them.

Multi Window has a menu that you can pull up even when you're not using Multi Window. Press and hold the Back key, and you see a small semi-circle on the left side of the screen. Tap it to bring up the menu: tap it again to make the menu recede. If you'd like to stop the semi-circle from appearing, hold down the back key. That won't turn off Multi Window; it just makes the semi-circle stop appearing. To bring it back and display the menu, hold down the back key once more.

To turn Multi Window off, pull down the status bar and swipe through the widgets at the top of the screen, and then tap the one for Multi Window.

You'll learn to:
- Use the two S4 keyboards
- Have your S4 take dictation
- Copy and paste text
- Send and receive text messages
- Search the Web

Typing, Texting, and Searching

A SMARTPHONE LIKE THE Galaxy S4 wouldn't be very smart without the keyboard. Of course, the S4 is great for voice calls, but for text messaging, email, and web surfing, you need an easy way to enter text, and the S4 comes through with flying colors. It gives you two onscreen keyboards—but three ways of entering words into your phone. You can tap to type the usual way, swipe your way through words without lifting your fingertip from the screen, or use the S4's built-in microphone to speak what you want to type.

Whether you prefer to use your fingers or your voice, this chapter is about all the things the S4 lets you do with text. From basic typing, you move on to editing, text messaging, and chatting. Another important thing you need typing for is searching through all your stuff on the phone, so the chapter finishes off with that.

NOTE The S4 offers still two *more* ways to capture text: handwriting recognition and "scanning" for text with the camera. At this writing, these features are nothing to write home about (no pun intended), but they may improve with future Android updates. If you'd like to give them a try, see page 54 for handwriting recognition and page 55 for text recognition.

Whichever keyboard you use, it automatically pops up when you tap somewhere you can enter text, like an email message, a text message, a web browser's address bar, and so on.

The two keyboards are:

- **Samsung.** The Samsung keyboard is typically the one you see when you first turn on your S4. As with every keyboard in history, you tap a key to enter a letter.

  But you're not limited to tapping individual keys. Instead, you can tap a key, and then drag your finger over each letter in the word, in order. This feature—called Swype—captures all the letters in the word using built-in intelligence to figure out what you're entering. It's much faster than tapping individual letters. It takes some getting used to, but you can master it in a few minutes. Once you get used to swiping, you may never go back.

  If even swiping feels like a bit too much effort, the Galaxy S4 understands. It lets you speak to enter text just as if you were talking on the phone.

NOTE If you've ever used another Android-based phone, you're already somewhat familiar with the Samsung keyboard. It's much like the one built directly into the Android operating system, and so is similar to the on all Android phones.

- **Swype.** Back in the day, the standard keyboard didn't have Swype (or a talk feature, for that matter). If you wanted to use Swype, you had to switch to the special Swype keyboard. On the Galaxy S4, a separate Swype keyboard isn't truly necessary, but it's still there. Swyping works a little differently on each of the phone's two keyboards, so this chapter covers both ways. Choice is good.

To switch between the two keyboards, pull down the Notification panel, press the Settings icon, and then select My device→"Language and input." Just underneath the "Keyboards and input methods" heading, you'll see a setting labeled Default. That tells you which is your current keyboard. To change it, tap Default, and choose the keyboard you want to use.

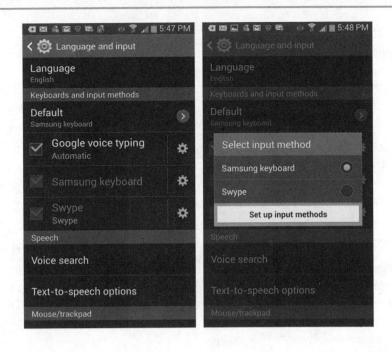

Using the Samsung Keyboard

TAP WHEREVER YOU CAN enter text, and the keyboard appears. When you first tap in the text-entry box, a blinking cursor appears, indicating that you can start typing text. When you tap a key, a kind of "speech balloon" pops up just above your finger, showing you a larger version of the letter you've just tapped.

Surrounding the letters are five special keys:

- **Shift.**  Tap this key, and the letters all change to uppercase. After you type a key, though, the keyboard changes back to lowercase. To turn on Shift Lock so you can type multiple capital letters in a row, tap the Shift key twice in a row. The blue arrow turns white, and the gray background turns blue. Press Shift again, and you're back to the lowercase keyboard.

- **Del** . This key deletes letters to the *left* of the insertion point, like the Delete key on a Mac keyboard. If you use a PC, where the Delete key is a *forward* delete key, you may find this behavior confusing at first. Just use the direction of the arrow icon on the key as a guide: Think *backspace*.

  Tap the Del key once, and it deletes the letter to the left of the insertion point. Hold it down, and it keeps deleting letters to the left until you let it go.

- **Sym** . This key reveals a keyboard full of symbols, punctuation marks, and numbers. When you tap it, the same key changes to read 1/2. Tap it, and yet more symbols appear, including shapes such as stars and hearts. The 1/2 key then reads 2/2; tap it to get back to the previous numbers, symbols, and punctuation keyboard.

- **Return** . Tap and you move down to the next line, just as on a computer.

- **Microphone** . Don't want your fingers to do all the work? No problem. Tap this key, wait for the words "Speak Now" to appear, and then speak into the Galaxy S4. For more details, see page 53.

Auto-Suggestions and the Dictionary

As you enter text, the Galaxy S4 helpfully suggests words that might match what you plan to type. As you type, the phone S4 changes its suggestions based on the letters you enter. The suggestions appear just above the keyboard. Tap any one of the choices to enter it.

The S4 even makes suggestions if the text you've entered is obviously misspelled—great if you're ham-handed. So, for example, type *meeyinv*, and auto-suggest offers a variety of options, including *meeting*.

But there are more suggestions than the ones you see. Tap the down arrow at the right of the screen, and more suggestions appear. Also, the keyboard fades out so you can't use it. All you can do is select one of the suggestions. To go back to writing, tap the arrow—which has now turned into an up arrow—and the normal keyboard appears again. Or, simply tap in the text input box to get the normal keyboard back.

You may notice something more amazing still: The Samsung keyboard doesn't just suggest words that you're current typing, but it even suggests words *before you type them*. That's right, it's as though the phone is a mind reader of sorts. So if you type *I am going out of*, before you can even start typing the next word, the keyboard helpfully shows you the word *town*. Tap it if you want to use that word. The keyboard even helpfully adds a space before it.

Moving the Insertion Point

Once you get the hang of entering text, you'll come across another challenge—how to move the insertion point if you want to go back and edit, delete, or add words or letters. You can tap where you want to place the insertion point, but that's not always effective. Even if you have tiny fingers and fine-tuned hand-eye coordination, you'll rarely be able to tap in the precise spot where you want the insertion point.

There's a better way: Tap anywhere in the text, and you'll see a big arrow beneath the blinking cursor. Move that arrow to place the insertion point precisely.

Accented and Special Characters

You can easily type accented characters with the Galaxy S4 keyboard. (After all, don't we all have a friend named René Müller-Strauß?). When you press and hold certain keys—the ones shown in the table—a palette of accented characters appears, with a box around the first accented character. Move your finger to the one you want to use, and it gets inserted.

KEY	ACCENTED AND SPECIAL CHARACTERS
A	å, æ, ā, ă, ą, @, à, á, â, ã, ä
C	:, ç, ć, č
D	!, ď, đ
E	ê, ę, ě, ĕ, ə, =, è, é, ê, ë, ē
G	/, ġ, ğ
I	ı, į, ī, ĭ, î, í, ì, >
K	ķ, (
L	ł, ĺ, ļ, ĺ,)
N	ñ, ņ, ń, ñ, ,
O	œ, ő, ø, ö, õ, ô, ó, ò, [

KEY	ACCENTED AND SPECIAL CHARACTERS
R	%, ŕ, ř
S	$, ß, ś, š, ş
T	\, þ, ť, ţ, ţ
U	ų, ű, ů, ū, ü, û, ú, ù, <
Y	ý, ǀ
Z	-, ź, ż, ž,

The Express Lane to Punctuation Marks

The Galaxy S4 letter keyboard doesn't have many punctuation marks on it, which can make for much annoyance as you have to constantly switch back and forth between the letter and number keyboards. There's a simpler way, though: Press and hold the period key. The most common punctuation marks and other common symbols, such as the @ sign, appear on the pop-up palette—11 of them. Tap the mark you want to use.

TIP If you want the keyboard—as well as all your menus, button labels, and so on—to use a language other than English, it's easy. Pull down the Notification panel, tap the Settings icon, and then select My device→"Language and input"→Language and then select the language you want to use. You've got plenty of choices, including German, Spanish, French, Italian, and more.

Swipe Your Way to Better Text Input

The Samsung keyboard has an even niftier piece of magic built into it, one that you likely won't immediately notice: You can move your finger across the keys rather than tapping them, and input text that way. Rather than tap each letter individually, you put your finger on the first letter of the word, and then with a single motion, move your finger from letter to letter of the word you want to input. As you do so, you'll see the path that you've traced. Don't worry too much about accuracy, because the keyboard does an exceptional job of interpreting the word you want to input, using its dictionary. Just try to get near each letter; it's OK if you're off a little bit. When you've finished tracing the word, lift your finger.

There are times when the keyboard might not know precisely what you're trying to trace, and the trace might match multiple words. If that happens, just choose from the word choices that pop up. Tap the word you want. That's all it takes. Then keep swiping your fingers.

Tips for Swiping Text

Entering text this way can be much faster than tapping. Here's how to get the most out of it:

- **Don't use the space key.** After you enter a word, lift your finger and enter another word. The keyboard automatically puts a space between the two words.

- **Circle or scribble for double letters.** If you want to enter the word *tennis*, then when you get to the "n," make a circle on the key with your finger, or scribble back and forth across the key. Then glide with your finger to the next letter.

- **Work quickly.** Don't slow down in an attempt to be more precise. Swype is built for speed. Move your finger quickly; you'll be surprised at how well Swype recognizes words.

The Magic of the Microphone Key

REMEMBER THE MICROPHONE KEY (page 48)? Tap it, and you can dictate text to your Samsung S4. But that's just the beginning of what this key can do. Tap and hold it instead of just tapping it, and a menu bar appears just above.

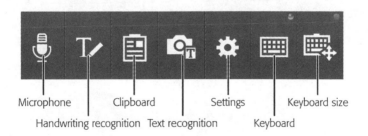

Microphone   Clipboard   Settings   Keyboard size
     Handwriting recognition Text recognition   Keyboard

There are a bunch of cool things you can now do by tapping the appropriate icon. Here's what they do, from left to right:

- **Microphone.** Does what the icon says—lets you dictate text. Tap this key, and the words "Speak now" appear on the screen. Say a few words. The Galaxy S4 thinks for a few seconds, and then types what you dictated. If you decide you'd prefer to type than speak, tap the little keyboard symbol.

TIP Speak clearly and distinctly. The S4's microphone works well for words and short phrases, but not so well for long sentences. You can, however, speak part of a sentence, let it input the text, and then speak the next part.

- **Handwriting recognition.** Tap this key, and the keyboard goes away, and in its place will be a large gray area. Use your finger or a stylus to write letters on it, and the Samsung S4 does its best to recognize what you're writing. It is fast? No. Is it effective? No. Is it fun? It might be for you. In any event, it's there if you want to use it.

- **Clipboard.** This lets you paste in something that you've previously copied to the Clipboard. (For more on copying and pasting, flip to page 58.) When you tap it, a list of your last several clips appear. Tap any to insert it.

- **Text recognition.** Tap this, and you can take a photograph of any text—a portion of a page of a book, let's say—and the Galaxy S4 does its best to recognize the words. First, take the photo; you're then prompted to select the portion of the photo that you want to grab text from. After that, the S4 tries to recognize the text and then pastes it into your message.

> **NOTE** Text recognition sounds like magic, but it doesn't always work like magic. It works best when you're taking a photo of very large, clear, easily recognizable text.

- **Settings.** Takes you to a screen that lets you change the S4's keyboard settings.
- **Keyboard size.** The next two choices let you select what size keyboard to use. If you look closely, you'll see there's a small green dot above one of the two keyboard icons, meaning that it's the keyboard currently being used. The leftmost one is the normal-sized keyboard, the one you're using out of the box. If you want to use the much smaller keyboard, tap the icon all the way to the right. A wee little keyboard appears, one you need mini-fingers to use. You can drag it around the screen by dragging the little tab at its top. When you're tired of working so small, hold your finger on the microphone key and from the menu that appears, select the larger sized keyboard.

Using the Swype Keyboard

THE GALAXY S4 HAS a second Swype keyboard—one that's all Swype, all the time. Now that the S4's regular keyboard allows for swiping, this second keyboard isn't quite as necessary. Still, it's there, and there are some differences between its keyboard layout and features and the S4's built-in one. If you've used the Swype keyboard on an earlier model phone, this one will make you feel right at home. If you prefer this Swype keyboard, switch to it by pulling down the Notification panel, tapping the Settings icon, and then selecting My device→"Language and input"→Default. From the screen that appears, select Swype.

Swype Keyboard Layout

The Swype's keyboard is laid out a bit differently than the Samsung keyboard. The basic keyboard is the same, although some special keys are in different locations. The real difference, though is in two keys:

- **Swype.** This key does double-duty. Tap and hold it, and a screen appears that offers help and lets you edit Swype settings. If you simply tap the key, it highlights the word directly to the left of the insertion point, and brings up the Word Choice menu, so you can correct the word if you want.

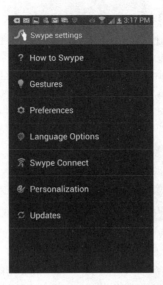

- **123.** Similar to the SYM key on the Samsung keyboard (page 48), it works a bit differently. Tap it when you want to type numbers or punctuation marks. To display a keyboard with still more special characters and symbols, tap the Shift key on the symbol keyboard. The Shift key then changes to a 1/2 key; tap it to access a second number, punctuation, and symbol keyboard.

NOTE If you're entering numbers or special characters with Swype, you have to tap them. You can't move your finger across the keys in order to input them.

Adding Words to the Swype Dictionary

To make suggestions about what words you might be typing, the Swype keyboard looks in its dictionary. But the dictionary isn't a static thing; you can easily add new words to it, which then join the suggestion list. In fact, the S4 even offers to add them for you. When you type a word that Swype doesn't recognize, it pops up a message asking if you want it added to the dictionary. Tap the + sign if you want to; simply ignore the message if you don't want the word added.

Copying and Pasting Text

WHAT'S A COMPUTER WITHOUT the ability to cut, copy, and paste? A computer at heart, the Galaxy S4 lets you do all that, even though it has no mouse. For example, you can copy directions from Google Maps into an email to send to a friend, paste contact information into a note to yourself, and so on.

You copy and paste text using the same basic techniques you use on a PC or a Mac. You select it, and then copy or cut, and then paste it.

To select text in an input box, double-tap the text that you want to select. If you're lucky, the exact words you want to select are highlighted in blue with brackets on either side. Just above the keyboard, you'll see the words as well.

There's a good chance, though, that you won't be that lucky. No problem—just drag either or both brackets to select the exact text you want.

When you select text, a menu bar appears at the top of the screen. Here's what you can do from this menu:

- **Select all.** Selects all the text and graphics in the input box and pops up the same menu of choices you have when you select a word. The selected text is highlighted and contained within the brackets. Move any of them to limit the selection.

- **Cut and copy.** Copies the text to the clipboard so you can paste it somewhere, and deletes the text.

- **Copy.** Copies the text to the clipboard so you can paste it somewhere, but doesn't delete the text.

- **Clipboard.** Replaces the text you've selected with the latest text you've pasted to the clipboard.

As for pasting text once you've copied it to the clipboard, it's a snap...well, a tap. Hold your finger where you want to paste the text, and then tap the Paste button that appears. You can also paste text by holding your finger on the microphone key and selecting the paste icon, as outlined on page 55.

Copying Text from a Web Page

Chances are when you're browsing the Web, you'll eventually come across some text that you want to save for later use. The Galaxy S4 has a specific—but simple—procedure for copying text from a web page to the Clipboard:

1. **Hold your finger on the text you want to copy.** A magnifying glass appears, and the word is highlighted in blue.

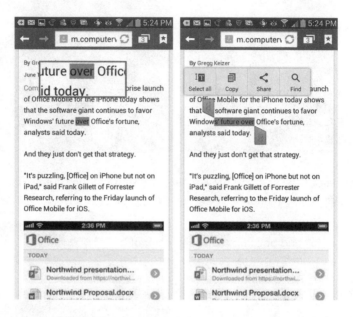

2. **Take your finger off the screen.** The word is bracketed and a menu appears above the text. Move either one or both of the brackets to include all the text you want to copy.

3. **Tap the Copy icon.** The text is copied to the Clipboard. You can also tap the Select All icon to select all the text on the page, tap the Search icon to perform an Internet search for the text, or tap Share to share it via Bluetooth, email, Facebook, or several other ways.

Text Messaging

WHAT!? YOU SAY YOU use your smartphone to make phone calls? That's *so* early twenty-first century! By 2008, as reported by the Nielsen Mobile research group, the average mobile phone user sent and received more text messages than phone calls—357 text messages a month compared with 204 calls. Fittingly, the Galaxy S4 is a messaging monster. Not only can you send and receive plain old text messages, but you can send and receive pictures and videos along with them as well.

When you send text messages, you use the SMS (Short Message Service), which limits you to 160 characters (including spaces and punctuation), which comes out to a sentence or two. That may sound short, but in a world where Twitter limits you to messages of 140 characters, 160 characters can suddenly seem like a lot of space.

NOTE Text messaging is different from a chat program. A chat program establishes a direct connection between you and another person or people, and in addition to letting you chat with one another via the keyboard, you can do videochats and more. For details on how to chat with Google Hangouts and Samsung's ChatON program, see page 286.

Text messaging doesn't come free. You'll have to pay extra, either for a monthly plan or for individual text messages. Check with your wireless provider for details.

NOTE The charges for text messaging are for messages you *receive* as well as those you send.

Receiving a Text Message

When you get a text message, the S4 plays a notification sound. What happens next depends upon whether the phone is active or asleep:

- **If you're using the phone,** you hear a notification sound, and a message appears across the top of your screen. A notification also appears in the status bar.

- **If the phone is asleep,** it wakes up, you hear a notification sound, and you get a notification that you've got a text message (at the top of your screen).

In either case, pull down the Notification panel and tap the notice. If you've got more than one text message, the notice tells you so. You go straight to a list of your most recent text messages, those you've sent as well as those that have been sent to you. You see only the last text message in a conversation. So if you exchanged four text messages with someone three days ago, you see only the last message listed here.

To read the message you were just sent, tap it. You see the message in a text balloon, and if it's part of an ongoing conversation of messages, you see each message.

NOTE Text messagers are encountering an unpleasant fact of texting life—spam. It's not nearly as prevalent as email spam, but you'll most likely get some at some point in your messaging life.

To respond, tap in your message using the keyboard, and then press Send. Off your message goes, instantly. You see the record of your message appear in a text balloon. If your friend texts back, you see it in a text balloon...and so on.

Sending a Text Message

To send a text message if you haven't received one, tap the Messaging icon on the Home screen or the App Drawer. The list of all your messages appears. Tap the envelope icon at upper right, and a screen appears where you create your text message. There are several ways to tell the Galaxy S4 where to send your text message, both accessible from the To field:

- **Type a name into the field.** The phone looks through your contacts and displays any matches. Tap the contact to whose cellphone you want to send a text message.

- **Tap a phone number into the field.**

- **Tap the icon of a person** next to the recipient field, and you're sent to your Contacts list, where you can choose a recipient.

After that, type your message in the message field and tap Send, and your message goes on its merry way.

> **TIP** If you prefer to talk rather than type, press the microphone key on the keyboard, and then speak your message (page 53). Yes, it's odd to send a text message that starts out as the spoken word, but welcome to the twenty-first century.

There are plenty of other places on the Galaxy S4 where you can send text messages. Here are the most common ones:

- **When you're viewing a contact.** Tap the Message icon next to a phone number to address a text message to that number. Anywhere you view your contacts, you're only a tap or two away from sending a text message.

> **NOTE** Make sure when you tap the Message icon that the phone number is a *cellphone* number. If it's a landline, the message won't go through.

- **When you're viewing pictures or video.** You can share these things via text messaging much same way you can share them via email. When viewing the picture or video, tap it so the top menu appears, then tap the Share button. From the screen that appears, tap the Messaging icon. The photo will be embedded into a text message. Type any text you want, then add the recipient and send it as you would any other text message.

NOTE If the photo or video is too large to send, the S4 will compress it for you. It will take a few seconds to compress, depending on its size.

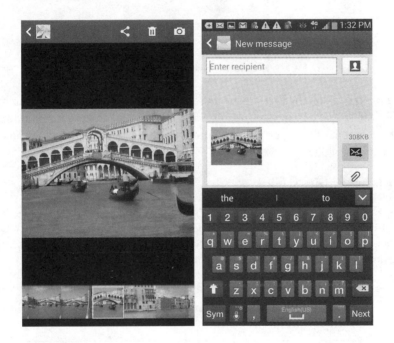

Adding Pictures, Audio, and Video

On the Galaxy S4, the term "text message" is an understatement, because you can send a whole lot more than text using the SMS service. It's a breeze to send a photo, an audio snippet, a video, an entire slideshow, a name card with contact information on it, and more. When you're composing your text message, tap the Insert icon (it's the picture of a paper clip) to choose any of these items and others from a menu that appears. Depending on what you choose, you'll come to a different menu—for example, all your photo albums if you choose to include a photo. From the menu, you can also take a picture, or record audio or video, which you can then send.

You end up back on the text-messaging screen, where you see an attachment icon on the left side of the screen. Tap Send, and the S4 sends your picture. After a moment or two, you'll see the message you just sent, including the picture, audio, or video.

Text Messaging Tricks

When you're composing a text message, you're in the text input box, and you press the Menu key, you have more options than just inserting a picture, audio, or video. You can even create a slideshow. Here are your primary options when you press the Menu key:

> **NOTE** These options don't appear unless you're in the text entry field. Also, other options may appear as well, depending on the person you're contacting.

- **Insert Smiley.** If you're a fan of smileys, also called *emoticons*, tap here to see a long list of ones you can insert. (If smileys set your teeth on edge, avoid this option.)

- **Add text.** You can add more than just ordinary text—you can add information from a contact, a calendar item, and more. Select the item you want to add from the screen that appears, and follow the instructions.

- **Add slide.** This tricky option is fun once you get used to it. Tap it and a slide doesn't actually get added—instead you see a dotted line of text with 1/2 at the right. Tap it again, and another dotted line appears below that, with 2/3 at the right. All you're doing at this point is creating blank slides, with no content in them. To add a picture, video, or audio, to a slide, put your finger at the appropriate point and tap the Insert icon, then select what you want to add, as described in the previous section. You'll see the photo added. Soon you'll see all your slides, with pictures in them.

- **Edit or preview the slide show.** Press the Menu key, and you can add more slides and remove slides. You can also preview your slideshow by tapping the Preview button. And you can control how long each slide displays by selecting the Duration option. When you're done, send the text message as you would normally—you've just sent a slideshow!

Searching Your Galaxy S4

LOOKING TO FIND THE proverbial needle in a haystack on your Galaxy S4? It can seem like an insurmountable problem. After all, the S4's haystack is rather large, including contacts, maps, social networking sites like Facebook, and the entire Web.

It could take you quite a long time to find a needle in all that hay if you didn't have the S4's universal search, which searches all the above in one fell swoop. Here's what universal search scans to find matches for you:

NOTE This list will vary according to the apps installed on your S4.

- **Contacts.** Search through first and last names, and also company names. It lists names as well as phone numbers in the results.
- **Browser.** Looks through your bookmarks and web history.
- **Music.** Searches artist names, album names, and track names.
- **Kindle.** If you have the Android Kindle book-reading app from Amazon on your S4, universal search looks through the titles and authors of the books you've downloaded.

NOTE When you first unpacked and used your Galaxy S4, it may not have had the Kindle app on it, and you may never have downloaded it. Yet the app may be on your Galaxy S4 all the same. If so, that's because it may have been installed during one of the software updates performed on your phone wirelessly. (It's called an *over the air* update, or OTA.)

- **Google search.** Lists popular Google searches that include your search term. It also includes search terms you've already used on Google, even those that you've used on a computer, not on your phone.
- **Titles of installed apps.** It searches through the names of apps you've downloaded. Tap a name to launch the app.

- **Contacts on social media sites.** Universal search doesn't just search through the contacts on your phone—it also searches through contacts on social networking sites whose apps you've installed, such as Facebook.

- **Text messages.** It searches through text messages you've sent and received.

Performing a Search

To launch a search from the Home screen, tap in the Google search box, or else tap the Menu key and select Search. Tap in your text, and the Galaxy S4 does its magic. As you tap, search displays its results, narrowing the results as you type and your search term gets more specific. In addition, you'll also see Google recommendations for your search.

As you type, just beneath the search box, you'll see Google recommendations for searching the Web, and then any partial matches of apps on your phone, contacts, and other matches from your phone. Underneath that you'll see text in blue: Search Phone.

To search the Web, tap Enter; to choose any Google suggestions, tap them; and to launch any matching app, open a contact, and so on, tap it. And to search your phone, tap Search Phone (naturally). Why do you need to search your phone, when the S4 has just searched it? Tapping Search Phone does a deeper search. It lists the search results by category. If there are too many to show for each category, there's a Show More button at the bottom of the category. Tap it to see more matches.

Look down at the bottom of the screen. There's a set of icons for Web, Images, Places, More, and Phone. You won't be able to see them all, so swipe to the side to see more. Tap any to launch a search. The search, though, will be Web-focused—for example, tapping Images uses Google image search, and tapping Places searches Google Places. Tapping Phone, though, searches your phone yet again. And tapping More brings up a whole host of new Google searches, ranging from News to Books to Shopping to Video and more.

Controlling Searches

You're given some control over what Search looks through on your phone. When you're in Search, tap the Menu key and then select Settings→Phone Search. From the screen that appears, you'll see a list of all the content and apps on your phone that Search looks through. Check the boxes next to the content you want it to search through, and uncheck the boxes you don't want it to search.

Voice Search

WANT TO SAVE WEAR and tear on your fingers? Use voice search. It works like regular search, with one very important difference: Rather than typing your search, you speak it. Other than that, everything is the same.

To perform a voice search, tap the microphone icon to the right of a Google search box, or else press the Search button and choose Voice Search from the screen that appears. Talk into the phone clearly. Your S4 gamefully tries to interpret them. It then displays results. (For more detail on searching by voice, see page 70.)

The S4 can also perform a very nifty trick—listen to a piece of music, then tell you what it is, and link to it. If when you do a voice search you're playing music, it shows a small note icon with the word next to it "Listen to Music." Tap that, and hold the phone close enough to the music source so it can hear it. After a little bit, if Google can figure out the music, it shows a match, including a link to buy the music, or to listen to it if you own it. This feature is really useful if you're listening to music and want to know who is singing.

You'll learn to:
- Use the dialer and Contacts app to make calls
- Use Favorites as your speed dialer
- Manage, add, and delete contacts
- Use the S4 for conference calls
- Use caller ID, call forwarding, and call waiting

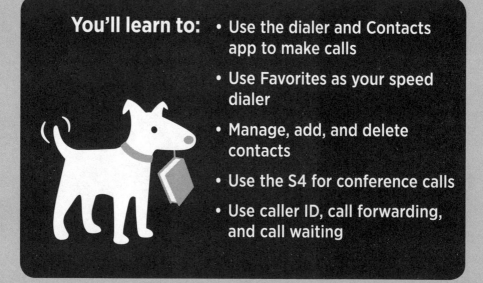

CHAPTER 3

Phone Calls

THE SAMSUNG GALAXY S4 can do so much, you may forget it's a phone as well. Among all the amazing things this device can do, though, it's great for making phone calls. When texting just won't do, the Galaxy S4 offers everything from simple voice calls to nifty features like Visual Voicemail and Call Waiting—and that's what you'll learn in this chapter.

Once you see by the bars in the Galaxy S4's upper-right corner that you've got cellular reception, you're ready to make calls. You can place a call in any of five ways. Don't be daunted by the variety—all methods are easy, including a "Look, Ma, no hands" approach to calls that lets you call someone by talking into the phone rather than by using your fingers to tap keys.

Placing a Phone Call

THE GALAXY S4'S PHONE App is Command Central for making phone calls. On the Home screen, tap the phone icon (at lower-left). The Phone app opens, with four buttons at the top, representing the four ways you can make a call:

(619) 232-8856

Add to Contacts

- **Keypad.** You'll be pleased to see that the virtual buttons on this dialer are a whole lot bigger and easier to tap than the cramped keypads on most cellphones. Even if you have fat fingers or iffy coordination, tapping the right number is a breeze. Tap the number you want to call, and then tap the green Call button at the bottom.

- **Recents.** On this list of recent activity, icons indicate calls that you've made ➔ ⛟, received ⟵ ⛟, or missed ⤬. You also see more information about the call, like the date and time. To repeat or return a call, tap its listing in the log. When the call screen appears, tap the green phone button.

TIP You can also send a text message from the Logs area. Tap the listing and then tap the text message icon on the screen that appears.

- **Favorites.** The Galaxy S4's version of speed dial. The Galaxy S4 lists the people you call or contact frequently. Tap the person's name, then on the screen that appears, choose how you want get in touch—phone, email, text, message, and so on.

- **Contacts.** Tap a contact, and you can choose from among making a call, sending a text message, sending an email, sending an instant message via Google Talk, and more. The options you see here depend on the information you have for that contact. If you don't have someone's email address, for example, you won't get that option. You'll find out more about all these options later in this chapter.

You may see more contacts here than what you originally tapped into your phone. That's because, if you have a Gmail account, S4 imports those contacts into its Contacts list. It can also import contacts from other services, like Facebook. You'll see how it works later in this chapter (page 80).

TIP You don't need to go to the Phone app first any time you want to call or text someone. Instead, you can tap the orange Contacts icon on the Home screen, the App Drawer, or anywhere else you see it.

Dialing a Call

MAKING A CALL WITH the dialer is straightforward: Tap the virtual buttons, and then tap the green phone button to place the call. You'll find the keypad easier to use than a normal cellphone keypad because its buttons are larger.

If you want to call in to your voice mail instead (see page 90), tap the voice mail button at lower-left. (It looks like a cassette tape from an old-school answering machine.)

When you make a call, the Dialing screen pops up showing you the phone number you're dialing. If you have a picture of the person in your Contact list, you see that photo here. A timer begins, showing you the elapsed time of the call.

There are also buttons for putting the call on the Galaxy S4's built-in speaker, muting the call, and connecting to a Bluetooth headset. And, of course, to end the call, tap the "End call" button.

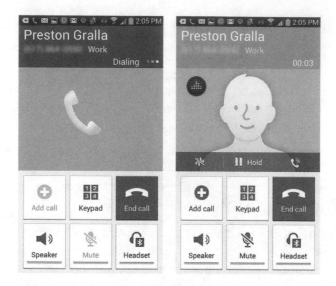

Next to the "End call" button is another button whose purpose seems baffling at first—Keypad. Why would you need a keypad when you're already on a call? For that most annoying means of modern communications—the phone tree. Press the keypad button, and you can experience all the joys of having to "Press 1 for more options."

The Dialing screen offers a bit more Galaxy S4 phone magic. Hit the Add button and presto—you've created your own conference call. For details, check out page 89.

Choosing from the Recents List

The Recents list shows you every call you've made or received—and lets you make phone calls right from the list. Tap the Logs button at the top of the screen, and you see your call history listed in chronological order. You see the name, phone number, and time each call was made. Icons next to each call listing provide further details:

- ➡📞 means a call you made.

- ⬅📞 means a call made to you.

- ✂ means a call you didn't answer.

You can also get more information about each call in the Logs list by tapping anywhere in the log entry (except on the contact's picture—more on that in a minute). A screen then appears with more details about the call, including the exact date and time it was made and its duration. You even see all your recent history of calls and communications with that person. From here you can also call her (tap the phone icon), send her a text message, add her to your Contacts list, view her info in Contacts if she's already there, and more.

Back on the to the Recents list, if you tap the contact's picture (or if there's no picture, the person icon), a pop-up screen appears. Tap any of the icons on it to contact the person in the following ways, among others:

- Call the person.

- Open his record in Contacts.

- Send him a text message.

- Send him an email.

- Contact him via a social networking site such as Facebook. You only see this option if you've installed the appropriate social networking app on your Galaxy S4 as described in Chapter 11.

- Locate the person on Google Maps by using the address information in his address book.

TIP Tap the Menu key for ways to manage the Logs list, including deleting individual entries, changing the list order, choosing whether to display the call duration, and so on.

Choosing from Your Contacts

The Phone app gets phone numbers, pictures, and other information by tapping into your main Contacts list. The Galaxy S4 gets these contacts from multiple places. For example, if you use Gmail, the S4 automatically imports your Gmail contacts into its list. And if you use S4 along with Facebook, your Facebook friends join the party as well. If you use Google+ and have people in your circles, it includes them as well. It marks Gmail contacts with a G icon and Google+ ones with a G+ icon.

You can also add contacts directly to the S4. You'll learn all the ins and outs of Contacts in the next section. Suffice it to say, if you've ever interacted with someone by email or social media, chances are your S4 already has her phone number.

NOTE You may notice that on your Contacts list, many people have pictures next to their names, even though you never took their pictures. Is the Galaxy S4 pulling hidden camera tricks? Of course not. If you use Facebook on your Galaxy S4, it pulls in pictures from Facebook for any of your contacts who have them.

When you first load Contacts, you'll notice something odd and potentially annoying—the S4 arranges your contacts alphabetically by first name, not last name. So if you know a lot of Joes and Marys, you're going to spend a little more time than you'd like scrolling.

NOTE   Why does the Galaxy S4 alphabetize by first name, rather than by last name? It's a Google thing. Google wrote the Android operating system that powers the phone, and Gmail alphabetizes its contact list by first name. As Gmail does, so does the Galaxy S4.

You likely know more than one screenful of people, and you can navigate through the list in several ways:

First, you can flick through the list. Also, you'll see the alphabet down the right side of the screen, and you can tap any letter to get sent to that letter immediately.

You can also search the list. Type letters into the search box at top, and as you type, the list gets pared down, hiding everyone whose first name, last name, company name, or title doesn't match what you've typed. It's a great time-saver for quickly paring down a big list. You also see the words you're typing, just above the keyboard, so you can more easily track what you type.

When you've gotten to the person you want to call, tap the person's contact listing. You'll see all the information you have about him—phone numbers, email addresses, home and work addresses, and more. From this screen you can make a call, send an email or text message, and so on by tapping the appropriate icon.

Managing Contacts

THE GALAXY S4'S PHONE, Messaging, and IM apps all use the same master Contacts list. In fact, you can go directly to the list by tapping the Contacts icon on the App Drawer.

The Galaxy S4 is nothing if not thoughtful. If you use Gmail, the phone grabs all your contacts from there and pops them into your Contacts list. And it's not just a one-time transfer of contacts, but it happens every time you add, edit, or delete a contact. Whenever you change or add a contact in Gmail, those changes are synced to your S4, and vice versa. So if possible, it's better to create new contacts in Gmail on your computer, and then let the phone import that new information when you sync up. It's much easier to type on a keyboard than it is to tap away on your S4.

Adding a Contact

No matter where you are you can always add a contact right on your Galaxy S4. Tap the + button at the top of your Contacts list (the button stays there even when you scroll) and a screen pops up asking where you want to save the contact. The available locations may vary depending on the apps you have and your S4 setup, but at minimum you'll be able to choose from saving to your SIM card, to the device, or to your Google account. No matter where you save the contact, though, it'll show up in your Contacts list. However, if you save to your device or SIM card, the contact won't sync with your Google account, so your best bet is to go for the Google option.

After you choose where to create your contact, you arrive at a screen where you fill in contact information. Type the person's first name, last name, address information, and so on. If she has more than one email address, phone number, or address, tap the + button next to the entry to add more. Make sure to scroll through this whole screen—there's plenty of information you can add here.

One more trick—you can add a photo to the contact information. At the top of the screen, tap the icon that looks like a person's head with a + on it, and a screen appears that lets you add a photo. If you already have a photo on your phone, tap Image and you can browse through the Gallery (page 119) for the picture. If the person happens to be right there with you, tap "Take picture," and the Camera app launches. Use it to take a photo. There are several other options available for adding pictures, but none are as easy as browsing the Gallery or snapping a photo on the spot.

> **NOTE** If you want to change the location of where you're saving a contact, tap the same triangle on the right side near the top of the screen that shows the location you're saving to. When you tap the triangle, you'll get a choice of other locations where you might want to save.

The Contact screen also lets you do way cooler things than typing in basic information. You can choose a specific ringtone and even tell your phone to vibrate in a certain way when that contact calls. So pay attention to those fields. And there are plenty more fields you can add as well. Tap "Add another field," and you'll get plenty of options, like Relationship, Notes, and so on.

Editing Contacts

Already have a contact and want to edit his information? Tap the Edit button at the top of a contact, then edit to your heart's content. You can change or add any of the same things as when you first added the contact.

Tap here to edit the
contact information

For even more contact-handling options, tap the Menu key when you're viewing a contact. You'll be able to do things like:

- Combine two different bits of contact information into one (if one comes from Gmail, for example, and another from Facebook)

- Add a shortcut to the contact to the Home screen.

- Print the contact information to a wireless printer.

- Share the contact information via Bluetooth, email, text message, and other ways.

Working with Groups

Like most folks, you probably have a long list of contacts, and although the Contacts lets you flick through them quickly, you may can have a hard time zeroing in on the person you want. There's a simpler way—Groups. The Galaxy S4 lets you put contacts in various groups—Family, Work, and so on—making it easier to find the person you want. You can view just the group rather than the entire Contacts list.

The Groups button appears at the top of the screen when you're viewing your contacts. Tap it to see your Groups. Tap any group in the list to see all its members. To create a new group, when you're viewing the list of your groups, press the Menu key and tap Create. Type a name for the group and then start putting people in it. Tap Add Member, and your entire contact list appears, with a checkbox next to every contact. Tap that box for each contact you want to add to the group, and when you've added everyone, tap Done.

TIP From the screen that lets you create a group, you can also select a ringtone for when anyone from that group calls you. (Beyoncé for your ring-theory group, perhaps?)

Fancy Tricks with Contacts

The Galaxy S4 has a few more tricks up its sleeve when it comes to working with contacts. To see them, press and hold your finger on a contact, and then press the Menu key. The choices vary according to the contact information you have. Here are the choices you'll see, and what each does:

- **Edit.** Lets you edit the contact's name and other information.

- **Delete.** Deletes the contact from your Galaxy S4.

- **Join contact.** Combines two separate listings for a contact into a single listing. For example, if you've imported a contact from both Gmail and Facebook, they'll usually show up as separate contacts until you combine them using Join.

- **Share contact via message.** Lets you send information about a contact using text messaging. You can send all the information about the contact, or just some of it. Follow the onscreen prompts for making your choice.

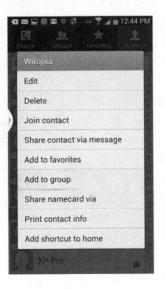

- **Remove from favorites.** This option only appears if the person is in your favorites list.

- **Add to favorites.** Adds the person to your Favorites—the Galaxy S4's version of speed dial.

- **Add to group.** Lets you add a contact to a group.

- **Add to reject list.** Puts the person on a list of callers you don't want to hear from. Your phone won't answer calls from numbers on this list.

- **Send namecard via.** Lets you share the contact's namecard—an electronic file that contains all the contact's information. You can send it in a variety of ways, including email, text messaging, Bluetooth, and others.

- **Print contact info.** If you have a wirelessly enabled printer that works with your Galaxy S4, you can print the person's namecard.

- **Add shortcut to home.** Puts a link to the contact on your Home screen.

TIP If you're viewing a contact, you can get to some of the same choices by tapping the Menu key. The Menu key reveals some choices you don't see when you hold your finger on a contact. For example, you can view a history of your communication with the contact—phone calls, emails, text messages, and so on.

Designating Favorites

WHAT IF YOU WANT to quickly call your best friend, your spouse, your lawyer, one of your children, or your weekly tennis partner? Scrolling through hundreds of contacts is a complete waste of time. You need a way to quickly jump to the contacts you frequently call.

That's where the Favorites list comes in. Think of it as the Galaxy S4's speed dial. The S4 puts people on the list based on how often you communicate with them. Other than that, it works the exact same way as the normal Contacts list.

Although the S4 automatically adds your frequently used contacts to the Favorites list, you can also add your own. Just open the contact and tap the star at the top of the screen. The star turns gold, and the person shows up on your Favorites list.

NOTE To remove someone from your Favorites list, open the contact, and then tap the gold star. It loses its gold color, indicating that the person is no longer one of your Favorites.

Answering Calls

ONE RINGY DINGY, TWO ringy dingies...when you get a call on your Galaxy S4, you'll know in no uncertain terms that someone's trying to reach you. Depending on how you've set up your S4 to handle incoming calls, you'll hear a ring, feel a vibration, and see the caller's name, photo, and phone number onscreen.

NOTE For information about how to choose a ringtone, and whether to use Vibrate mode, see page 400.

The way you find out when a call is coming in, and the way you answer it, depends on what you're doing when you get the call:

- **If you're doing something else on the Galaxy S4,** you'll hear a notification, and a screen appears telling you that you've got a call. Slide the green button from left to right. When the call is over, tap "End call." If you don't want to answer the call at all, drag the red button from right to left.

- **If the Galaxy S4 is asleep or locked,** you get the same call screen and the same red and green buttons. Even if you've added a password to your phone, you answer the phone the same way—no password required to answer a call.

- **If you're wearing earbuds or listening to music on an external speaker,** the music stops playing and you hear the ringtone in your earbuds or speaker. Slide the green or red button. After the call ends, the music starts playing again.

Turning Off the Ring

If the Galaxy S4 starts to ring at an inopportune time, you can turn off the ringtone without turning off the phone or dropping the call. Just press the volume switch at the phone's upper-left side. The ring goes away, but you can still answer the call in any of the usual ways.

Ignoring the Call

Suppose you're just getting to the juicy part of a book you're reading, or you simply don't want to talk to the annoying person calling? You can ignore the call. After five rings, the call goes to voicemail. (It does so even if you've silenced the ring with the volume switch.)

If you prefer, you can send the call straight to voicemail, without further ado or further rings. And not only that, but you can also send a text message to the caller, explaining why you can't answer the call. To do it, pull up the "Reject call with message" button at the bottom of the screen, and select from any of the pre-created messages that appear, such as "I'm driving," "I'm in a meeting," and so on. The caller will be sent straight to voicemail, and he'll also get the text message from you. You can also write your own text—as long as, of course, you're *not* driving—by tapping "Create new message."

Conference Calling

HERE'S A FANCY PHONE trick that's great for business and personal use—conference calls. Sitting at a Starbucks, but want people on the other end to think you're in an office with a fancy phone system? The Galaxy S4 lets you conference in multiple people with no extra charges or software, depending on your carrier. And you can also use it for conferencing in friends when you're all trying to decide whether to meet at 6 p.m. before the Red Sox game so you can catch Big Papi at batting practice.

To make a conference call, first make a call as you would normally. Then tap "Add call." The phone places the second call and switches you to it. When the person answers, you'll see a visual representation of both calls. Tap either picture to switch to that line. To create a conference call, tap Merge.

When you're done conferencing, tap "End call" to disconnect everyone from the call.

Voicemail

YOUR GALAXY S4 HAS built into it all the usual voicemail capabilities you'd expect. You know the drill: Dial in to your voicemail, enter a password, and listen to voice messages. To dial in to voicemail on the Galaxy S4, tap the Voicemail icon 📼 on the Home screen. If you're using voicemail for the first time, follow the prompts for setting up your voicemail box, including choosing a password and selecting or recording a message.

Visual Voicemail

Looking for something niftier? Depending on your carrier, the Galaxy S4 may have *visual voicemail*, which lets you see, listen to, and manage all your voicemails in a neat, chronological list instead of dealing with a bunch of prompts. For example, if you've got 17 messages, and you want to listen to number 17, you don't need to listen to the other 16 first. Just tap message 17.

When you're playing a voicemail, you get visual controls for pausing and restarting and calling back. Tap the menu button at the top of the screen, and you can forward the call. There are several ways to delete a call. While you're listening to it, or after you've heard it, tap the Delete button at the top of the screen. When you're viewing the complete voicemail list, you can also delete any by holding your finger on it, and selecting Delete from the menu that appears.

For details, check with your carrier. You may be charged extra every month to use this service, often a fee of about $3.

Call Waiting

THE GALAXY S4 OFFERS Call Waiting, so it lets you know when you have an incoming call while you're already on a call. You can choose to either answer the new call—and put the first call on hold—or ignore it and let it go to voicemail. If you're a real fast talker, you can even keep both calls going at once and switch back and forth.

When you're on a call and another call comes in, your screen shows you the phone number of the second caller. The phone won't ring or vibrate, and at that point, you're still on the call with your first caller.

You have two choices:

- **Answer.** Answer the call as you would normally, and you can accept the incoming call. You get an "Accept call" notification message on your screen that gives you two choices: Put your first caller on hold and answer the call, or end the first call and answer the incoming call. If you answer the call and put the first caller on hold, you'll see the same screen as you do for conference calling, and can switch back and forth between the calls or merge them.

- **Ignore.** You can ignore the call as you normally ignore an incoming call, and proceed with your first call.

Call Forwarding

CALL FORWARDING LETS YOU have your Galaxy S4 calls rerouted to a different number. That way, when you're at home, you can have your cellphone calls ring on your landline and only have to deal with one phone. Even if the S4 is out of commission, you can still forward its calls to another phone and never miss a call.

If you haven't used call forwarding before, first make sure that the service is available from your carrier and activated. Check with the carrier for details.

Once you've done that, turning on call forwarding is a breeze. On your Galaxy S4, dial *72, and then, using the dialpad, enter the number where you want your calls to be forwarded. Press Send, and then wait to hear a confirmation tone or message. Once you've got confirmation, press "End call."

To turn off call forwarding, dial *73, press Send, and wait to hear a confirmation tone or message; then press "End call."

Caller ID

CALLER ID IS BUILT into the very guts of the Galaxy S4. That's why you see the phone number, and at times the caller's name, every time you get a call. And when you call someone, she sees your phone number as well. There's a way to block your number from being displayed, although as with call forwarding, you can't do it on the phone, but have to go through your carrier. Check your account to make sure you have the capability. Then when you want to block your phone number from being displayed when you make a call, tap *67, and then make the call. Your number won't be displayed on the receiving end. Instead, the person will see "Private" or "Anonymous" or something to that effect. When the call ends, Caller ID is reactivated; you'll have to tap *67 again to enable it on your next call.

You can also turn off outgoing Caller ID on your carrier's website, log into your wireless account and turn it off there. You may see an "Add/Change features" section, for example, where you can turn on the checkbox for Caller ID Blocking.

Bluetooth Earpieces

BLUETOOTH IS A SHORT-RANGE wireless technology designed to let all kinds of devices connect with one another, exchange or sync files and photos, or let a cellphone serve as a wireless modem for a computer.

With a little work you can get the S4 to do all that. Mostly, though, the phone's Bluetooth capabilities come in handy for hands-free talking with an earpiece.

If you've ever seen someone walking down the street, apparently talking to an invisible friend, you've seen Bluetooth in action (unless he really *was* talking to an invisible friend). The small device clips to your ear, and you talk into its microphone and listen in the tiny speaker in your ear.

The earpiece you use for making phone calls is typically monaural, and not designed for listening to music. If you're a music lover, invest in a *stereo* Bluetooth headset.

Pairing with a Bluetooth Earpiece

To use a Bluetooth earpiece with your phone, you'll need to *pair* them—that is, get the two of them talking to each other. The process is a bit geeky, but not difficult. The exact steps may vary a bit depending on the earpiece you're using. But generally, these are the steps you'll take:

1. **On the earpiece, turn on Bluetooth and make it discoverable.** In other words, set the earpiece so your Galaxy S4 can find it. Check the earpiece's documentation on how to do so.

2. **On your S4, turn on Bluetooth there, too.** You have several ways to do this. For example, pull down the Notification panel and tap the Bluetooth icon, if Bluetooth isn't already turned on. On the Home screen or a pane, press the Menu key, select Settings→Connections and then tap Bluetooth. Once Bluetooth is on, the S4 will start scanning for any nearby Bluetooth equipment. Your earpiece should show up on the list.

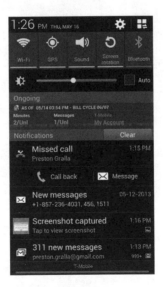

3. **Tap the earpiece's name and type a passcode.** You'll find the passcode in the earpiece's manual. The passcode is for security purposes, so that no one else can pair with the device. The number is usually between four and six digits, and you'll need to type it within a minute or so. You only need to enter the passcode once. After that, the pairing will happen automatically.

You should now be connected. You still dial using the Galaxy S4, but you can talk through the earpiece. Check the earpiece's documentation on how to answer calls, control the volume, and so on.

TIP Having trouble getting your new Bluetooth earpiece to work? Search the Internet for the make, model number, and the word *setup*. If you're having trouble, someone else likely had trouble as well, and you'll probably find a solution.

Bluetooth and Car Kits

An increasing number of cars include built-in Bluetooth so that you can pair your S4 with it. This way, you can make calls directly from your car's control panel, and hear calls over your car's speakers. You can do other nifty things, such as play music from your phone on your car's entertainment system.

If your car doesn't have built-in Bluetooth, there are plenty of Bluetooth car kits out there. Generally, pairing your S4 with a Bluetooth car kit is much the same as pairing it with a Bluetooth earpiece. How you use the car kit varies, of course. In some instances, you can dial a number on the car's touch-screen or answer the phone by pressing a button on the steering wheel.

TIP Don't be lulled into thinking that driving with hands-free calling is safe. Studies show that the danger in talking on a phone while driving isn't related to holding the phone—it's the distraction of holding a conversation while driving.

The Built-In Features

You'll learn to:
- Use the built-in Music app
- Create playlists
- Play Internet radio stations
- Play music on nearby devices
- Use the Google Cloud Music Player

CHAPTER 4

Music

THE GALAXY S4 DOES a great job of playing and managing music, so much so that you may no longer feel the need to carry around another music player. It includes an excellent built-in music player and manager, and a 3.5 mm headset stereo jack that you can connect to headphones or external speakers. You can connect wirelessly to Bluetooth speakers as well. Read this chapter and get ready to plug in and turn up the volume.

Where to Get Music

Before you play music, of course, you first need to get it onto your Galaxy S4. For details about how to do that, turn to page 336.

You can also buy or download music via S4 apps, such as the Amazon MP3 app. It may come with your Galaxy S4. If it doesn't, download it from Google Play (page 301). Tap the Amazon MP3 icon from the App Drawer to run the app. You'll need to have an Amazon account to pay for and download music, so set one up first if you want to use the app.

NOTE If you tap a download link on a web page for a music file in the Galaxy S4 browser, the file doesn't download to your phone. Instead, the S4 plays the music file, but doesn't add it to your collection.

Using the Music App

YOU PLAY AND MANAGE your music by using the Galaxy S4's Music app. Tap the Music icon in the App Drawer to launch it. The app organizes your music into seven different lists, through which you scroll like all other lists on your phone. Simply swipe to the right and left to see all of them, and then tap any you want to view or play:

- **Songs.** An alphabetical list of every song in your music collection. It shows the song name and artist. Tap a song to play it.

NOTE When you're in the music app, at the bottom of the screen, you see the name of the song you're playing. If you're not playing a song, you see the last song you played along with a control for playing the song. Tap it, and you're sent to the full player. (See page 106 for details.)

- **Playlists.** Here's where you'll find all your *playlists*—groups of songs that you've put together in a specific order, often for a specific purpose. For example, you might have several party playlists, a playlist of songs you like to listen to while you work, another for the gym, and so on.

NOTE In addition to the Music app built into the S4, Google also has a *cloud-based* music player app. With it, you can upload music from your PC or Mac to big Google computers (called *servers*), and then play that music on your phone, without actually having to store it on the phone. (Because your music lives in the cloud—get it?) The service and app are free and work like a charm. The app is called Play Music and is likely already on your S4. If it's not, though, download it from Google Play. There's also a for-pay version that's a streaming music service in which you pay a monthly fee and can stream music to your S4. See page 116 for details about the cloud music player.

To see the contents of a playlist, tap the playlist. Tap any song to play it from that point until the end of the playlist. To add a song to the playlist, press the Menu key, tap "Add to playlist," and then select songs to add from the list that appears. (You can also add songs to playlists while you're playing them, and in other ways as well. See page 112 for details.) When you press the Menu key, you get other ways to manage your playlist, including removing songs from the playlist, searching through the playlist, and changing settings (for the entire music app, not just for playlists).

- **Albums.** Lists all the CDs (albums) in your music collection. If a thumbnail picture of the album is available, you see it next to the album listing. Each album lists its name and its singer, composer, band, or orchestra. Tap the album to see a list of all the songs in the album. To play any song, tap it. The music app then plays from that point until the end of the album.

To add songs from an album to a playlist, when you're viewing an album, press the Menu key and select "Add to playlist." A list of all the songs in the playlist appears. Tap any you want to add to a playlist, and then select the playlist you want to add it to or create a new one.

• **Artists.** Lists every singer, composer, and band in your collection. Tap the artist's name, and you see a list of all her songs. To play any song, tap it.

The Galaxy S4 can play a wide variety of music files, including AAC, MP3, WAV, WMA, OGG, AAC+, and MIDI. Android by itself won't play WMA (Windows Music Audio) files, but Samsung gave the S4 a special piece of software called a *codec* so it can play them. For the same reason, it can also play WMV (Windows Media Video) videos.

- **Music Squares.** This unique-to Android feature examines all your music, and arranges tracks in different squares onscreen depending on the type of music—Calm, Exciting, Passionate, and Joyful. It lets you suggest to the S4 the sort of music you want to listen to without having to come up with specific songs or artists. You choose a mix of these music moods by swiping your finger across the grid.

Music Squares is a notoriously flaky feature, with many people complaining that it simply doesn't work. The ways in which people have fixed the problem are various, with some as simple as tapping the Menu key when you're in Music Squares, and then selecting "Library update," and others mind-bogglingly complex, including moving music to an external SD card, turning off the phone and removing the card and the battery, replacing them, rebooting...well, you get the picture. If Music Squares doesn't work for you and you've got your heart set on using it, do a Web search for *Music Squares*, and you'll find plenty of advice. There are also apps you can download that do much the same trick. Look in Play Store for Songza or Stereomood.

- **Folders.** Lists all your music by folder. Tap the folder to display all its files, and then tap a track to play it. The track will play, as will all the others from that point until the end of the listing.

- **Nearby devices.** Lists all nearby devices on your network that have music on them. Tap a device see the music on it. You can then play the music on the device, using the player, by tapping the music using the normal controls.

Playing Your Music

TAP A SONG TO play it. At the bottom of the screen, you see the usual controls for playing and pausing music and moving to the next track or the previous track. If you want to play your music in random order, tap the Shuffle icon at the top of the screen.

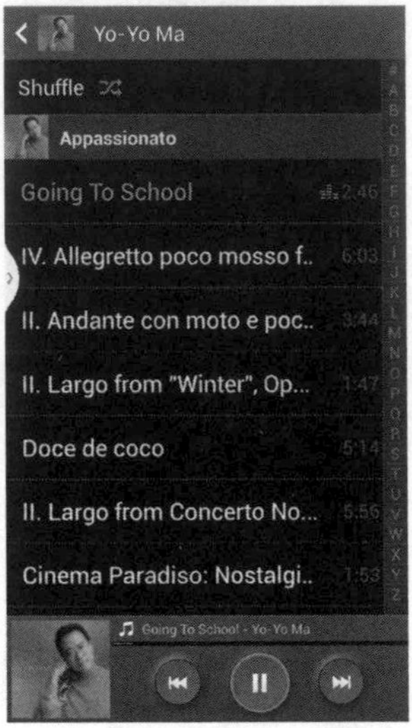

That's the simple, stripped-down version of the music player. Not satisfied with just playing, pausing, going to a next track or previous track, or shuffling your music? Then the S4's got just what you want. Tap the picture on the left side of the screen, either a picture of the album cover or a music-note icon. If you hold the screen sideways, you'll get the same features, but with a different look.

The full-blown music player appears. Its screen is loaded with extra controls and widgets. Among other controls, you'll find:

- **Pause/Play.** When music is playing, the button looks as it normally does on any music player. Tap it to pause; tap it to play again.

- **Previous, Next.** These controls work just as you'd expect. Tap Previous to skip to the beginning of the song you're playing or, if you're already at the beginning, to go back to the last song you just played. Tap Next to skip to the following song.

    Hold down one of the buttons, and you rewind or fast-forward through the song. As you hold, the rewinding or fast-forwarding accelerates. You'll hear the music as you speed forward or backward, sounding like a bizarre foreign language.

- **Slider.** Underneath the picture of the album from which the song is taken, you'll see a slider that shows you the song's progress. It includes the song's total length, and how much of it you've already played. Move the slider to go to a specific location in the song. To make the slider appear or disappear, tap the picture of the album.

- **Song and album information.** Up at the top of the screen you'll find the name of the singer, the name of the album, and the song being played.

- **List.** Tap the small musical note at lower right, and the big album image or musical note changes to the current song list. For example, if you're listening to a playlist, you'll see the entire playlist, and if you are playing an album, you'll see the whole album. From here, you can tap any other song to play it. To bring pack the picture of the album or musical note, tap the button again.

- **Shuffle.** The Galaxy S4 music player normally plays the songs in your playlist or album in order, from first to last. Tap the Shuffle button at lower left to play the songs in your current album or playlist in random order—you never know what's coming next. Tap it again to stop the shuffle.

- **Loop.** Can't get enough of the current album, playlist, or song? Tap the Loop button. This button starts out as an A with an arrow next to it. Tap it, and it changes into an A with a loop around it, signifying that the album or playlist will keep repeating. Tap it again and that changes to a number 1 with a loop around it, signifying that the track you're currently playing will keep repeating. When, you've had your fill, tap it again, and you get back to the A with an arrow, which means that looping is off.

- **Volume button.** Tap this upper-right button, and a volume slider appears. Drag to increase or decrease the volume. Tap the small icon at the bottom of the volume slider and you can select from a variety of built-in sound modes—from Normal, Pop, Rock, Dance, Jazz, Classical, and so on.

- **Other buttons.** Three other buttons reside here. Tap the down arrow at bottom left to return to the mini player. Then, tap the button at upper left to see nearby devices on your network whose music you might want to play. Tap the star just above the slider to turn it gold and identify the track as a favorite. That puts it on a playlist called, unsurprisingly, Favorites, that you can then play when you want. (See page 112 for more details on Favorites.)

More Music Controls and Features

Want even more music controls and features? Tap the Menu key and you'll be able to do all the following:

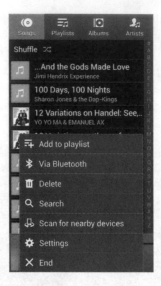

- **Add to playlist.** Lets you add a song or songs to a playlist. See page 112 for more details.

- **Via Bluetooth.** Lets you share the song via Bluetooth (see page 93).

- **Delete.** Deletes a song, playlist, and so on.

- **Search.** Lets you search for music.

- **Scan for nearby devices.** Looks for nearby devices that have music you might be able to play.

- **Settings.** Lets you change many settings; sound effects, music menu items, and so on.

- **End.** Exits the music player.

More Song Options

And yes, you've got even more options when you play songs. Hold your finger on a track, and a menu pops up:

- **Set as.** Lets you set the song as your ringtone, a caller ringtone, or an alarm tone.

- **Add to playlist.** Adds the song to a playlist. (See page 112 for details.)

- **Delete.** Deletes the track.

- **Details.** Shows you lots more details about the track, such as its genre, date it was first recorded, file format, size, and plenty more.

Creating Playlists

WHEN YOU TRANSFER MUSIC from your PC or Mac to your Galaxy S4 by using Windows Media Player, you also transfer over your playlists. But you're not dependent on that WMP to create playlists—you can also create and edit them from your phone.

The easiest way to do so is to tap the Menu key when you're playing a song, and then select "Add to playlist." A new screen appears that lists your music. Turn on the boxes next to the music you want to add to a playlist, and then tap Done. If you haven't created a playlist yet, tap the "Create playlist" button. Type a name for the playlist, tap OK, and voilà—a playlist with those songs on it. The playlist then appears in the Playlist area. If you've already created one or more playlists, select the playlist to which you want to add the music.

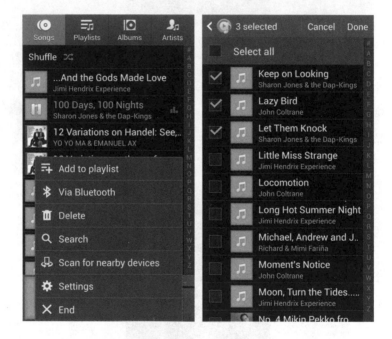

Even if you haven't imported or created any playlists, the S4 creates several automatically for you—"Favorite," "Recently added," "Most played," and "Recently played." These playlists don't show up when you try to add music to a playlist, because they're created and managed by the S4.

To edit a playlist, when you're in the list, hold your finger on a song. A menu appears that lets you remove the song from the playlist (it still stays in the Music app, but is removed from the playlist), add it to another playlist, set it as a ringtone, or see more details about the song.

Galaxy Radio

Another way to play music by using your Galaxy S4 is to use an app that turns the phone into an FM radio or streams music to the phone wirelessly. To use your S4 as an FM radio, head to Google Play and download any one of many apps, like Tune-In Radio (*www.tunein.com*).

There are also many apps that play streaming music to your S4, like Pandora (*www.pandora.com*) and Spotify (*www.spotify.com*); search for them by name in Google Play. In fact, if you already have a Pandora account that you use to play music from the Web, all your stations will already be set up when you use the S4's Pandora app. How's that for convenient?

Services like Pandora and Spotify have the seemingly psychic ability to learn what kind of music you like from the choices you make, and play similar songs for you. Spotify also lets you share music over Facebook, Twitter, and other means. With the S4, you can truly enjoy and share your tunes wherever you go.

Using Your Galaxy S4 While Playing Music

BECAUSE THE GALAXY S4 is built for multitasking, you can play music even when you're doing something else. Open the Music app, start the music, and then feel free to use other apps and features. The music keeps playing. While music is playing, a small button appears in the status bar. Drag down the Notification panel and tap the song playing, and you see a miniature set of controls for playing, pausing, and jumping forward and back in music. To head to the music player, tap the picture of the album.

Even when your phone is locked, if you were listening to music before the Galaxy S4 locked itself, it keeps playing. Turn on the screen, even though the phone remains locked, and you'll see music controls. You can pause and play music, as well as skip to the next song or go back to a previous song, without having to unlock the Galaxy S4.

Playing Music and Media on Other Devices

THE GALAXY S4 LETS you share, view, and play music, videos, and photos, using a standard called DLNA—short for Digital Living Network Alliance. The S4 is DLNA-compliant, which means that it can share media with other DLNA devices, such as TVs, computers, and mobile devices. When you buy a device, look in the documentation to see if it's also DLNA compliant. You can also look for this logo on packaging or documentation:

NOTE If you're not sure whether you have a device that's DLNA-compliant, go to *www.dlna.org*. In addition to finding out more information about DLNA, you can do a search for your device and see if it supports DLNA.

Here's just some of what you can do with your Galaxy S4 and other DLNA devices:

- Stream your music, videos, and photos from your S4 to a DLNA device, such as a TV, PC, Xbox, or Playstation 3.

- Transfer music and picture files from your phone to your PC.

- Stream videos from the phone to your TV.

- Browse any videos you have stored on your PC, using the Galaxy S4, and then stream the video to your TV by using an HDMI cable (see page 145 for details about HDMI).

And that's just a few of the possibilities and permutations with your Galaxy S4 and DLNA; this section can't cover them all.

Out of the box, the S4 is set up to use DLNA. In the Music app, when the phone scans your network to see if there are nearby devices from which it can play music, it's actually using DLNA.

For sharing with other devices such as TVs, check the device documentation for how to share via DLNA. And you can also customize your DLNA settings on your S4. To do it, pull down the Notification panel, then tap the settings icon and tap "Nearby devices." You'll then be able to change your DLNA settings, such as what media content you want to share, what devices you want to share with, and so on.

Google Music Cloud Player App

THE GOOGLE MUSIC CLOUD Player may forever change the way you manage—and even think about—your music. It lets you play music on your phone that isn't actually *on* the phone, but instead lives in the *cloud*—basically big Google computers called servers that store your music and stream it to your Galaxy S4 (or any other device, for that matter).

The app's official name is Google Play Music, and it should come installed on your S4. If it isn't, you can download it from Google Play. Then, install the Play Music software on your PC or Mac (whichever computer houses your music collection). You then tell the software to upload the music to the cloud. After that, you install Play Music on your S4 (or, indeed, any other Android device). At that point, you can listen to your music from the cloud—as long as you have a 3G, 4G, or WiFi connection.

Once you've got everything installed, just tap the Play Music app and start playing. It integrates with the S4's normal music player, so it plays any music you've got installed there, as well as music from the cloud.

And you can also subscribe to unlimited music streaming, and can play thousands of tracks for a monthly fee, much like the streaming Spotify music service. Play Music will give you all the details.

Keep in mind that there will be times when your music isn't available from the cloud—because you're not connected to the Internet—so you can choose to hide streamed music at that point. You can also set a variety of other options, such as whether to only stream music when connected via WiFi rather than via 3G or 4G. That way, you won't eat up data from you data plan.

The cloud player is a fabulous player, especially if you have a digital music collection on a PC or Mac. Check it out and listen to your beloved music anywhere!

You'll learn to:

- View photos and videos in the Gallery

- Create slideshows

- Take photos and videos

- Use Drama mode, Dual mode, and other modes

- Use the S4 as a universal remote

CHAPTER 5

Camera, Photos, and Video

THE SAMSUNG GALAXY S4 has a big 5-inch screen for a good reason—it's designed to excel at displaying photos and videos, and capturing them as well. It has a built-in 13-megapixel camera, so you can take photos in very high resolution, as well as a 2-megapixel front-facing camera for videoconferencing. It can shoot even and play HD (high definition) video. (For techies, it records video at 1080p.)

In other words, you've got more than just a phone in your pocket—you've got a multimedia marvel as well. And with a bit of mucking around and tweaking, you can even watch videos from it on a big-screen TV.

This chapter gives you all the details about taking and viewing photos and videos with your Galaxy S4, viewing pictures and videos transferred to your S4 from your computer, and viewing photos and videos from your phone on TVs and other monitors.

Opening the Gallery

THERE ARE FIVE MAIN ways to see photos or videos into your Galaxy S4:

- Transferring them from your PC or Mac (see Chapter 13 for details).

- Taking a photo using the Galaxy S4's built-in camera.

- Downloading them from the Web.

- Getting them in email attachments.
- Using Google's Picasa app.
- Using the DropBox cloud-based file storage service.

No matter how you get them, though, you view them the same way, by using the Gallery app. Here's how:

1. **In the App Drawer, tap the Gallery icon.** The Gallery app launches. You'll see photos organized by individual albums. Even if you haven't yet taken a single photo with your S4 (or transferred any), you may still find albums there, because the S4 automatically imports photos from Google's Picasa photo service and the DropBox cloud-based file-storage service. So if you've used those services, you've got photos.

   When you first run Gallery, it organizes your photos by album. But you can view them in other ways as well—by the time they were taken, by location, by your favorite photos, and so on. To change your view, tap the drop-down triangle next to Albums and choose how they're organized. For a bit of fun, choose Spiral, and you'll see them spiraling across your screen. No matter how you organize them, though, the way you view them is the same.

TIP If you use photos a lot, drag the Gallery icon to your Home screen (page 30).

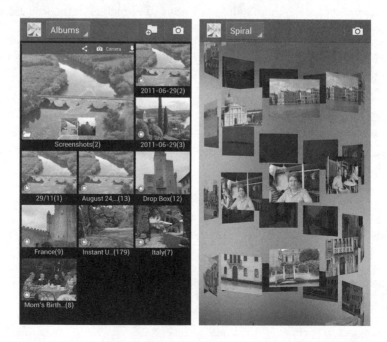

2. **Tap any of the albums or other sources that contain your photos— DropBox, Picasa, or whichever.** The screen fills with thumbnails of photos in the album. You can view the thumbnails, as well as entire albums and individual photos, either vertically or horizontally. Just turn the phone in the direction you wish to view them.

3. **Tap the photo you want to view.**

The phone displays the photo on its big, beautiful screen. Now you can see why you wanted the Galaxy S4—that extra screen real estate pays off when viewing photos.

A variety of buttons appear onscreen for a moment or two, then disappear. Tap the photo to make them appear again.

Depending on the photo's length-to-width ratio, it may not fill the entire screen. If it doesn't, you'll see black space along the sides or at the top and bottom.

4. Tap the Gallery button at the top right  and you're sent back to the Gallery. Tap the Share button  and you share your photos in many different ways, from email to text messaging, via Bluetooth, using social media, and more. The exact ways you can share will vary according to what apps you've got on your S4.

The next button is the Camera button: ◎ Tap it to launch the camera to take photos or videos. (You'll learn how to do both later in this chapter.) The next button you come to varies according to whether the photo is on a cloud-based storage service Picasa or DropBox, or physically on the S4. If it's on a service like Picasa, you're actually looking at the photo over the Internet, not on your phone. But you can download it to your S4, if you want. Just tap the download button ⬇. The photo then downloads. You'll be able to see it in the Download album in the Gallery. If the photo is on your S4, then you won't see a Download button. Instead, there will be a button for deleting the photo 🗑. Tap it, and then tap OK to delete it, or tap Cancel to rescue it.

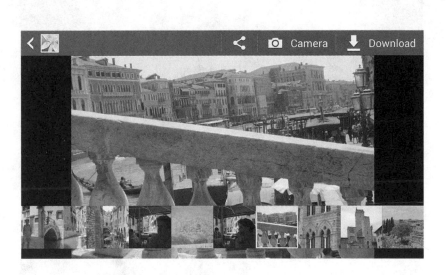

Look down at the bottom of the screen when the icons appear on the photo. You'll see thumbnails all of the photos in the album you're viewing. Tap any thumbnail, and you'll jump straight to that photo.

Viewing Pictures

Now that you've got photos on your screen, the fun begins—viewing them in different ways and flicking through them:

- **Zooming** means magnifying a photo, and you've got the power to do that at your fingertips—literally. Double-tap any part of the photo, and you zoom in on that area; double-tap again and you zoom out. You can also use the thumb-and-forefinger spread technique to zoom in more precise increments. Once you've zoomed in this way, you can zoom back out by using the two-finger pinch technique. (Flip back to page 37 for a refresher on all these techniques.)

- **Panning** means to move the photo around the screen after you've zoomed in, so you can see different areas. Use your finger to drag the photo around. As with Zooming, panning works the same whether you're holding the phone horizontally or vertically.

- **Rotating** means to turn your phone 90 degrees so it's sideways. When you do so, the photo rotates and fills the screen using the new orientation. This technique is especially useful when you have a horizontal photo that looks small when your S4 is in its normal vertical position. Rotate the phone, and like magic, the picture rotates and fills the screen properly. Similarly, if you're viewing a vertical picture while holding the phone horizontally, simply rotate the phone 90 degrees, and your photo rotates as well.

- **Flicking** advances you to the next or previous photo in your list. Flick from right to left to view the next photo, and from left to right to view the previous one.

Tagging Faces in Photos

ONE OF THE NIFTIEST things you can do on social media sites such as Facebook are to share *tagged* photos of yourself, family, and friends. It's a great way to share. In any photos on the G4 with pictures of people's faces, you can identify the people in the photo by name—that is, tag them. Then, when you put the photo up on a social media site people can see the names of the people in the photos. More amazingly, people who've been tagged in the photos get a notification that a tagged photo of them is available, and they can then view it.

Tagging photos is easy. Open the photo as you would normally, and then tap the photo. Boxes appear around the faces of every person on the photo. The S4 will then do some photo magic, and will automatically tag any people whose faces it knows—for example, you. For other photos, tap the "Add name" and follow the instructions for tagging the person.

That's all it takes. Now when you and your friends look at photos on your favorite social media site, you'll be able to remember who's who.

More Photo Options

WHEN YOU'RE VIEWING A photo, you've got even more options, available when you press the Menu key:

> **NOTE** All these options are only available for photos that are on your S4. If a photo is in the cloud, you only get a small subset of these options—creating a slideshow, scanning for nearby devices to share photos with, seeing photo details, and changing settings.

- **Edit.** Gives you a solid set of tools for editing photos, including dropping, rotating, changing colors, adding effects, and more. When you choose the Edit option, things get a bit confusing at first. A screen appears, telling you that you need to select a picture area in order to edit the photo. That's not really true; you only need to do that if you want to edit only a section of the photo, rather than the entire photo. So go ahead and click OK to get to the main color tools. However, if you *do* want to edit only a section of the photo, hold your finger on the photo, and a screen appears that lets you select only a section of the photo, or the entire photo. When you do that, a different set of tools appears, for selecting a portion of the photo. After you select a piece of the photo, you can edit in the same way you can the entire photo. You can also do add some cool effects—see the box on page 128.

Edit Away

The S4 gives you surprisingly powerful photo-editing tools right on the phone. They're worth checking out. True, they're not up to the level of a high-powered, expensive piece of software like Photoshop, but you can't beat free.

For a start, you can crop any photo and rotate it. The Rotate tool is surprisingly robust. Tap it and you can rotate the photo to the right or left, as well as flip it horizontally or vertically.

The Color tool is similarly useful. Tap it, and you get eight ways to edit the color, adjusting the brightness, the contrast, the color saturation, and so on. Perhaps most useful of all is the Autoadjust tool that analyzes the photos and makes the changes automatically that the S4 thinks will improve it.

Finally, there's the Effect tool. You can add nearly two dozen instant effects, like sepia, grayscale, negative, fish eye, engraving, and more.

Favorite. Marks the photo as a Favorite. Once you've designated Favorites, you can then hop to them quickly in the Gallery. If you're viewing a photo already marked as a Favorite, the menu will let you remove it.

- **Slideshow.** Runs an onscreen slideshow of your photos in your current album or view. You can choose transitions between slides, choose music to accompany the show, adjust how long each photo should display, and choose whether to show the oldest photo first or the newest one first.

- **Photo Frame.** Lets you put a frame around the photo, and draw on the photo as well.

- **Photo Note.** Lets you draw directly on the photo and annotate it.

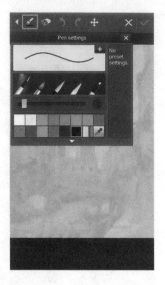

- **Copy to clipboard.** Does just what it says: Copies the entire photo to the clipboard so that you can paste it somewhere, like into an email.

- **Print.** If you've got a wireless printer to which you can connect your S4, this will print the photo. You may have a printer connection without knowing it, for example, if you're connected to a home network that has a printer connect directly to the network.

- **Rename.** Lets you rename the photo.

- **Set as.** This nifty choice lets you do lots of things with the photo, such as setting it as your home or lock screen, or as a contact photo. Make your choice, and you can then crop the section of the photo you want to use (page 33). After that, the S4 does its magic.

- **Buddy photo share.** Detects whether the photo has a face on it. If it does, you can tag the photo and then share it via social network services and other ways.

- **Rotate left.** Rotates the photo to the left.

- **Rotate right.** Rotates the photo to the right.

- **Crop.** Lets you crop the photo.

- **Detect text.** Tap this one and wait for the magic. It examines your photo in search of any text in it. If it finds any, it recognizes the letters and words, and turns it into text that you can then save or share with others.

- **Scan for nearby devices.** Looks around to see whether there are any other wireless devices with which it can communicate. If it finds any, you can share the photo with it.

- **Details.** Shows you all the details you've ever wanted—and more—about the photo. You'll find the size, resolution, time it was taken, focal length, exposure time...you get the idea.

Details

Title: Venice 055
Type: JPEG
Time: 05/26/2009 3:28PM
Album: 2009-06-28 Venice
Size: 385 KB
Resolution: 1500x2000
Orientation: 0°
Manufacturer: Canon
Model: Canon PowerShot SD780 IS
Flash: Off
Focal length: 17.9MM
White balance: Auto
Aperture: 5.8
Exposure time: 1/625
ISO: 125
Path: /storage/emulated/0/

OK

- **Settings.** This is a somewhat weird option to put in the Gallery. It lets you change your account settings. But there is some method to the madness, because it also lets you turn the photo tag options on and off.

Working with Multiple Photos

IN THE PREVIOUS SECTION, you learned about ways to work with individual photos. But what if you want to work with multiple photos at once—delete them, share them, and so on? On the S4, it's easy.

When you're viewing photos in an album, by time, or other grouping, press the Menu key and tap "Select item." Small checkboxes appear at the top of each photo. Tap the photos you want to select—the boxes turn green when selected.

When you select photos, the top of the screen displays the number of photos you've selected. Tap that top box, and on the screen that appears you can select all the photos, or deselect them all. To deselect individual ones, tap the green box, and the check-mark goes away.

Now you can perform actions on the photos you're selected. You've got two options at upper right for sharing the selected photos or deleting them. Press the Menu key for many more choices, including many that you get when you are looking at an individual photo (page 127). But you also get a few others:

NOTE When you tap Details you'll see information about all the photos you've selected, including how many items you've chosen, and the dates of the first and last photos taken.

- **Move.** Lets you move them to a different album.

- **Copy.** Lets you copy them to a different album.

- **Create collage.** Creates a collage out of photos you've chosen. You can select from a variety of collage styles, add and remove photos, and so on. The S4 saves it in an album called Collage.

NOTE You can only create a collage when you select four or fewer photos. Select five or more and the Create Collage option doesn't even appear on the menu. Strange, but true.

- **Create a story album.** Creates a very cool album out of the photos you've chosen. It uses one photo for the cover and artistically arranges multiple photos on each album screen.

- **Hide items.** Hides the selected photos from view. Don't worry, though, they don't vanish forever. If you want to see them again, select the album, press the Menu key and select "Show hidden items." That will display just the items you've hidden. If you want to unhide the items, you can do that, too. When you're showing the hidden items, select them all and then choose to display them.

Videos in the Gallery

THE WAY YOU VIEW and work with videos in the Galaxy S4 is essentially identical to the way you work with photos, with a few minor differences:

- You can spot videos in the Gallery by a right-facing triangle on their thumbnail.

- Rotate your S4 by 90 degrees when you're viewing videos, since they're usually taken with a horizontal orientation (as are the ones you shoot on your S4).

Do you, a friend, or a loved one suffer form "vertical video syndrome?" This fictitious disease afflicts people who hold their phones vertically when taking videos, which means that they will look small and squashed when played the way videos are supposed to be viewed—in horizontal orientation, like on a television or in a movie theater. In June 2012, a tongue-in-cheek Public Service Announcement was uploaded to YouTube warning about this threat. In a little over its first year, it received more than 3.3 million views.

- When you tap a video, it opens with a right-facing triangle—the Play button. Before you play the video, buttons appear at the top right of the screen to let you share the video with others, trim the video, and delete it. If you press the Menu key, you'll get a selection of options, including making the video a Favorite, renaming it, scanning for nearby devices to share it with, getting details about it, and changing video settings. These are the same options as for photos; see page 127 for details.

- Tap the triangle to play the video. When the video plays, a circle moves along a progress bar to show where you are in the video. Drag the circle forward or back to move forward or back in the video. Tap the Pause button to pause the video; tap the Play button to start playing it again. You'll also see the total time of the video, and for how long the current video has played. You can also mute the video. There are also buttons for playing the video full screen, and playing the video on another device such as a TV. (For details about connecting your S4 to a TV, see page 145.)

Here's a handy video feature for multitaskers: Tap the video when it's playing to bring up the player controls, and then tap the small icon on the lower right hand side of the screen. The current video plays in a small screen inside the larger screen. That way, you can use the Gallery to look at photos, for example, and keep watching the video. Tap the X on the mini video window to close it.

Press the Menu key for a variety of options, including sharing the video, getting details about the video, turning off the video's audio, and seeing a *chapter preview*, which lets you see just the video's main sections. You can then tap any section to jump to it.

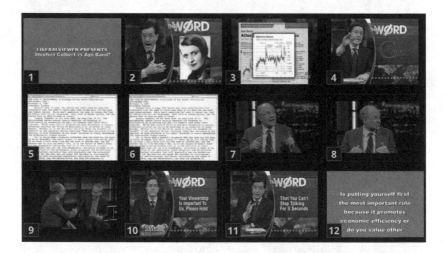

Taking Still Photos

IF YOU'RE USED TO no-frills smartphone cameras that do little more than let you point and shoot grainy, low-resolution photos, you're in for a surprise with the Galaxy S4. It sports a 13-megapixel camera that takes sharp, vivid photos. And it also has a front-facing camera that takes photos at 2 megapixels. Although you'll mainly use it for videochats, it's also useful for taking selfies and the S4's great Dual mode feature that lets you take a combined photo with both cameras simultaneously. (See page 140 for details.)

Camera lens   Camera lens

Fortunately, using the camera is still point-and-shoot simple. Frame your shot on the screen. You can use the camera either in the normal vertical orientation, or turn it 90 degrees for a wider shot. Zoom in and out by using the Galaxy S4's volume control button, which now miraculously acts as a zoom control. Then tap the button on the right side of the screen to take the photograph.

TIP The camera also includes a handy onscreen zoom feature, which features 4X zoom. To zoom in, pinch your fingers together; to zoom out, spread them apart.

You'll hear the familiar snapping sound of a photo being taken. A small thumbnail of your new photo is displayed in the lower left-hand corner of the viewfinder. Tap it to view the big image.

NOTE When you're not taking pictures, you can also get them onto your S4 by transferring them from your computer. See page 332.

Using the Onscreen Controls

THE CAMERA HAS A variety of convenient onscreen controls.

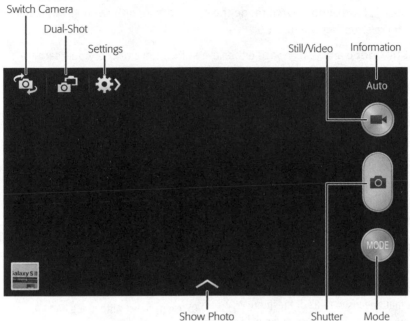

- **Switch camera** toggles between the normal camera and the camera facing you. Use the camera facing you for a self-portrait (think of it as the "selfie" button) or during video chats.

- **Dual-shot** lets you take a composite photo of what the front- and back-facing cameras currently see. (For more, see the box on page 140.)

- **Settings** lets you choose from a variety of settings, including the shooting mode (single shot, panorama, and so on), the scene mode (portrait, landscape, and so on), and more.

- **Information** shows you current information about the photo or video you're taking, for example, what mode the camera is in, or how much space a video you're shooting will take up.

- **Still/Video** lets you choose either the still camera or the video camera.

- **Shutter** snaps the picture.

- **Mode** lets you select from many different modes of taking photos—for sports photos, night photos, panoramas, and more. (For details, see the next section.)

- **Show Photo** that shows a photo strip of other photos you've taken. Tap any to open it.

GEM IN THE ROUGH

Challenge to a Dual Shot

Dual shot lets you take photos of images with your front and back cameras simultaneously. Think of the interesting effects you can come up with—a picture of the band onstage juxtaposed with your own rapt reaction. A picture of the summit that includes you in your climbing gear. Imagine a kind of postcard effect, in which you get a scenic vista as the background (taken with the camera you normally use to take photos), and then put a frame that looks like a stamp around the photo that the front-facing camera takes.

To use it, select Auto mode and tap the Dual Shot icon—it's an overlapping image of the front and back of the camera symbol. You can play around with choosing borders other than a stamp for the image you take with the front-facing camera. To do so, tap the arrow at the bottom of the screen and choose which one you want to use.

Using Different Modes

THE CAMERA'S PRESET SHOOTING modes represent one of its most powerful features. They automatically take the best pictures for what you're currently shooting. Tap the Mode button to see them all. To use them, just follow the onscreen directions. Make sure to play around with them, because you get a number of amazing ones.

- **Auto** mode chooses what the camera thinks are the best settings for the current conditions. For example, on a bright, sunny day it will adjust to prevent the picture from getting washed out.

- **Panorama** mode lets you stitch together a panorama from multiple photos so that you'll literally get the big picture.

- **Night** mode adjusts the settings for night shooting so your photos will be legible and it will be easy to pick out details, even though you did your shooting at night.

- **Sports** mode is ideal for taking pictures of fast movements, so that rather than showing a blur of motion, your photos will be crisp.

- **Drama** mode creates a truly striking effect. It lets you take a series of photos of a moving subject and then merges them into a single shot with multiple images showing the movement over time.

NOTE Only people who also have a Galaxy S4 will be able to hear the sounds from Sound & Shot mode.

- **Sound & shot** mode lets you can add a few seconds of background sound to a picture. It's like an audio photo. (What's next—smellavision?)

There are a lot more modes as well, so make sure to check them all out. The others are Beauty face (makes your face look as good as possible), Best photo (takes a series of photos and choose one to save), Best face (takes five pictures quickly, and the software will automatically select the best photos of faces in all five, and save them), Animated photo (makes a photo move), Rich tone (takes pictures of a scene or person at different exposures and combines them into a single image), and Eraser (lets you erase moving objects from a photo).

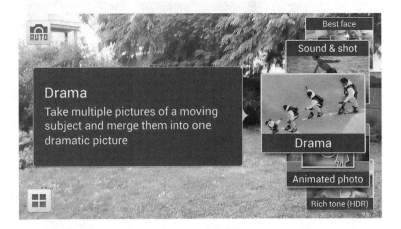

Drama Mode

Drama mode is a bit hard to describe, but once you get the hang of it, you may get hooked. Turn it on, and the S4's camera takes a continuous set of frames of a location for about five seconds— for example, your daughter doing a handstand. The S4 detects the person moving in the photos, and stitches together multiple pictures of the person against the static background, so you see the person's movements over time in a single photo. Sort of a time-lapse effect.

To get the best results with Drama mode, you need to make sure that the person in the frame isn't too large or too small, and that they don't move too slowly or too quickly. But it should only take you a few minutes to get it right. Once you do, you may never stop playing with it.

Customizing Your Camera Settings

NOT A POINT-AND-SHOOT TYPE? Like to fiddle with your camera's settings for true photographic control? Then you've got a friend in the Galaxy S4, because it's got ways to customize them seven ways to Sunday. When you're using the camera, press the menu key. You've got two choices for customizing your settings. A Help button also appears.

- **Edit quick settings.** Brings up a grid of icons that let you alter the most common settings you'll likely use, such as changing the white balance, using a GPS tag or not, using the anti-shake and video stabilization features, changing your exposure value, and more. Just tap the icon of the feature you want to customize, and follow the instructions.

- **Settings.** Gives you access to some of the same settings that "Edit quick settings" does, plus some extras, such as whether to use face detection, a smart feature that recognizes faces and focuses the camera on them. (Nothing ruins a picture more than a blurry face.)

Taking Video

TO TAKE THE VIDEO, tap the camera/video button at upper right. The video immediately starts recording. At the upper left, a red button with the word REC appears, and a number next to it tells you how much time in your video-taking has elapsed. At the upper-right, a number tells you how much memory the video is taking up as you shoot.

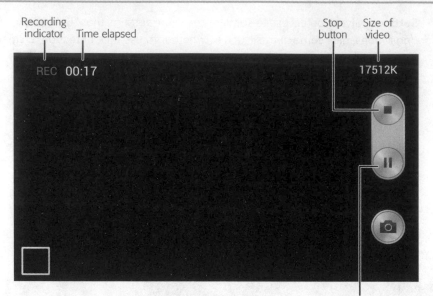

Recording indicator · Time elapsed · Stop button · Size of video

REC 00:17 · 17512K

Pause button

The Pause and Stop buttons let you discontinue recording. When you do that, you return to the still camera. You can zoom in and out in the same way that you can with the still camera, by pinching or spreading your fingers, or using the volume buttons.

NOTE If you want to change video options, such as using a video stabilizer, you can't do it from video mode. Instead, you have to switch back to the still camera and select your options, as outlined on page 142.

Playing S4 Video on Your TV

THE S4 INCLUDES A somewhat secret feature that you might find extremely useful: You can play video from it on your TV. And it's not just video you can play there. You can also display photos on your TV and even play games on your S4 and see them on your TV. In fact, anything that you see on your S4, you can send over to your TV.

To do it, you rig up a way to connect your S4 to a TV. Alternatively, if you have a Samsung TV, you may be able to connect wirelessly.

Connecting to the TV by Cable

First, you need to buy a special cable from Samsung, an MHL-to-HDMI adapter. (Get it at this URL: *http://bit.ly/15m7rD6*.) Then buy an HDMI cord, available from any electronics store or online. Now follow these steps:

1. **On the S4**, pull down the Notification panel and tap Settings→My device→⚐ Accessory, then turn on the checkbox next to "Audio output mode."

2. **Plug your normal wall charger into the USB port at the bottom of the S4**, and then plug one end of the MHL-to-HDMI adapter into that. (Only one end of the adapter fits.)

3. **Plug one end of the HDMI cable to the MHL-to-HDMI adapter**, and the other end to an HDMI port on your TV. You've now made a connection between your S4 and your TV.

4. **On your TV**, switch the input to the HDMI port where you've just plugged in the MHL-to-HDMI adapter. You should now see whatever is on your S4 mirrored onto your TV.

This method generally provides better audio quality than a wireless connection, and you also won't tend to experience laggy video. On the other hand, your S4 will have to be near enough to your TV so the wires reach.

Connecting to a Samsung TV Wirelessly

This method only works if you have a specific kind of Samsung TV—called a Smart TV. Even then, setting up a wireless connection is a bit dicier. In theory, you merely need to change a setting on your S4, and like magic, its screen gets mirrored to your nearby TV. But theory rarely works as well as practice. Suffice it to say, don't go buy a Smart TV just for this one purpose. And if you do, double-check the documentation to ensure that it will work.

Say you do have the right Samsung TV. On the S4, pull down the Notification panel and tap Settings→Connections→Screen Mirroring. Your S4 automatically looks around, searching for a device that will let it do screen mirroring. Your TV will show up on the list. Tap it, and you'll be mirroring what's on your S4 onto your TV.

Using Your S4 As a Universal Remote

THERE'S ONE MORE PIECE of TV magic your S4 can perform—you can use it as a universal remote to control your TV, streaming music player, and more. It's not always easy to do, and it may not work at all, but it's worth a shot. To do it, make sure your TV turned off. Then launch the WatchON app. You'll be walked through a series of screens asking you your location, your cable provider, and so on. You'll also have to either sign into your Samsung account, or if you don't yet have one, sign up for one (page 22).

Once that's done, you pair your S4 with your TV and cable box by following the onscreen instructions. If it works, you'll not only be able to use it as a remote, but take advantage of extra features as well. For example, you can use the WatchON guide rather than your TV guide for finding what you want to watch, you can stream from your Netflix account, and plenty more.

You'll learn to:
- Use Google Maps to map anything
- Fly around the world with Google Earth
- Get directions for walking, driving, biking and for public transportation
- Use the GPS with turn-by-turn navigation

CHAPTER 6

Maps and Navigation

WHAT'S THE MOST-USED SMARTPHONE feature these days? Quite possibly maps and navigation. And they can do much more than show you where you are or how to drive to your next destination. They can help you find a great nearby restaurant, pull up the fastest route to your friend's house via public transportation, show you which highways are clogged with traffic, and more.

Google Maps

Google Maps on the Galaxy S4 is the mobile version of the renowned Google Maps website (*http://maps.google.com*). In fact, the S4's Maps app is even more powerful than the web version, since it can incorporate GPS information.

Type any address or point of interest in the U.S.—or in many places all over the world—and you see a map. You can choose a street map, an aerial satellite photo, or a combination of the two (more on that on page 152).

But don't settle for looking around. You can also find nearby businesses, points of interest, and traffic congestion. Maps also offers turn-by-turn directions, even including public transportation in some cities. There are even bike-friendly maps.

Browsing Google Maps

Tap the Maps icon on a pane or in the App Drawer, and Google Maps launches. At first launch, if it finds your location, it will show a map of your neighborhood, with a pointer to your location. If it can't find you, you'll likely see a map of the United States, but you can work your way down to street level.

Navigate the map by dragging or flicking. Rotate the map's orientation by putting your thumb and second or third finger on the map and twisting. Zoom in by spreading your thumb and your second or third finger or tapping twice with a finger. Zoom out by pinching your fingers, or by tapping the screen once with two fingers (the amazing two-finger tap).

NOTE If you've turned on GPS (page 20), instead of displaying a map of the United States, Google Maps locates you and displays a map of your current location.

As you zoom in on the map, you'll see locations of interest—museums, libraries, schools, parks, restaurants, and so on. Tap any, and a balloon appears over it ,and at the bottom of the screen you see information about it, including ratings if people have reviewed it. There's also an icon of a car that you can tap to get driving directions to it.

Tap the balloon or the description at the bottom of the screen, and you get a lot more details, including a Street View photo of the location (if available), photos people have taken, and more. You can also call the establishment, read (and write) reviews, get directions, search for nearby businesses, and so on.

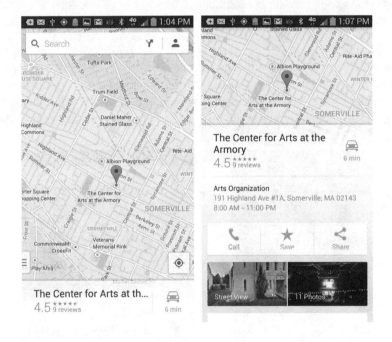

NOTE Google frequently updates its Maps app. The Maps app described here is the latest version as of the writing of this book. So if you have an older or newer version of Maps, it may vary from what you see here.

Changing Your View

Just being able to zoom in and out of a map down to the street level, or all the way out to the continent level, is pretty cool, but you have still more view options, which Google Maps calls *layers*. A layer is a specific type of view, or information superimposed over a view. To change a view to a different layer, look down at the bottom left of the screen for a small vertical rectangle with three lines inside it. Swipe that rectangle to the right. A menu swoops in from the left that shows you a bunch of choices, including a satellite view, a real-time traffic map, a link to Google Earth (more on that on page 154) and so on. Your current view will be highlighted with a dark band it. To switch to any other view, tap it.

NOTE In some views, such as the terrain view, you'll see a virtual compass needle at the top of the screen, showing you north, so you'll never lose your orientation no matter how bad your sense of direction.

The satellite view, unsurprisingly, is an actual satellite photo of the location. Layered on top of it is the normal Google map, making it easy to see streets, street names, and landmarks. As you zoom in, the photo may at first appear blurry, and it may take a little while for the image to resolve itself, so be patient.

The layers on Google Maps sometimes change, as Google adds new information, and as it makes deals with other companies to add their layers. So check layers often, to see what new things you have in store.

Traffic

The map can show you how bad the traffic is on highways and major metropolitan thoroughfares. Turn on the Traffic layer, and, where available, the app indicates traffic congestion by the following color-coding:

- **Green** means the traffic is flowing very nicely—at least 50 miles per hour.

- **Yellow** indicates slower-moving traffic, between 25 and 50 miles per hour.

- **Red** means a traffic jam; avoid it if you can. It means that traffic is moving at less than 25 miles per hour.

Make sure to look for small orange icons with a symbol of a man at work. They show where there is construction or maintenance going on. Tap any of the symbols, and you get a description of the work.

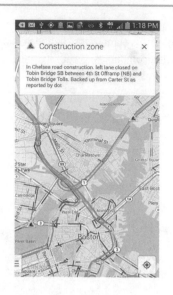

NOTE You can help Google get more accurate information about traffic in your area. Before you start driving, turn on the GPS on your phone and turn on the My Location feature. When you do that, anonymous information about your location and driving speed is sent to Google, which uses that to help figure out the current traffic conditions.

Google Earth

For a truly awesome piece of mapping technology, check out the Google Earth layer. Google Earth lets you fly over anywhere on the planet in full, realistic 3D. It uses satellite photography, so you virtually visit realistic pictures of anywhere on earth. Want to visit the Coliseum in Rome, the Grand Canyon in Arizona, the Taj Mahal in India? You can do that and more. It also integrates with Google Maps so that you can overlay street names on top of satellite maps. There are even built-in "tour guides" to take you on tours of many places on earth. Make sure to look at the bottom of the screen for a small tab. If it's there, pull it up. You'll see photos of interesting places to visit. Tap any to see a video tour of it.

Street View

Street View is a full, 360-degree panoramic, photographic view of streets and an entire area—an entire city, if you like. Street View is a great way to plan, for example, a walking tour of downtown Boston. (Make sure to visit the State House and its golden dome on top of Beacon Hill if you head there.)

To use Street View, hold your finger on any location on a map, until the address appears at the bottom of the screen. Pull up the location from the bottom and select Street View.

Once you're in Street View, drag and flick to move around to change your view, or explore nearby streets. You can also drag around the little human figure to move through the streets. It's simple to do. You can also try Compass Mode, in which all you need to do is move the phone to get different views. To get into Compass Mode, press the Menu key when you're in Street View, and then select Compass Mode.

More Layers

As Google updates Maps, it continually adds (and sometimes takes away) layers. So you'll find plenty of layers to try out. Transit Lines shows public transportation on the map, and Bicycling shows bike paths.

Layers also changes depending on how you use Google Maps. If you use Google Maps to find businesses (see page 159 later in this section), it puts listings of businesses you've viewed online in layers. And if you've searched maps, it lists those searches as well, so you can quickly relaunch the search directly from layers.

The Compass Button

See that compass button on the bottom right corner of the screen? It's a magic find-me button. If you're looking at a map that isn't your current location—for example, if you're in Boston and you're looking at a map of San Francisco—just tap the compass, and it shows a map of your current location, with an indicator in the center of the map showing where you are. So if you're viewing a map of a place halfway across the world, you can always tap this button, to go to your current location.

For even more magic, if you're already looking at a map of your current location and tap the compass, becomes a *live* compass so you can see the direction in which you're viewing your map. Not only that, but you can also tilt your Galaxy S4, and the map orientation follows the direction of the tilt.

How the Galaxy S4 Finds Your Location

Google Maps' usefulness really comes into play when it's combined with the S4's ability to find your location. The phone finds where you are in one of three ways:

- **GPS.** The S4's built-in GPS chip works just like the one in a Garmin or TomTom, although it's not quite as accurate. (Hey, those devices *only* do GPS, not phone calls or games, so cut your phone some slack.) GPS works best when you have a good view of the sky. If not, the S4 switches to one of the following two location methods.

- **WiFi positioning.** The phone's WiFi chip can do more than just connect you to a WiFi network—it can also help determine your location. It does this by using information (from a large database) about WiFi networks near you. Then, using the information about the WiFi locations and your distance from them, it calculates your location. It's not as accurate as GPS, but it still works pretty well.

- **Cellular triangulation.** If GPS or WiFi doesn't do the trick, then the S4 calculates your location based on how close you are to various cellphone towers near you. It's not as accurate as GPS or WiFi positioning, but it's nice as a backup.

> **TIP** GPS and WiFi can use up a lot of juice from your battery. When you don't need them, turn them off.

Now that you know how the Galaxy S4 finds you, it's time to tell it to do its tricks.

You'll need to tell the S4 to find your location if you're going to use any of its location-based services, such as giving you turn-by-turn directions. Doing it is simplicity itself: As explained earlier, tap the compass button in the lower right. Google displays a blinking blue arrow to show your location.

> **NOTE** If the Galaxy S4 is not exactly sure about your precise location, it draws a blue circle around the blinking arrow, to show that you may be anywhere inside that location. The larger the circle, the less certainty Google has about your location.

As you walk, drive, bicycle, or move in some other way, the blue arrow moves as well. The arrow changes direction to show the direction in which you're moving.

Searching Maps

Google Maps makes it easy for you to search for a business or other location. Given that Google is the premier search site on the Internet, would you expect anything less?

To search, tap the Search button at the top of the screen, then type your search term into the search box that appears at the top. When Maps finds what you're looking for, it displays the location and shows a little pushpin in it.

There are countless ways to search the maps. Here are some of the most common:

- **Address.** Just type an address, including the state or Zip code. Don't bother with commas, and most of the time you can skip periods as well. You can use common abbreviations. So, if you type *157 w 57 ny ny*, you'll do a search for 157 West 57th Street, New York City, New York.

- **Intersection.** Type, for example, *massachusetts ave and cogswell cambridge ma*, and Google Maps displays the location at the intersection of Massachusetts Avenue and Cogswell Avenue in Cambridge, Massachusetts.

- **City.** Type, say, *san francisco ca*, and you'll see that city.

- **Zip code.** Type any Zip code, such as *02140*.

Cambridge, MA 02140

NOTE As you enter search terms, Google Maps displays a likely list of matching results. You can speed up entering your search by choosing from the right search term when it appears, rather than tapping in the entire address.

- **Point of interest.** Type *central park, boston common frog pond*, or *washington monument*, for example.

- **Airport code.** If you know the three-letter code, you can type, for example, *sfo* for the San Francisco International Airport, or *bos* for Boston's Logan Airport.

When Maps finds the location, it marks it with a pushpin and shows the address at the bottom of the screen. Pull the address up from the bottom of the screen to get more details about it.

Finding Businesses and Contacts

GOOGLE MAPS CAN EASILY find local businesses. Any business that you can find with a Google search, Maps can find, too. But Maps can also find the home and business addresses of your friends, which it does by tying into your Contacts list.

If you want to search for a business near your current location or any other place, first navigate to the area where you're looking for businesses. Then do a search for the kind of business you're looking for—restaurants, for example. On the map, it shows icons representing all the businesses matching your search. And it also may put a pin on the one closest to you, with details about it at the bottom of the screen.

To see a list of all matching searches—again, in this example, restaurants—tap the icon of a row of arrows next to the search box. It shows a listing of all matching businesses, including ratings and recommendations from various services or users of those various services such as Zagat (which Google happens to own). To get more information about any business, tap the listing. Information appears at the bottom of the Maps screen. Pull that information up and you'll see complete details about the business.

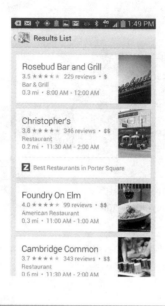

NOTE You may notice that when you search for a business, ads sometimes appear in various locations—for example, at the top of the screen that gives you a business's details. That's one of the ways Google makes money—by selling ads related to your map searches.

Which details you get varies according to what the business is and what information Google has about it. For restaurants and other businesses that have been reviewed by Zagat, for example, you'll get a detailed review. For a restaurant, you'll also see an overall rating; cost; and category ratings for food, décor, and service. There may be photos of the restaurant, and you can also upload photos yourself.

All businesses have three buttons associated with them: Call, Save, and Share. Tapping Call takes you to the S4's phone app and places the call. Tap Save, and the Save star turns gold. You also see the star on the map, in gold. From that point on, whenever you're using Maps, you'll see the gold stars of all businesses you want to visit again, right onscreen. Tap the star, and you see the description of the business in the usual way. To take away the star, when you're viewing its description, tap the gold star to turn it back to blue. Tap Share, and you can share information about the business via email, Bluetooth, chat, and other means. Next to the name of the business you'll see an icon of a car. Tap it, and you get you turn-by-turn directions to the business by foot, car, bicycle, or public transportation.

Locating the address of your friend's home or business is easy. You can do it, though, only if the address is in your Contact list. In Maps, search for the friend's name. If you have an address for the friend, it appears in the search results. Tap it, and you'll see the location on a map.

Gralla Preston
No reviews   2 min

You can also do it straight from the Contacts list. Find the person in your Contacts list (see page 78 for details). Next to the person's address or addresses, you see a small pushpin icon. Tap the pushpin to go to the location on Google Maps, complete with another pushpin.

Getting Directions

YOU'VE HEARD THE OLD cliché: Ask a Maine resident for directions, and the answer is inevitably, "Can't get there from here." Fortunately, Google Maps is much more helpful. Ask it the same question, and you get to choose how you want to get there: driving, walking, biking, or public transportation. Google provides directions for all four, or as many as it can find. (Not all types of directions are available to all places, but you'll have more choices in major metropolitan areas.)

You can get directions in many places throughout Maps, and throughout the Galaxy S4, because that capability is embedded very deep in the phone. So expect to find directions in many different places; for example, when you search for a business, find the location, and look at the page that gives you information about the business.

One surefire way to get directions anywhere in Maps: Tap the Directions icon just to the right of the search box at the top of Google Maps. A screen appears with a starting point, destination point, and icons for finding directions via car, public transportation, bicycle, and on foot. You'll also see a list of places you've just been to or searched for.

If the S4 knows your current location, it uses that as the starting point, and puts the words "My Location" in the starting point box. If you want a different starting point, tap My Location and then type an address into the text box that appears.

Next, choose your destination. Either choose from the list of recent searches and locations, or tap "Choose destination" and type where you want to go. Once you've set the starting point and destination, you're ready to go. Tap which kind of directions you want. You'll see a list of various options for getting there, each showing the amount of time it will take, the distance in miles, whether there's traffic, and the main routes you'll take. To choose one of the routes, tap it. You'll see a map with the directions laid out. Pull up the directions from the bottom of the screen to see a list of the turn-by-turn directions.

This example uses driving directions, but the other types of directions work much the same way. You can scroll through the entire list of directions. To zoom in on a specific section of the route, tap it on the direction list.

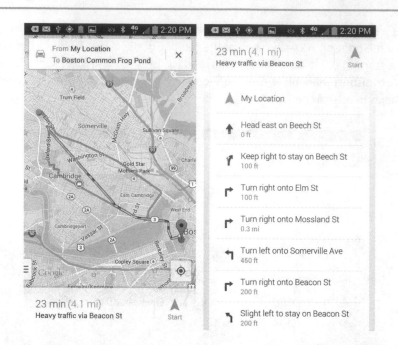

Tap the arrow buttons to get to the previous or next driving instructions. You can also return to your master list of instructions by tapping the S4's back button. In this way, you can switch back and forth between your overall directions and your current one. When you're looking at the list of overall directions, tap any instruction, and you'll see a close-up of the directions on the map.

Turn-by-Turn Navigation

GETTING TURN-BY-TURN DIRECTIONS IS helpful, but the Galaxy S4 offers something even more powerful—turn-by-turn navigation, just like the GPS gizmos made by Garmin and TomTom.

To use it, when you've typed in your location and final destination and are on the screen showing you the map view of your directions, tap the Start button at the bottom right of the screen (or, in the App Drawer, select Navigation).

You've turned your phone into a full-blown GPS navigator, complete with the usual annoying robot-like female voice. But it does the job. It tracks your location as you drive and displays it on a map. When you're approaching a turn, it tells you what to do ahead of time. It shows you all the information you need, including distance to your next turn, current location, time to your destination, and more. So forget buying that $300 GPS unit—it's built right into the S4.

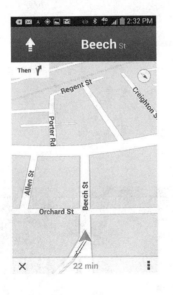

NOTE The turn-by-turn navigator requires your GPS to be turned on. You don't need your GPS turned on if you want to get normal directions on Google Maps, though.

Turn-by-turn navigation includes lots of other nice features built into it. Want to avoid highways or avoid tolls when you drive? Press the Menu key while you're in the Navigation app, and select Options. You can choose to avoid either or both.

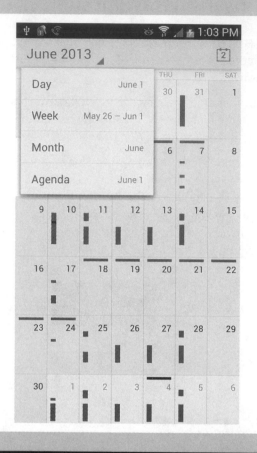

You'll learn to:
- Use different calendar views
- Create new appointments
- Accept an invitation
- Use multiple calendars
- Sync your calendar with Outlook

CHAPTER 7

Calendar

OF ALL THE WAYS you can use your Galaxy S4 to keep track of your life, the calendar may be the most important. Need to remember the meeting this afternoon, the dinner date tonight, the tennis game tomorrow morning? Forget paper-based calendars—the S4 puts them to shame.

Better still, Galaxy S4's calendar is actually Google's Calendar, so whether you're looking at your calendar on your phone or on your PC, you see the exact same thing, because the S4 syncs with Google Calendar. So no matter where you are, you know where you need to be today, tomorrow, and beyond.

Using the Calendar

TO RUN THE CALENDAR, tap the calendar icon in the App Drawer....well, things aren't quite that easy. The S4 comes with two calendar apps. One is the true-blue Google Calendar, and that's the calendar this chapter teaches and recommends. The other is a calendar from Samsung. The Samsung calendar can sync with Google Calendar, so they can work together.

NOTE The calendar that you see on the Home screen itself is likely to be the Samsung calendar, with a green icon. The Google calendar has a blue icon, and you can run it from the App Drawer—or drag its icon to the Home screen.

Samsung Calendar
Google Calendar

When you tap the calendar, it immediately opens. You're looking at events from Google Calendar, so if you're already using Google Calendar, you see your appointments instantly. If you've never used Google Calendar, you see a blank calendar.

You should see the most up-to-date calendar information on the Galaxy S4 calendar, because it syncs with Google Calendar on the Web. Syncing means that not only will your S4 calendar grab the latest information from your Google Calendar on the Web, but when you make any changes to your calendar on the S4, Google Calendar gets updated with that information as well.

Google Calendar Versus Samsung Calendar

On your S4, you've got a choice of which calendar to use, the Samsung Calendar or Google Calendar. This book strongly recommends going with Google, for several reasons. Perhaps most important is the fact that Google Calendar has become a standard for working with others, and using the same calendar that coworkers, family, and friends use is a big plus. Although the two calendars sync automatically, there's a lag when you use the Samsung Calendar rather than the Google Calendar, which could prove problematic if you need to update your events with others quickly.

In addition, Google Calendar is designed to work with all of Google's services—not just today's services, but tomorrow's as well. There's no guarantee how well the Samsung Calendar will work with all of Google's services, including future ones.

Google Calendar is one of Google's most important services, and so Google spends plenty of time adding new features. But calendaring is far from being one of Samsung's most important services, so it's not as likely that Samsung will update it as frequently as Google updates its calendar.

One final note; Google Calendar may not be on your S4 when you first run it. Each cell phone provider decides which apps go on and which don't. So if it's not on yours, head to Google Play and download it.

If you have more than one calendar in Google Calendar, you can see information from all calendars in one unified view.

NOTE When you first set up your phone, you either chose to set it up with an existing Google account, or create a new one. If you set it up with an existing account, your Galaxy S4 Calendar automatically syncs with your existing Google Calendar and displays all its events. If you created a new account, you start with a blank Google Calendar.

Calendar Views

There are four different ways you can look at your calendar, all within easy reach: Day, Week, Month, and Agenda. To get to any of them, tap the triangle to the right of the date on the top left of the screen.

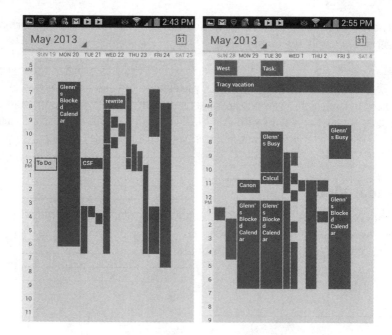

Here's what each does:

- **Day.** Tap here to see the calendar for the day you've highlighted, arranged by hour. Flick up and down to go through all hours of the day. Swipe your finger to the left or right to see the next day's calendar, or the previous day's calendar.

- **Week.** Here you get a weekly view. Swipe left or right to see the next week or previous week, and flick up and down to see later or earlier in the day.

- **Month.** This view shows you the entire current month. Horizontal colored bars indicate appointments and events, and show you their duration. Flick up and down to see the next or previous month.

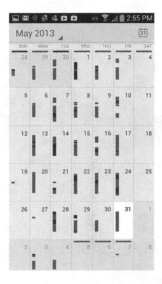

- **Agenda.** This scrolling view displays a list of all your events and appointments, not just for today or this week or next month, but years into the future, and years back in the past. It's a great way to see what's on the horizon or to get an overview of where your time is going. Scroll through them all by flicking. To see the details of any event or appointment, tap it, and the appointment opens.

Making an Appointment

There are two ways to create an appointment (which Calendar calls an *event*):

- In Month, Week, or Day view, hold your finger on the time you want to make an appointment. Then follow the instructions

NOTE When you run the Galaxy S4 calendar, you're not actually looking at Google Calendar on the Web. Instead, the Galaxy S4 calendar syncs with Google Calendar on the Web, but holds the information in the Galaxy S4 itself. So if you're in an area without reception, and you've previously updated Google Calendar on the Web but not yet synced it to your phone's calendar, the S4 calendar won't have any information you added since the last sync.

- In any view, press the Menu key and select New Event.

In some instances, like when you create a new event from the Month view, you only need to fill in a name and a time. In other instances, like when you create a new event from the Day view or from the Menu, a much more detailed form pops up, with plenty of information to fill in:

- **Event name.** Type a name for the event.

- **Location.** Tap here and enter the location for the event. As you type, Calendar looks in your address book for places that match the location as you're typing. That way you don't have to type an entire address. Type part of it, and then pick from the list.

- **From and To.** Tap this to choose the starting and ending times.

- **Time Zone.** Choose your time zone.

- **Guests.** Type in the name or names of the people you're inviting. As you type, the Calendar looks in your Contacts to find matching names. Select any that match to cut down on your typing.

- **Description.** What will you be doing? Having lunch? Meeting with your accountant? Skydiving? Tap in a description. If you're inviting other people, keep in mind that the invitation will be sent to them, so make the description clear (and keep it clean).

- **Repetition.** Will this be a one-time event, or one that repeats? If it repeats, the Calendar gives you a lot of flexibility about how to choose that. You can choose an event to repeat every day at the same time, every weekday at that time, once a week at that time and day of the week, monthly, or even yearly on that date. And there are more options as well.

- **Reminders.** After you create the event, the S4 can flash reminders before the event, letting you know that it's about to happen. You can choose at how far in advance to send the reminder, in any increment you want. Create as many reminders as you like by tapping the "Add reminder" button and filling in the details.

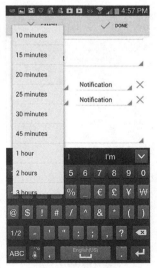

When you set a reminder time, you get a notification in the Notification panel when the time comes. Tap it to see the full reminder details. You can then Snooze the reminder so it'll disappear, and then pop up later according to what interval you've set. Or you can dismiss it, which means it will vanish forever, never to be heard from again.

To get even more event details, tap the reminder, and you see who orga-nized the appointment, who will be attending, the time, and the reminder interval. You can also accept the invitation, decline it, or tentatively accept it.

- **Show me as.** This option lets you choose whether you appear to be avail-able or not, if someone else wants to schedule you for an event held at the same time. Unless you change the default setting, the calendar assumes that you're not available—after all, you're already attending an event. But you can choose to make yourself available. For example, you may want to schedule an event for yourself tentatively, but be willing to change it in case someone needs to schedule an important appointment with you.

- **Privacy.** Sometimes, you want others to see an event you put on your calen-dar ("Board meeting"), and other times you won't want them to see it ("Dog grooming"). This option lets you make the event private, so only you can see it, or public, so others in the group calendar can see it.

Now you're ready to save your event. But there's one more thing you can do—color-code it. Tap the small icon of the palette near the top of the screen and from the colors that appear, choose one.

When you've done all that—and don't worry, it goes a lot faster than it sounds—tap the Save button. Your event now shows up on your calendar.

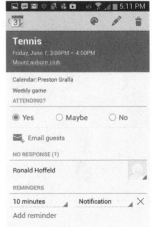

> **NOTE** For more information about using a group calendar and how to set all its options, head to your Google Calendar on the Web: *www.google.com/calendar*.

Getting Notifications About Who Has Accepted

If the appointment you created includes someone else—a dinner companion, let's say—he gets an email, and either accepts the invitation or not. You don't need to do anything to send the email; it gets sent automatically. (All of life should be so easy.) Once someone has accepted, you get a notification, and the acceptance is noted in the calendar.

Editing, Rescheduling, and Deleting Events

To look at one of your appointments, tap it. You see a summary of the appointment, including the date and time, place, attendees, and any reminders you've set. You also see whether attendees have confirmed that they'll attend.

To edit something you've scheduled, tap the Edit button at the top right of the screen. (It looks like a pencil). You're now at the familiar screen you used to create the event. You can edit everything about the event—name, location, place, duration, and so on. When you're done, tap Save.

Accepting an Invitation

If you're a social kind of guy or gal, you'll not only invite other people to events, but people will also invite you. If they use Google Calendar (or the Samsung calendar), they can use it to invite you to events.

You'll get the invitation by email, and it'll contain all pertinent information about the event, including the time and place, who scheduled it, who else is attending, and so on. Tap "More details" to get still more information. When you do so, you can choose to get more details via either your web browser or the calendar itself. In practice, both options have the same result—they launch your browser and take you to a Google Calendar page showing more details about the event.

Down at the bottom of the screen, you can say whether you're going—Yes, No, or for those unable to commit to anything (you know who you are), Maybe. Tap your response, and you go to a Google Calendar page confirming your choice. There you can write an additional note or change your response. The person creating the event gets notified of your status via email (or Outlook or whatever calendar program she uses).

You can accept invitations sent via email not only in your S4's email program, but also via your normal email service. So, for example, if you're a Gmail user, you can accept the invitation on Gmail either on the Web or on your phone.

Calendar and Geolocation

THE GALAXY S4 CALENDAR beats a paper-based one in many ways, and none better than geolocation. When you create an event, send an invitation, or receive one, the S4 turns it into a live link that, when clicked, shows its location in Google Maps—as long as an address is provided, or it's located at a business or landmark such as a restaurant, park, health club, and so on. Tap the Maps link to see it.

So when folks get your event invitation, they can see exactly where to go on Google Maps. And you can use all of Google Maps' capabilities, including getting directions, getting additional information about the business or area, seeing in in Street View, and more. (For more details about using Google Maps on the Galaxy S4, see page 150.)

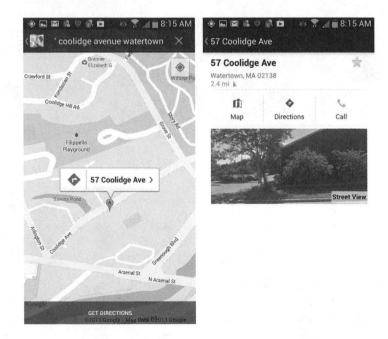

Working with Multiple Calendars

Got more than one Google Calendar? You can use them on your Calendar app on the S4 the same way you can use them in Google Calendar on the Web.

Whenever you create a new event, you see a down arrow next to your name in the Calendar area at the top of the event screen. Tap the arrow, and you see all your Google Calendars. Tap the calendar where you want the event to appear.

NOTE When you look at all your available calendars, you may notice one you don't remember creating, the Samsung Calendar. That's a calendar created for you automatically if you create a Samsung account (page 22). It's also the main calendar used by Samsung's built-in Calendar app. It syncs automatically with your Google calendars.

Your calendars are color-coded, so as you look at your schedule, you can see at a glance which calendar each event is on. The color appears just to the left of the event itself.

If you'd like, you can turn off the display of one or more of your calendars. When you're in the calendar, press the Menu key, and then tap "Calendars to display." You see a list of all your calendars, along with the color-coding for each. Next to each calendar is a checkbox. If there's a green checkmark next to it, the calendar is visible. If there's no checkmark, it's hidden. To make it visible, turn on the checkbox next to it, to hide it, take the check away. Don't worry; when you hide the calendar, you haven't deleted the calendar itself. You've just hidden it.

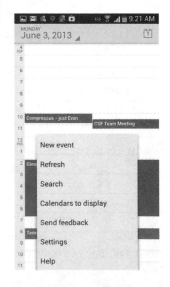

You can't change which calendar automatically appears in the Calendar area when you create a new event—it's the same one every time. So even if you choose a different calendar to create an event, the next time you create a new event, that first calendar is the one that automatically shows up. The same holds true for Google Calendar on the Web. Whichever calendar you created first is the calendar that automatically shows up.

More Calendar Options

PRESS THE MENU KEY, and you'll find a few more options for your calendar:

- **New event.** Tap here to create a new calendar item as described on page 171.

- **Refresh.** In theory, this should sync your calendar with Google Calendar on the Web. In practice...well, it's a bit mysterious what it actually does in practice. You may end up with a blank new event at a random time on the day you're viewing. As the saying goes, your mileage may vary.

- **Search.** This option gives you a nifty way to search your calendar. Tap it and type a search term. As you type, your calendar pulls up matching calendar entries. Select any calendar entry to search your calendar, or type in a different term. The calendar then displays matching results. Tap any calendar entry to go to the event.

- **Calendars to display.** As explained in the previous section, this option lets you decide which calendars to show.

- **Send feedback.** Got a problem or complaint with Google Calendar? Here's a way to get in touch with the folks at Google about it. You may or may not hear back from them. (Still, it's always good to get something off your chest; you'll live longer that way.)

- **Settings.** Settings, settings, and more settings. That's what you'll find here. You'll be able to change settings for all your calendars (choose General settings for that), or for individual calendar accounts (choose an individual calendar account for that). You can also create a new account by tapping "Add account" at the top of the screen.

General settings controls options such as whether to hide events that you or others have declined, determine which day should display as the first day of the week, whether to receive calendar notifications, whether your phone should ring and vibrate when you get a calendar notification, and so on. The settings for individual accounts are as bare-bones as it gets: You decide whether to show the account or any individual calendars in the account.

There's a difference between an account and an individual calendar. It's possible to have multiple calendars under a single account. (Confusing, isn't it?) So your main Google Account, for example, may have three calendars if you've set up three of them: Work, Home, and Travel. So what's an account? If you have more than one Google Account, each is a separate account. And if you've signed up for a Samsung Account, that's a separate account as well.

Google Calendar on the Web

THE WEB-BASED VERSION OF Google Calendar lets you set many of the options for your calendar that you can't set on the Galaxy S4. So in your S4's browser, head over to *www.google.com/calendar* to set those options. Sign in, and you'll see a version of Google Calendar on the Web specifically designed to display nicely on the Galaxy S4. You can create new events, but you won't be able to change all the options that you can change if you use your computer to visit; it's somewhat stripped down.

What happened to Google Tasks?

If you're already a Google Calendar or Gmail user, you may have used Google Tasks, a very simple and very useful way to keep track of all your to-dos. When you use Google Calendar on the Web, your task list appears at the right side of the screen.

But the Tasks feature is nowhere to be found on either the Galaxy S4 calen-

dar, or on the Google Calendar version designed to be viewed on the Web with your phone's browser.

Ah, but that doesn't mean you can't get to it on the S4. You can. It's just that Google has put it somewhere you didn't expect. Go to *http://gmail.com/tasks*. You'll find Google Tasks there, in all its glory.

Synchronizing Your Calendar with Outlook

WHEN YOU SET UP your Galaxy S4 calendar, you either hooked it to an existing Google Calendar or you had to create a new one. But not everyone in the world uses Google Calendar. Plenty of people use other calendars—notably, Outlook.

There's no direct way to synchronize your S4 Calendar with Outlook, so you may think you have to manually keep two sets of calendars in sync, by adding and deleting appointments in both places.

You don't—there's a workaround. It's a bit kludgy, but it works. First, synchronize Outlook with Google Calendar on your PC. That way, Google Calendar and Outlook will stay in sync. Then, sync your Galaxy S4 with Google Calendar. So you're essentially using Google Calendar as a go-between—it shuttles information between Outlook and your S4.

Here's where things get complicated. In the past, one way to do this calendar two-step was to download the free Google Calendar Sync app and use that to synchronize. Unfortunately, though, Google and Microsoft have been fighting like the Hatfields and McCoys, and so that app no longer works. However, if you use the Google for-pay service called Google Apps, you can use Google Apps Sync for Microsoft Outlook (*https://tools.google.com/dlpage/gappssync*) to do the trick.

An even better bet, if you're willing to pay a little bit of money, is Companion-Link for Google (*www.companionlink.com*). Not only does it sync your calendar, but it also syncs your Outlook contacts with your Gmail contacts, which means you can keep your contacts in sync between your Galaxy S4 and Outlook. You can try it for free for 14 days. If you decide it's worth paying for, it'll cost you $49.95, or $14.95 per three-month subscription.

TIP Neither of these pieces of software work for syncing Google Calendar with Macs and iCal. However, Google has posted instructions for syncing iCal with Google Calendar at *http://bit.ly/a2if0E*.

Corporate Calendar and Microsoft Exchange

WOULDN'T IT BE NICE if we could all get along? Yes, it would. And wouldn't it be nice if your Outlook calendar at work synced with your Google Calendar? Yes, it would.

Sigh. But it probably won't work...unless it does. That pretty much sums up the confusing state of the conflict between Microsoft and Google when it comes to having their calendaring technology work with one another. Once upon a time, a piece of technology with the daunting name Microsoft Exchange ActiveSync worked with Google Calendar. The IT gods could set it up so that if you used an Outlook calendar at work, you'd be able to view that calendar right on your Android phone (like a Galaxy S4).

Ah, those were the days. Back in early 2013, though, Google stopped supporting Microsoft Exchange ActiveSync. So any company looking to use it for the first time to sync Outlook with Google Calendar is out of luck. However, companies that were already using it may still be able to keep doing so.

Does yours? There's only one way to find out. Call up IT and ask them. Then cross your fingers, hope for the best, and follow their instructions.

The Galaxy S4 Online

You'll learn to:
- Connect to a WiFi network
- Turn your S4 into a WiFi hotspot
- Configure WiFi Direct
- Use Airplane Mode

CHAPTER 8

Getting Online: WiFi, 3G/4G, and Mobile Hotspots

THE SAMSUNG GALAXY S4 is filled with plenty of cool features, but it really comes to life when you take it online. With it, you've got the whole Internet in your hand—and on a screen larger and more vivid than on other smartphones, along with a blazing fast 4G Internet connection. Whether you need to search, get maps and directions, watch YouTube videos, or do pretty much anything else on the Internet, the Galaxy S4 lets you do it.

But first, of course, you need to get connected. You'll get the rundown on how to do that in this chapter, along with learning about one of the Galaxy S4's more amazing capabilities—the ability to turn into a WiFi hotspot to give computers and other devices an Internet connection.

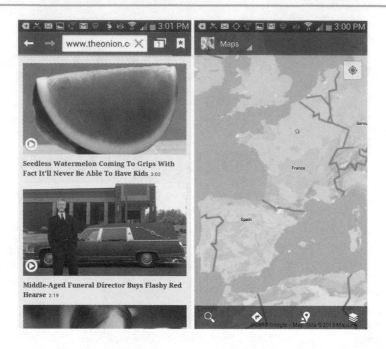

How the Galaxy S4 Gets Online

WHENEVER IT'S POWERED ON, the Galaxy S4 is ready to hop onto the Internet. Whenever your carrier's high-speed third-generation (3G) network or even faster, state-of-the-art 4G network is available, the phone uses it—you can tell by the symbol in the status bar. The 3G and 4G networks were built for data and the Internet, so you can quickly send and receive good-sized email attachments, download music, watch YouTube videos...pretty much everything Internet.

With your carrier's 3G or 4G coverage, you'll be able to hitch a ride in most places you use the S4. When the 3G or 4G network isn't available, the Galaxy S4 drops down to the older network used for voice calls, indicated by the bars in the status bar. It's much slower than 3G or 4G, but at least you're not cut off from civilization completely. 3G and 4G connections do run through your battery charge pretty quickly, which was a problem on earlier smartphones, but Samsung gave the S4 a battery that's up to the challenge. (If you are worried about running out of juice, however, you can carry a spare. Try that with an iPhone!)

To connect via 3G, 4G, or the voice network, there's nothing you need to do. The Galaxy S4 connects automatically depending on what's available. WiFi, the fastest connection of them all, takes a little more work, as you'll see in the next section.

Connecting via WiFi

WHEN YOU CONNECT TO the Internet via a WiFi hotspot, you've hit the mother lode of connection speeds. WiFi hotspots can be as fast as your cable modem connection at home.

If you've ever taken a laptop on the road, you may already know where the best WiFi hotspots are. Some coffee shops and hotels, for example, offer customers free WiFi, while others make you pay for it. More and more, you'll find WiFi coverage in airplanes, libraries, and even entire cities. In fact, if you connect your computers to the Internet at home using a wireless router, you have your own WiFi hotspot, and you can connect your S4 to the Internet via your home network.

Your actual connection speed varies from hotspot to hotspot. When you're at a public hotspot, you're sharing the connection with other people. So if a lot of people are using it at once, and the hotspot isn't set up to handle that many connections, your speed may suffer. Also, WiFi isn't a good bet when you're in motion. Hotspots have a range of only about 300 feet, so you and your phone can quickly move right past them.

NOTE When you're connected to a WiFi hotspot, the S4 uses it for more than just Internet access. It also uses WiFi for finding your current location in apps like Google Maps (unless you turn on GPS, as described in the box on page 20). The phone uses a clever technology that finds nearby WiFi networks and uses fancy algorithms to determine your location. It's not as precise as GPS, but it's still pretty good.

Unlike the 3G/4G connection, which happens automatically, WiFi doesn't work unless you turn it on. That's a good thing, since WiFi connections sap much more battery power.

Once you're ready to hook up to a hotspot, here's how:

- **Use the widget.** To get to it, pull down the Notification panel, and it's at the upper left of the screen. The leftmost button controls your WiFi radio. If the button is gray, tap it, and it turns green, meaning you've turned on WiFi. If it's already green, you don't need to do anything. (If it's on and you want to turn it off, tap it.)

- **Use connection settings.** Pull down the Notification panel, tap the Settings icon, and from the screen that appears, tap Connections. Toward the top of the screen you'll see your WiFi status. If it's green and reads "On," there's nothing you need to do—you're already connected. If it's gray and reads "Off," you'll need to turn it on: flick the Off button over to the right. Voilá Instant WiFi. To turn it off, flick the On button over to the left.

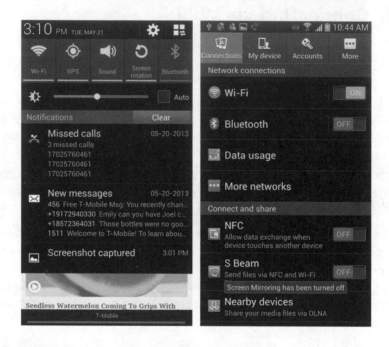

What happens next varies according to whether you're connected to a WiFi network. If you're already connected, and your settings are all aligned, you don't need to do anything—you'll automatically connect to one of your preferred WiFi networks, like the one you use at home.

However, if you've never connected to a network before and you're in range of an open WiFi network, or if networks you've connected to before are out of range, then the S4 needs to ask you which network you want to join. When you turn on WiFi, a list of all nearby networks appears. For each network, you see its name, as well as the relative strength of the connection: the more blue waves, the stronger the connection. In addition, some networks have lock icons on them. A lock means that the network is encrypted and password-protected, and so you'll need the password for it in order to connect to it. No lock means that you can connect without a password.

On the screen that lists all nearby WiFi connections, you'll also see a list of networks you've connected to in the past, even those out of range. Those networks won't show an icon with waves on it, and the words "Not in range" appear underneath them in the listing.

NOTE In some instances even though a network shows that it doesn't require a password, you'll need a password in order to use it. In those cases, you can connect to the network without typing in a password, but in order to use the network, you'll have to open your browser, and register or type in a password. Ask the manager or whoever owns the network. Often, these kinds of networks are for-pay, so you'll have to use a credit card. In some instances, a business (like a coffee shop) will give you a password for free, sometimes for a limited amount of time.

Tap any network on the list, and a connection screen appears. Tap Connect if it's open, or, if it's protected, type the password and tap Connect. Either way, after a few seconds, you make the connection. The network to which you just connected shows up in your list with the word "Connected" underneath it.

If you find yourself getting disconnected from WiFi networks, try adjusting your connection settings. From the Home screen, pull down the Notification panel, tap the Settings icon, and then select Connections→Wi-Fi. Press the Menu key and select Advanced. Make sure the "Keep Wi-Fi on during Sleep" setting is set to Always. That way, your WiFi won't go to sleep when the S4's screen turns off. Select "Only when plugged in," and WiFi won't go to sleep as long as your phone is plugged in.

What if for some reason a screen doesn't appear showing you all the available nearby networks? That might mean that there are no networks within range… or it might just be some odd temporary glitch. To check whether there are any available networks nearby, on any page, pull down the Notification panel, tap the Settings icon, and then tap Connections→Wi-Fi. You come to the screen that shows you all the nearby WiFi networks so you can make a connection.

TIP If your cellphone plan includes a limit on the amount of data you can use every month, and charges you more if you go over the limit, the S4's WiFi capabilities can be your best friend. When you're sending or receiving data via WiFi, it's not counted as part of your data plan. So using WiFi whenever possible can help make sure you don't bump up against your limits. And if you know you're going to be downloading large files, such as songs or movies, try to do it via WiFi. In addition to not racking up data use, it'll be faster than 3G or 4G as well.

Disconnecting and Reconnecting

To disconnect from a WiFi network, turn off WiFi. If you want to keep WiFi on, but want to disconnect from the network, go back to the screen that lists the nearby WiFi networks, tap the network to which you're connected, and then tap Forget. Boom—you're disconnected.

There's a downside to disconnecting this way, though. Normally whenever you connect to a WiFi network, the Galaxy S4 remembers that connection. So the next time it's in range, it automatically connects you, including using the network's password. If you tap Forget, though, it won't log you in automatically the next time you're in range.

NOTE The S4 tells you in the Notification panel that there's a nearby WiFi network if that network is an open one—that is, one that doesn't use security. It won't notify you if you've previously connected to the network, and your phone is set to remember it and connect automatically. If you want to turn off ever being notified, on any pane, press the Menu key, and then select "Wireless and network"→"Wi-Fi settings." Then tap "Network notification" so the green checkmark goes away.

Connecting to For-Pay WiFi Networks

Some WiFi hotspots require you to pay a fee for their use. In those instances, you'll have to take one more step when connecting. First make the connection in the normal way. Then launch the Galaxy S4's web browser by tapping its icon on the Home screen or in the App Drawer. A screen appears, delivered by the network, asking you to first register and pay.

Some free WiFi networks require you to first agree to terms of service before you can use them. In that case, when you launch the browser, those terms of service will appear. So if you're at a free WiFi hotspot and connect to it, but can't get an Internet-based app like Pandora to work, it might be because you haven't yet launched your browser and agreed to the terms of service.

Connecting to an "Invisible" Network

For security reasons, some people or businesses tell their network not to broadcast its name—its *Service Set Identifier* (SSID). That way, the network may appear invisible to people passing by. (Dedicated hackers, though, can easily detect it.)

If you need to connect to a network that isn't broadcasting its SSID, you can still connect, as long as you've been provided with its name, the type of security it uses, and its password. Pull down the Notification panel, then tap the settings icon and from the screen that appears, tap Connections→Wi-Fi. Scroll to the bottom of the screen, and tap "Add Wi-Fi network." Type the network's SSID, choose the security type, type the password, and then tap Save to connect to the network.

The WPS Alternative

All this fiddling around with WiFi network connections can be confusing and time-consuming. So the Galaxy S4 has a built-in feature for making the connection easier—as long as the WiFi hotspot to which you want to connect uses a standard called WPS (WiFi Protected Setup). Find out from your provider whether your home router has it, and if it does, follow the instructions that came with the router for setting it up. Then on your phone, pull down the Notification panel, then tap the settings icon and from the screen that appears, tap Connections→Wi-Fi. Tap the Menu key, and from the menu that appears, select either "WPS push button" or "WPS PIN entry," depending on the way you've set up WPS on your router. (Again, check the WPS instructions for doing this.) Then just follow the S4 instructions onscreen. You'll make the connection automatically, no muss, no fuss.

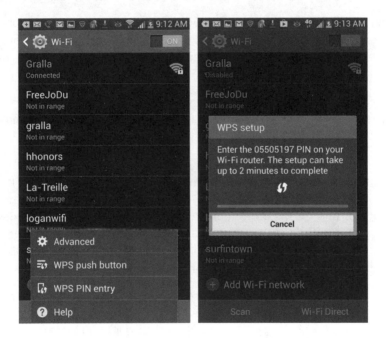

Turning Your Galaxy S4 into a WiFi Hotspot or Tethering It

The Galaxy S4 can do more than just connect you to a hotspot. It can create its own hotspot, so other computers, cellphones, and devices can connect to the Internet through it. That means, for example, that if you've got a computer that you want to connect to the Internet but there's no WiFi hotspot or Internet service nearby, you can connect using your phone. So from now on, wherever you are, you've got Internet access as long as you've got your Galaxy S4 with you. The S4 calls this setting up a *portable hotspot*.

Doing this, you can provide Internet access not just for one PC, but for up to five—that's right, count them, five—devices. (Note: the number of devices you can connect to may vary according to your carrier, so check with it for details.)

Not only that, but a related feature lets you share your Internet connection by simply connecting a USB cable between your computer and your S4. That's called *tethering*. And you can also connect the devices to the WiFi hotspot via Bluetooth as well.

> **NOTE** If you don't have a 3G or 4G connection, you won't be able to set up a mobile hotspot. So try doing this only when you see the 3G or 4G signal in the status bar.

To perform this magic, the Galaxy S4 connects to a 3G or 4G network as it normally does, using its 3G or 4G radio. Then it uses its WiFi radio to set up a WiFi hotspot, and lets up to five computers, phones, tablets, and similar devices connect to it as well. They connect to it as they would connect to any other hotspot, and share its single 3G or 4G connection. So don't expect blazing speed if several people use it simultaneously. Still, it's a high-speed connection.

Be aware that this does come at a price. As of this writing, you'll generally have to pay an extra $20 per month or so in addition to your normal data fee to be able to use this feature. (Again, check with your carrier.) And there may be maximum data limits imposed as well. That will apply only to data sent and received via the 3G or 4G hotspot, not toward your normal data plan.

OK, enough introduction. Here's how to do it: First, make sure WiFi is turned on and you've got a 3G or 4G connection. Once you've done that, pull down the Notification panel, tap the Settings icon, and from the screen that appears, tap Connections→"More networks"→"Tethering and Mobile HotSpot." What you do next varies according to whether you want to tether your phone or turn it into a hotspot.

Setting Up a Hotspot

If you want to set up a hotspot, slide the Mobile HotSpot to On so that the button turns green. First you'll come to an introductory screen telling you what a portable hotspot is. If you don't want that screen to appear every time you set up a hotspot (and you certainly don't), tap "Don't show again," and then tap Cancel.

A screen appears titled "First time HotSpot configuration." As the name implies, you'll only see this screen once, so don't despair—you won't have to fill it in every time you want to set up a hotspot.

Here's what you'll fill out:

- **Network SSID.** Type the name that you want your Hotspot to have. The box will be filled in for you already, with something really exciting like "Samsung Galaxy S 4 4494." Make the name anything you want. Go crazy....or don't. But make it something that you'll remember.

- **Broadcast network name (SSID).** This box will already be checkmarked for you. It means just what it says: Anyone will be able to see the network's name because it's being broadcast, which is the way networks normally work. But if you're paranoid, uncheck the box. No one will be able to see that your network exists. However, you can still connect to it. For details, see page 196.

- **Security.** This drop-down menu lets you choose the type of security you want your network to have. WPA2 PSK will be chosen for you. Most of the time, you'll want to stick with it, because it gives you a high level of security. Whatever you do, though, don't choose Open. If you do that, anyone can connect to your hot spot. Not only will they suck up your bandwidth, but they could also possibly steal your files.

- **Password.** Select the password that you or anyone else will have to type in in order to connect. Please, whatever you do, don't use the word "password" as a password. When choosing a password, use a mix of numbers and letters, including capital letters. You'll have to make it at least eight characters long.

That's it. Tap Save, and you'll be ready to go. If you're feeling super-techie, tap the "Show advanced options" box. A number of new options appear, including choosing the network's broadcast channel (if you need to ask what that is, you don't need to select it), the maximum number of devices that can connect to the hotspot, and the timeout settings, which is the number of minutes of inactivity it takes before the connected device will get bumped off the network.

Changing the maximum number of devices that can connect using the "Show advanced options" menu may not actually change the number of devices that connect. The maximum number of connections is set by your carrier, so increasing the number beyond that won't actually change how many devices can connect.

When a device connects to your hotspot, you'll get a notification.

When you don't want the hotspot to be active anymore, get back to the screen where you set it up, then flip the On switch to Off.

Setting Up and Using Tethering

If you're only going to connect one device to your phone in order to give it Internet access, such as a PC, you might instead want to use the USB tethering feature. With it, you connect your PC and your phone with a USB cable, and your PC then uses the phone's Internet connection.

There is a caveat, though. It doesn't work with Macs, and not even with all Windows PCs. It only works with PCs with Windows Vista, Windows 7, or Linux.

TIP If you use Windows XP and you're feeling techie, you may be able to get a Windows XP PC to tether to your phone. To do it, follow instructions found here: *http://bit.ly/fYxSOl.*

To tether your PC to your phone, first connect your PC to your S4 (page 332). Windows will install a special driver that lets your PC recognize your phone. Next, tap the Menu key and select Settings→"Wireless and network"→"Tethering and Mobile Hotspot" and turn on the box next to USB Tethering. You'll now be able to use the S4's Internet connection. Your phone can be connected via 3G, 4G, or Wi-Fi, and your PC will share that connection.

When you connect your S4 to your PC with a USB cable, you can't use tethering and transfer files at the same time. So if you turn on tethering, you can't transfer files. Also, when you use tethering, you won't be able to use the S4's memory card.

Configuring Wi-Fi Direct

YOUR GALAXY S4 CAN use a helpful technology called WiFi Direct that makes it easy to connect directly to other WiFi devices *without* having to use a WiFi network. So, for example, you can connect directly to a PC that also uses WiFi Direct in order share files, as described in Chapter 13.

Only devices that meet the Wi-Fi Direct standards and certifications can use WiFi Direct, and your Galaxy S4 does that. To use Wi-Fi Direct to connect to another device, on any pane, tap the Menu key and select Settings→Wi-Fi and tap the Wi-Fi Direct button at the bottom of your screen. You'll get a warning that you'll be disconnected to your current WiFi network (if you're connected to one). Tap OK. On the screen that appears, tap Wi-Fi Direct. Your phone scans for nearby WiFi Direct devices. Once it finds any, follow the onscreen prompts to connect.

NOTE For more information about Wi-Fi Direct, and to see what other devices use it, go to *www.wi-fi.org/Wi-Fi_Direct.php*.

Airplane Mode

AIRLINES BAN THE USE of cellphone signals during flights. But they don't actually ban the use of phones. So you can still use your Galaxy S4 to run apps, play games, and so on, as long as its radios aren't turned on.

That's where Airplane mode comes in. It turns off all your S4's radios but lets you use your phone for everything else.

NOTE You might also want to use Airplane mode even when you're not in flight in order to save power.

There are two ways to turn on Airplane mode:

- **Use the widget.** To get to it, pull down the Notification panel. At the top of the screen you'll see a variety of widgets, such as for turning WiFi and GPS on and off. Slide all the way over to the right until you see the Airplane mode icon —the one that looks like an airplane. Tap it and it turns green and turns off all the S4's radios.

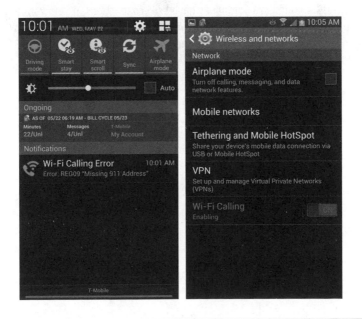

- **Use "Wireless and networks" settings.** Pull down the Notification panel, tap the Settings icon and on the screen that appears, tap Connections→ "More networks." Check the box next to "Airplane mode" to turn it on, and uncheck the box to turn it off.

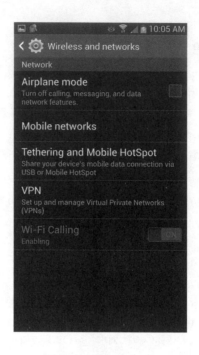

TIP   An increasing number of airplanes have WiFi connections. If you want to connect your S4 to the plane's WiFi network, turn on Airplane mode, and then turn on WiFi alone. Make a connection as you would normally. That way, you've turned off all the S4's radios except for WiFi.

You'll learn to:
- Browse the Web
- Use multiple browser windows
- Create and manage bookmarks
- Save and view online pictures and graphics

CHAPTER 9

The Web

ONCE YOU'VE USED YOUR Samsung Galaxy S4 to skim movie reviews on your way to the theater, check out an online menu before you choose a restaurant, or find a newspaper to read on the train, you may wonder how you ever got along without having the Web in the palm of your hand. The big 5-inch screen gives you an awesome Web experience wherever you go. At 4.3 inches, even the S4 MInI's screen makes the Web look great. With more and more web designers making their sites look good and work well on mobile devices like the Galaxy S4, you may find yourself using the Browser more than any other app.

The Galaxy S4's Browser

THE S4'S BROWSER HAS plenty of goodies, much like those in a computer browser, including bookmarks, AutoComplete for web addresses, cookies, password memorization, the ability to save and share pages, shortcuts, the ability to select and copy text...just about the whole nine yards. However, the browser itself is fairly bare bones, and its simplicity can at first be off-putting. But once you know your way around a bit, you'll be browsing at warp speed. Here are the main controls you need to know about:

- **Address bar.** Here's where you enter the URL—the web address—for a page you want to visit.

- **Windows open.** Tells you how many websites you've currently got open. Tap it to see thumbnails of them all. Then tap any thumbnail to visit it, and tap the–key to close any site.

- **Bookmarks.** Tap this button, and you'll add the current page to your Bookmarks list and also be able to see pages you've visited frequently, and the history of your Web browsing. See page 216 for more details.

- **Navigation buttons.** Tap these to go forward or backwards in your browsing session.

- **Menu key.** This key isn't on the screen itself—it's the button at lower left. Press it to get at most of the browser's features, including going back and forward, opening a new browser window, seeing and managing your bookmarks, and more.

There are plenty of choices when you tap the key. To open a new browser window, tap "New window." To share the page with others, tap "Share Page via." To change the brightness of the screen when using the browser, tap brightness and select your brightness level, or else keep it on Auto Brightness. There are also a Forward button and a More button, with plenty more options, as you'll see in the next sections.

Browsing for Browsers

The S4 gives you not just one, but two browsers: the standard one that runs right out of the box, and Chrome, which is the smartphone version of Google's house browser. They're similar, but with a few differences, notably in the way that Chrome handles tabs. This chapter focuses on the S4's built-in browser. It's the browser that runs whenever you tap the Internet icon. If you prefer to run Chrome, tap its icon in the App Drawer.

Another difference between Chrome and the built-in browser is that Chrome doesn't work with Flash, so you'll frequently run across videos that you can't play. On the other hand, if you use Chrome on other computers or devices, it will sync bookmarks and other information with Chrome on the S4.

If you use Chrome on a desktop computer, you may want to opt for using Chrome on the S4, and not just because it syncs information between the desktop and S4 versions. Its interface on the S4 is somewhat similar to the interface on the desktop version. For example, you can see and switch between multiple tabs, although unlike the desktop version, the tabs aren't arrayed horizontally, but instead vertically on top of one another.

There's also a nifty feature that lets you see all the sites currently opened on your other devices that use Chrome, like desktops and laptops or Android-based tablets. Not only can you see a list of sites, by device, but if you tap any, you head straight to it on your S4. To use the feature, press the Menu key and select "Other devices" from the screen that appears.

All that said, if you're not already a Chrome user, it can take some getting used to, particularly its tab handling. So which should you use? As the saying goes, you pays your money and you takes your chances—although in this instance, both browsers are free.

Furthermore, you're not just limited to the S4's built-in browser and Google Chrome. You can download other popular browsers—like Opera and Firefox—from Google Play.

These alternative browsers often add features that the built-in one doesn't have. Firefox, for example, will sync your Galaxy S4 bookmarks with the bookmarks on your PC or Mac. Opera is faster than the built-in browser because it compresses graphics before downloading them to your phone. It also syncs bookmarks with PC or Mac and offers other extras as well.

Basic Navigation and Managing Windows

Just as with a desktop browser, your phone's S4 browser lets you open multiple windows and visit multiple sites. It's just harder to tell that you're visiting multiple sites, because the S4's browser doesn't have enough room for tabs. Instead, the S4 opens multiple windows, one for each site you're visiting. When you're in the browser, tap the Menu key and select Windows, and you see thumbnails of your open windows. You'll see your current page in the thumbnail. Swipe up and down to see other open windows. Tap any window to view the site full screen. Tap the minus sign at its top to close the window. And tap "New window" at the top of your screen to open a new window.

Navigating a Web Page

Head to a web page, and most of the time you see an entire page, laid out with the same fonts, links, pictures, and so on, as if you were visiting it using a computer with a much larger screen. Of course, looking at an entire web page on the S4's screen isn't the same thing as looking at a web page on a 21-inch monitor. The type is minuscule, the photos small, the links hard to detect. But letting you see the entire screen at once makes a good deal of sense, because at a glance, you can see what section of the page you want to view.

That's where the fun begins. You can use the S4's zooming and scrolling capabilities to head quickly to the part of the page you want to view, and then zoom in.

You've got two ways to do so:

- **Use the two-finger spread.** Put two fingers on the screen on the area where you want to zoom in, and move your fingers apart. The web page stretches and zooms in. The more you spread, the greater the zoom. Pinch your fingers together to zoom back out. You may need to do the two-finger spread and pinch several times until you get the exact magnification you want.

- **Double-tap.** Double-tap with a finger on the section of the page where you want to zoom. Double-tap again to zoom out. You can't control the zoom level as finely with the double-tap as you can using the two-finger spread.

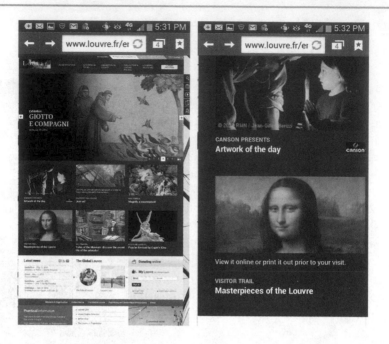

Once you've zoomed in, you scroll around the web page by dragging or flicking your finger—the same kind of navigation you use for other S4 apps.

Multiple Windows

THE GALAXY S4'S BROWSER doesn't confine you to a single window—you can use multiple ones, and easily switch among them. In fact, you may have multiple windows open without even knowing it. Press the Menu key, and look at the Windows entry on the menu that appears. It shows you the number of windows that are open in your browser.

Now tap the Windows button. You'll come to a page with a thumbnail of your current window. You may see the edges of other windows you have open to the right and left of it. Tap any window to open it. Tap the minus button on a window to close it. Tap the New Window button at the top right to open a new window, which will open to the browser's home page.

Web Pages Designed for Mobile Phones

AS YOU BROWSE THE Web, you may come across sites that differ significantly when viewed on the Galaxy S4 (or other smartphones) compared with the exact same sites viewed on a computer. That's because web designers have created pages specifically designed to be viewed with mobile phones, taking into account that mobile phones have smaller screens than computers.

CNN, for example, has sites designed especially for mobile viewing. Head to the same site at the exact same time of day with a smartphone and a computer, and you see very different pages, even though the content of the pages is much the same.

These pages are formatted to be read on the phone, so very often they don't include complex layouts, and instead present articles and other information in scrollable lists. They generally don't allow you to zoom in and zoom out. You'll navigate primarily by scrolling and clicking links.

The Address Bar

THE ADDRESS BAR IS the box at the top of the browser where you type the URL of the website you want to visit. As explained on page 208, there are buttons for managing bookmarks, seeing open windows, and going forward and backwards. When you type an address and head to a page, a small bar above the address bar shows you the status—how much of the page has loaded and how much is left to go.

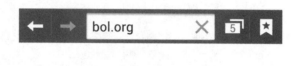

> **NOTE** The bar indicating your page's loading status is only an approximation, so don't take it for the absolute truth.

Typing an Address

To type a URL into the address bar, first tap the bar. The current URL is highlighted in blue. Then use the keyboard to type an address. As you type, the S4 displays sites you've visited that match the letters you type. So when you type the letter *C*, for example, it may display Computerworld.com (*http://Computerworld.com*), CNN.com (*http://CNN.com*), and so on. It will also display search terms you might want to use, because the Address Bar does double-duty as a search box. So it may be a very long list of URLs and suggestions you see.

> **NOTE** As you type, you'll also see suggestions for sites you might not yet have visited. Google is trying to be helpful, and displays popular sites that match the letters you're typing.

You'll notice, though, that it might also display URLs that don't start with the letter *C*. If you've previously visited a site about the international opera star Cecilia Bartoli, you may see that site come up when you type *C*. That's because the Galaxy S4's browser looks through your browsing history and Bookmarks list (see the next page), and looks for *all* matches to that letter, not just in URLs but also text in the page's title. When it displays its list as you type, it includes both the page's title and the URL.

As you continue to type, the list narrows down, and matches only those sites that match the letters you're typing. So if you type *com*, cnn.com (*http://cnn.com*) no longer appears your list, but computerworld.com (*http://computerworld.com*) does. When you see the site you want to visit, just tap its listing. You head straight there. If there's no match on the list, you'll have to type the entire URL.

You can also use the address bar to search the Web. Just type your search term, but don't add a .com ending. Your browser will search the Web for the term, using (what else?) Google.

NOTE Don't bother to type the *http://* part of a web address. The browser knows to put that in for you. You do, however, need to type in the .com or other ending, such as .edu. After you type in the address, tap the arrow button, and you head to the page.

Bookmarks

JUST AS WITH COMPUTER-BASED browsers, the
S4's browser lets you save your favorite sites as
bookmarks—sites you can easily visit again without
having to retype their URLs. In fact, before you even
use your browser, it has bookmarks for a few popular
sites, including Yahoo, Facebook, Twitter, CNN, ESPN,
and others. The exact bookmarks placed there will
depend on your cell phone carrier, because they're
usually in charge of that. Can you guess why? Right—
because they put their own Web page there as well.

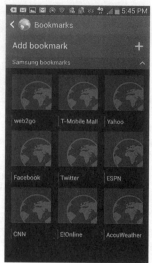

To see your bookmarks, tap the Bookmarks icon
at the far right of the Address Bar. You see all your
bookmarks, either displayed as a list or as a group of
thumbnails of each of the bookmarked pages, so that
you can distinguish them visually.

To switch back and forth between the views, when
you're viewing your bookmarks, press the Menu key and then select "List view"
or "Thumbnail view."

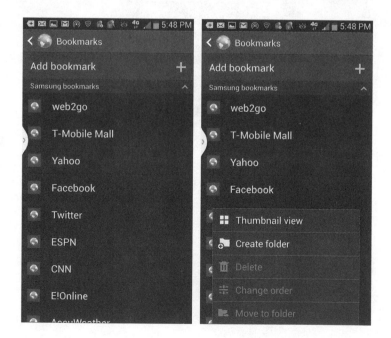

No matter which view you use, to go to a bookmarked site, tap the site. Voilà—you're there.

Adding a Bookmark

Whenever you visit a web page you want to add as a bookmark, tap the Bookmark button. The Bookmarks page appears.

TIP If you sometimes find yourself with a slow Internet connection, and wish there was a way to browse the Web faster, here's a bookmark you should add to your list: *www.google.com/gwt/n*. It hides most graphics, and lets you browse the Web much more quickly on a slow connection. In the small box near the top of the screen, type the site you want to visit.

Tap "Add Bookmark" or the + sign to add the page as a bookmark. A screen appears that includes the web page's title and its URL. In the Name box, type a different title if you wish, and in the Location box, type a different URL. Then tap OK. The bookmark is added to your list.

NOTE If you edit the URL, and the new URL differs from the page you wanted to bookmark, you'll go to the URL you typed, not the original one you planned to bookmark.

Managing Bookmarks

The Galaxy S4 lets you do more than just go to bookmarks. You can delete them, share them, edit them, and so on. There are several ways to do this, each of which has different options. For the first way, head to Bookmarks and then press the Menu key. You get these options:

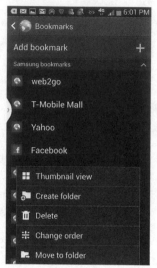

- **List view/Thumbnail view.** Switches between the list and thumbnail views.

- **Create folder.** If you've got a lot of bookmarks, you may want to organize them by folders—news, entertainment, and so on. Tap here and from the screen that appears, name your folder and tap OK. When you go to your Bookmarks, that folder will show up. Tap it to view any bookmarks in that folder. As you'll see in a little bit, it's easy to move bookmarks between folders.

- **Delete.** Select this and a screen appears that lets you select bookmarks you want to delete. After you select them, tap Delete to delete them, or Cancel if you change your mind and don't want to delete any.

- **Change order.** Lets you change the order in which your bookmarks appear in a list or thumbnails. Tap it, and from the screen that appears, drag the bookmarks to be in a different order on the list or thumbnail.

- **Move to folder.** Tap this and a screen appears that lets you select book-marks you want to move to a folder. Select them and a screen pops up with your list of folders. Put check marks next to any you want to move. Then move them to folder you want.

There's another way to manage your bookmarks. When you're on the bookmarks page, hold your finger on the bookmark you want to edit or manage. A menu appears with the following choices:

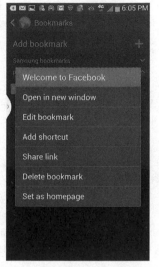

- **Open in new window.** Opens the bookmarked site in a new window. So if you're at *www.google. com*, open your bookmarks, and then choose *www.cnn.com*, *www.cnn.com* opens in a window of its own.

- **Edit bookmark.** Brings up a page that lets you edit the name and location of the bookmark. It looks much like the page for adding a bookmark.

- **Add shortcut.** Tap this option, and a shortcut to the bookmarked page is added to your Home screen. When you tap the bookmark, it opens the browser to that site. You can move and delete the icon after you add it, as you can see on page 30.

NOTE If you add a shortcut to your Home screen, and then delete the shortcut, the bookmark still remains in your browser's Bookmarks list.

- **Share link.** Tap to share the link of the bookmark by a variety of methods, including email, text message, Bluetooth, and more.

- **Delete bookmark.** After you tap this, you get a warning that you're about to delete the bookmark, just in case you want to reconsider or tapped this option by accident.

- **Set as homepage.** Tap this, and from now on whenever you open a new window, it opens to that site.

The History List

DID YOU VISIT A website earlier today, or sometime within last week, but can't remember what it was? No problem! The S4's browser keeps track of sites you've visited. It's a great way (in addition to Bookmarks) to head back to sites you've visited before without having to type—or even remember—the web address.

To see it, press the Menu key and select History. You'll see a list of websites you've visited today. The History list shows you not just sites you've visited today, but yesterday, in the last seven days, and a month ago. Rather than show you all the sites you visited before today, the browser shows the day (Yesterday, "Last 7 days," and so on), with an arrow next to it. Tap the arrow, and you see the full list of sites for that day.

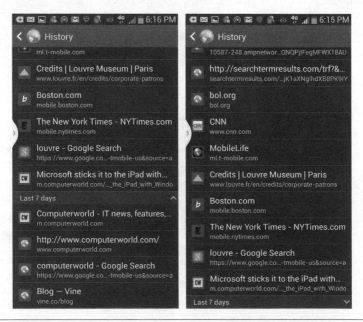

NOTE The History list doesn't give you the option of viewing sites as thumbnails, only as a list.

The list works much like the Bookmarks list—tap the site you want to visit. You'll notice one difference between these lists and the Bookmarks list: Some of the sites here have a gold star next to them. That indicates that the site is on your Bookmarks list.

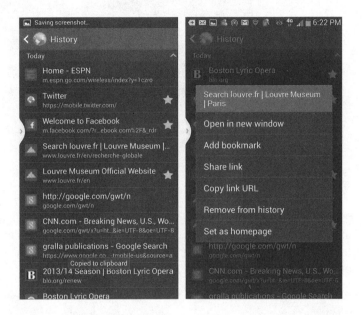

Editing and Managing the History List

You manage the History list just like you do Bookmarks. Hold your finger on the site you want to edit or manage, and a menu appears like the one you see for managing Bookmarks, although much smaller with fewer options. To remove the site from the History List, select "Remove from history."

There's one thing you can do to your History list that you can't do with the Bookmarks list: You can clear your entire history. If you feel guilty about visiting sites for any reason, you can get rid of them all. While in the History list, press the Menu key, and then select "Clear history." Your slate will be wiped clean.

Tapping Links

LINKS ON THE WEB couldn't be simpler or more convenient. Tap the link, and you get sent to a new web page. But this is the Galaxy S4, so there's a lot more you can do with links than just tap them. Hold your finger on a link, and a menu appears with these options:

> **NOTE** Sometimes when you click a link, instead of loading a web page, the Galaxy S4 may take a different action. For example, if the link is to an email address, it will open the Email app, with a new message addressed to the link's email address.

- **Open.** Opens the linked page in the current window.

- **Open in new window.** Opens the linked page in a new window.

- **Bookmark link.** Puts the link into your Bookmarks list.

- **Save link.** Saves the linked page to the Download folder. To view the link and anything else in the Download folder, see page 224.

- **Copy link URL.** Tap to copy the link's URL to the Clipboard, so you can paste it somewhere else, such as in a document or email.

- **Select text.** Most links are text links, that is they are words that when clicked, send you to a Web page. When you choose "Select text," you select that text, and then have options for doing more things with it, such as searching for the text, and more. For details, see page 228.

NOTE If you hold your finger on a graphic that's also a link, several other options appear, having to do with the image. You can save the image, copy the image to the Clipboard, or view the image.

Other Nifty Things to Tap

The Galaxy S4 is smart enough that you can take action based on what you see on web pages, without even having to use links:

- When you see a phone number on the Web and want to call it, just tap it. The Galaxy S4 dialer launches, with the number already entered. Tap the phone icon to make the call.

- When you see an address on the Web and want to see a map of its location, tap it. Google Maps launches, centered on the location.

- When you see an email address, even if the address hasn't been created as a link, tap it, and the Email app opens, with a new message already addressed to that address.

Saving Online Images

WHEN YOU'RE BROWSING THE Web, sooner or later you'll come across a picture you'd like to save. For example, if a friend posts a picture from your birthday party on Facebook, you can save it on your Galaxy S4 and then share it with others.

There's a quick and easy way to save that image. Hold your finger on the picture for a second or two, and a menu appears with the following three options:

- **Save image.** Downloads the picture to your Download folder card. See the next section to learn how to go back and view all the pictures in this folder.

- **Copy image.** Copies the image to your Clipboard.

- **View image.** Opens the image in its own page. As a practical matter, this option doesn't do much, because it doesn't make the image any larger or smaller—you're seeing the same image, just on its own rather than on a web page.

> **TIP** If the picture is also a link, the menu shows the usual options for bookmarking the link, saving the link, and so on.

Viewing Downloaded Images

Now that you've got graphics saved on your S4, how can you view them? It's simple. Open the Gallery (page 119) and go to the Download folder. Then view and manage them as you would any other pictures.

Finding Text, Sharing Pages, Getting Page Information, and More

THE GALAXY S4'S BROWSER has a lot more tricks up its sleeve than we've covered so far. To get to them, when you're on a web page, press the Menu key. You'll find a menu of options that lets you do any of the following:

- **Homepage.** Sends you back to your Homepage.

- **New window.** Opens a new window to your Homepage.

- **Add bookmark/Edit bookmark.** Tap this option and then add the bookmark in the usual way. If it's already a bookmark, you can edit it in the usual way.

- **Add shortcut.** Adds a shortcut to the web page on your Home screen. The shortcut will be to the specific page you're on, not to the general website.

- **Save page.** Saves the entire web page, graphics included, on your S4. How to view it once you've saved it? There's another option on the menu, Saved pages, that brings you there.

- **Share via.** Tap to share the page via email or text messaging, social networking, Bluetooth, and depending on what software you have installed, potentially several other ways as well. You don't actually share the page itself; instead, you send a link to it. Selecting this option copies the URL to an email message or a text message. You can then select an address and add explanatory text to the message as well.

- **Find on page.** Looking for text on a page? Tap this option, and a search box appears, along with the keyboard. Type the text or phrase you're searching for, and the Galaxy S4 finds the text, sends you to its location on the page, and highlights it in blue. To find the next time the text or phrase is mentioned, tap the down arrow. To find a previous mention of it on the page, tap the up arrow.

composer and pianist. A crucial figure in the transition between the Classical and Romantic eras in Western art music, he remains one of the most famous and influential of all composers. His best known compositions include 9 symphonies, 5 concertos for piano, 32 piano sonatas, and 16 string quartets. He also composed other chamber music, choral works (including the celebrated *Missa Solemnis*), and songs.

Born in Bonn, then the capital of the Electorate of Cologne and part of the Holy Roman Empire, Beethoven displayed his musical talents at an early age and was taught by his father Johann van Beethoven and Christian Gottlob Neefe. During his first 22 years in Bonn, Beethoven intended to study with Wolfgang Amadeus Mozart and befriended Joseph Haydn. Beethoven moved to Vienna in 1792 and began studying with Haydn, quickly gaining a reputation as a virtuoso pianist. He lived in Vienna until his death. In about 1800 his hearing began to deteriorate, and by the last decade of his life he was almost totally deaf. He gave up conducting and performing in public but continued to compose; many of his most admired

- **Incognito mode.** There are times that you want to browse the Web in privacy—you don't want anyone else to know you've visited. Not to imply that you have anything to hide, but no matter the reason, select this option. The site won't be saved in your History list, and there'll be no trace you've ever visited.

- **Saved pages.** Brings you a list of all the pages you've saved. Tap any to view it. It should look just like it does on the Web, except that it's saved on your S4.

- **History.** Brings you to the History list. For details, see page 220 earlier in this chapter.

- **Desktop view.** When you browse the Web with your S4, you'll often come to versions of sites optimized for its small screen. But there may be times when you want to see the full-blown site. If that happens, tap the checkbox in this option, and you'll see the whole shebang of the website. To switch back, get back to the menu and uncheck the box. When you select this option, it doesn't affect any other website, only the one you're visiting.

NOTE   Some sites don't have versions optimized for smartphone screens. When you're visiting one of those, you see the page just as you see it on a larger computer, and the Desktop view option is grayed out.

- **Brightness.** Lets you select the brightness level of your browser. You may want to select Automatic brightness, because that lets the S4 choose what it thinks is the best level.

- **Settings.** Here's how you can change many browser settings, including your Homepage, and many related to privacy.

- **Print.** If there's a wirelessly enabled printer nearby to which you can print, tap this to print the page.

Selecting and Copying Text

AS YOU BROWSE THE Web, you may also come across text on a website that you want to use elsewhere, say in an email or a document. It's easy. First, hold your finger on the text you want to copy. A magnifying glass appears. This tool makes it easy to maneuver to the exact text you want to copy. Move it by moving your finger, and then release it on the word you want to copy. If you want to copy more than one word (and you likely will), don't worry—just release your finger when it's on one of the words you want to copy.

When you release your finger, brackets appear around the word, and a toolbar appears with four icons: Select All, Copy, Share, and Find. Move the brackets until they surround the all the text you want to copy. Tap Select All to select all the text on the page. Select to copy the highlighted text to the Clipboard. You get a notification that the text was copied. You can now paste it into an email, a document, and so on. Tap Search to find other mentions of text on the page. Tap Share, and you'll be able to share your selection either as text, or as an image file. You'll be able to share it via Bluetooth, email, text message, and more, depending on what you've got installed on your S4.

But there are more options than first appear. Flick the menu to the right, and two more options appear: Translate and Web search. Tap Translate and you'll be sent to the S Translator app that will translate the text into any of multiple languages. This is great for when you're visiting a foreign-language website and want to translate phrases into English. If you instead tap Web search, you'll search the Web for the high-lighted phrase, using Google.

Online Privacy and Security

WHETHER YOU BROWSE THE Web with a computer or with the Galaxy S4, there are potential security and privacy dangers out there—cookies, pop-ups, and malicious websites. So the S4 browser, just like its big brother browsers on computers, includes the tools you need to keep you safe and protect your privacy when you browse the Web.

Pop-up Blocker

What's top on your list of web annoyances? Most likely at the pinnacle are pop-ups and pop-unders—ugly little windows and ads that either take an in-your-face stance by popping up over your browser so that you have to pay attention, or pop under your browser so that you don't notice they're there until you close a browser window, and then they demand your attention.

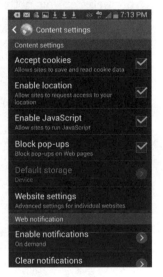

Sometimes these pop-ups and pop-unders are malicious, and if you tap them they attempt to install dangerous software or send you to a malicious website. Sometimes they're merely annoying ads. Sometimes, though, they may actually be useful, like a pop-up that shows a seating chart when you're visiting a ticket-buying site. The browser includes a pop-up blocker, and like all pop-up blockers, it can't necessarily distinguish between bad pop-ups and pop-unders and good ones, so it blocks them all.

However, if you're on a website that uses pop-ups that you want to see, you can turn off the pop-up blocker. When you're using the browser, Press the Menu key, select Settings→"Content settings," and then uncheck the box next to "Block pop-ups." When you leave the site and want pop-ups blocked again, go back to the setting and tap it to turn it on. A green checkmark appears next to the setting, and you are protected.

> **NOTE** When you turn off the pop-up blocker, it stops blocking pop-ups in *all* your browser windows, not just on one site. So be careful when you browse other places on the Web when the pop-up blocker is turned off.

Cookies

Cookies are tiny bits of information that some websites store on the Galaxy S4 for future use. When you register for a website and create a user name and password, the website can store that information in a cookie so you don't have to retype it every time. Cookies can also remember your habits and preferences when you use a website—your favorite shipping method, or what kinds of news articles you're likely to read. But not all cookies are innocuous, since they can also track your web browsing from multiple sites and potentially invade your privacy.

The browser gives you control over how you handle cookies—you can either accept them, or tell the browser to reject them. Keep in mind that if you don't allow cookies, you may not be able to take advantage of cookie-based features on many sites—like remembering items in your cart on a shopping site.

To bar websites from putting cookies on your S4, when you're in the browser, press the Menu key, select Settings→"Content settings," then tap the green checkbox next to "Accept cookies." The checkmark disappears, and from now on, no cookies will be put on your Galaxy S4. You can always turn this setting back on again, if it causes problems with web browsing.

Privacy Settings

If you're worried about privacy, there are a number of browser settings you can change. When you're in the browser, press the Menu key, select Settings→Privacy. From here there are a number of things you can do to make sure your privacy isn't invaded. For example, you can clear your browsing history so that others who use the browser can't see where you've been.

At many websites, you log in by typing a user name and password, and other information such as your address. The browser remembers those user names, passwords, and other information, and fills them in for you automatically when you next visit. That's convenient, but it also presents a privacy risk, because someone else using your Galaxy S4 can log in as you. So in the Privacy settings, turn off the checkbox next to "Remember passwords."

If you turn off "Search and URL suggestions," you won't be sending what you search to Google, but you also won't get suggestions, either. Also, normally when you type information into Web forms, your browser remembers it, so that it can put that information in other forms automatically. But if that worries you, uncheck the box next to "Remember form data."

You can also clear out website information your browser has stored on your S4. Tap "Delete personal data," and then select the kinds of data you want deleted from your phone, such as your browsing history, cookies, passwords, and so on. You also have a chance to clean out your *cache*. The cache is information the browser stored on your phone so it won't have to get that information from the Web the next time you visit that site. The cache speeds up browsing, since it's faster to grab the information—a website image, for example—from your phone than from the Web. Delete the cache if you want to clear all that information out, if you worry that the information there poses a privacy risk.

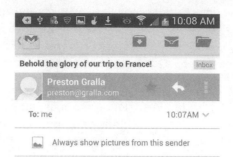

Behold the glory of our trip to France! | Inbox

Preston Gralla
preston@gralla.com

To: me 10:07AM ⌄

Always show pictures from this sender

Here's the view outside of our window in the cottage in Beynac:

ATTACHMENTS

1 of 20149 | Older

You'll learn to:

- Set up the Gmail and Email apps
- Compose and send mail
- Receive email
- Organize Gmail using labels
- Handle photos and attachments

CHAPTER 10

Email and Gmail

YOU WANT EMAIL? YOU'VE got email. The Galaxy S4 does a great job of handling whatever email task you throw at it. Want to send and receive attachments like pictures; Word, Excel, and PowerPoint files; and PDFs? The S4 can do that. How about working with just about any email service out there? It can do that, too. You can also manage your mail, sync your mail, and plenty more right on your phone. It's a great way to have your email always in your pocket.

Understanding Email on the Galaxy S4

THE GALAXY S4 RUNS on Google's Android operating system (page 27), so it comes as no surprise that it includes Gmail built into it. You don't have to use Gmail if you don't want to, though; you can use your current email service instead. Or you can use both. Gmail on the S4 works a bit differently from other email services, so this chapter covers Gmail as well as regular email.

NOTE The Email icon on your Home screen is Android's app for handling *other* email accounts, not Gmail. Gmail has its own app, which you can find in the App Drawer, as described in the next section. If you'd like to get started with a different email account (your work or home account, for example), flip to page 252.

Setting Up Gmail

ANDROID IS BUILT FROM the ground up to integrate with Google services—search, Google Maps, and Gmail. If you already have a Gmail account, then when you set up your Galaxy S4, you tie into that account. If you don't have a Gmail account, you first need to set one up.

NOTE When you first bring your S4 home, you may already be set up to use Gmail. Your wireless company's sales staff may have set up your Gmail account right in the store for you.

When you use the Gmail app on your S4, it synchronizes with your web-based Gmail. So when you delete an email on the phone, for example, it deletes it on the web-based Gmail; when you create and send an email on your phone, it shows up in your Sent folder on the Web; and so on.

Signing up for a Gmail account is free and takes only a few minutes. You can create it on the Web or on the S4. To do it on the Web, head to *www.gmail.com*. Fill in the usual information, such as first and last name, login name, and password. The login name you choose becomes your email address. So if you use the login name *petey.bigtoes*, then your email address will be *petey.bigtoes@gmail.com*. So make your login name something pleasant and easy to remember.

When you create a Gmail account, you're actually setting up an account for all of Google's services, not just Gmail. You use the same account to access Google Calendar, Google Plus, Google Drive, Google Play, and so on. In other words, if you have a Google Calendar account, then you already have a Gmail account. Use that information when setting up Gmail on your Galaxy S4.

Now that you have a Gmail account, you're ready to set up Gmail on your S4. When you set up your Gmail account, you'll also be setting up your Calendar account and importing your Gmail contacts into your Galaxy S4. In the App Drawer, tap the Gmail icon. After a brief welcome screen, Gmail asks whether you have a Google account. If you haven't already set one up, tap New, and then fill in the information required. Make sure to leave the box next to "Automatically configure account" turned on. That way, the S4 will do all the heavy lifting of properly configuring your new account.

If you plan to use Gmail a lot, drag its icon from the App Drawer to your Home screen.

If you already have a Gmail account, tap Existing. Enter your Gmail address and the other basic information. If you have a Google Contact list, the S4 automatically starts downloading it in the background, and also syncs your mail.

Reading Mail in Gmail

Once you've got your Gmail account set up, it's time to start reading mail. Launch the Gmail app by tapping it in the App Drawer. You see a list of emails, but the list you see depends on what you were doing the last time you were using Gmail. For example, if the last time you used Gmail you were in your Inbox, you see all the mail in your Inbox. If you were viewing mail in a different *label* (the term Gmail uses for a folder), you see just the mail in that label.

Most of the time, of course, you'll land in your inbox, which lists all your mail. Mail you haven't read is boldfaced and has a white background; the rest of your mail is in a normal font and has a gray background. The top of your screen displays the total number of messages in your inbox, and also your email address.

The S4 regularly checks your Gmail account for new mail, and if it finds any, it displays an email icon in the status bar. Pull down the Notification panel, and then tap the Gmail notification to launch Gmail.

When you're viewing mail in a list like this, each piece of mail shows the following:

- The sender

NOTE If the sender is one of your contacts and you have a photo for him (or if he's a friend on Facebook with a photo), you'll see a photo of him at the far left of each email. If he's not a contact, or is but you don't have a photo of him, you see a big letter—that's the first letter of his name.

- The subject line
- The date it was sent, or, if it was sent today, the time it was sent
- Whether it has an attachment
- Whether it has images

To open a message, tap it. Scroll up, down, and sideways in the message using the normal Galaxy S4 gestures of dragging and flicking.

All the links you see in the email message are live—tap them, and you go to the linked web page in the Galaxy S4's web browser. Tap an email address, and a new email message opens to that address. Tap a YouTube video, and the video plays.

In fact, in many instances, the text in the email message doesn't even need to be a link for the phone to take some kind of action on it. If there's a phone number in an email, tap it to call that number. Just tap the phone button to dial. If you tap a street address, the S4 shows you that location in Google Maps.

NOTE Gmail, Google Calendar, and your Gmail contacts are all set up to sync between your S4 and your various Google accounts on the Web. All this happens automatically, in the background, without you having to take any action. You can turn syncing off or choose to sync manually. For details, see page 408.

Handling Graphics in Gmail

There are two basic kinds of graphics you may get in Gmail. Some are embedded in the content of the message itself—for example, a company logo. Other times, the sender attaches the image to the messages, like a family member sending you Thanksgiving photos.

If the graphics are embedded in the content of the message, you see a "Show pictures" button. In some cases you don't really need to see the graphics (who cares what a company's logo looks like, really?). In that case, do nothing, However, in other cases, the graphic is an integral part of the message, like a graph or a map; tap "Show pictures." You see all the graphics on full display, right in the message. After you tap the "Show pictures" button, you'll be asked whether to always display graphics from the sender.

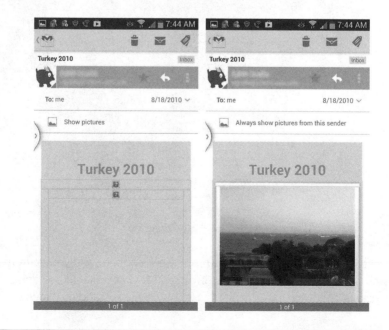

If someone has attached a graphic, you see the graphic displayed in the email message, a thumbnail of the image being sent. You also see the file name of the attachment.

To save the picture to your Galaxy S4, tap the thumbnail, and it gets down-loaded to the Gallery. You'll see a small blue indicator underneath the image, showing you the progress of the download. (For details about the Gallery, turn to page 119.)

Attachments in Gmail

Gmail lets you download graphics attachments, including those in the .jpg, .png, and .gif formats as well as Word, Excel, and PowerPoint files. It lets you preview those files and other file types as well.

If you get an attachment that you can preview, you see a paper clip icon near bottom of the message. The attachment's name appears next to the paper clip icon. Tap the paper clip to download it. If it's a Word, Excel, or PowerPoint file, it opens in an app called Polaris Office 5 that's built into the Galaxy S4.

Add the Sender to Your Contacts

If you're reading an email message from someone and want to add her to your Contact list, tap the small photo of her name or the icon next to her name. A screen appears that lets you create a new contact with the sender's name and email address, or add the information to an existing contact.

If the person is already in your Contacts list, when you tap the name, a list of icons appears that lets you respond to him in a number of ways, including by email, phone, and so on, based on the contact information you have.

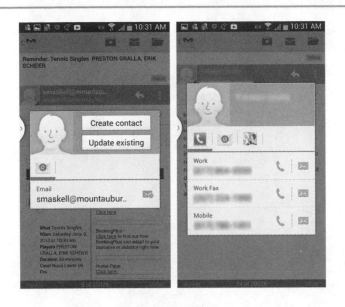

Replying and Forwarding in Gmail

Near the top of the screen in Gmail, next to the sender's name, you'll find a small toolbar of icons for replying to and forwarding mail:

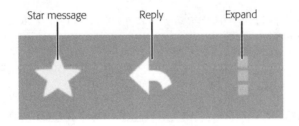

Star message   Reply   Expand

- **Star.** Adds a star to the message in the email list to call your attention to it later. You can use stars to flag messages that contain important information, say, or those that require further research. If the message already displays a star, tap it to remove it.

> **NOTE** For more information about starred messages, see page 250 later in this chapter.

- **Reply.** Replies to the message's sender only. A new email window opens, addressed to the sender, with the original email text quoted in it. (If there's an attachment in the original email, it won't be included.)

- **Expand.** Expands the toolbar to give you more options for replying and forwarding:

- **Reply all.** If the email was sent to multiple people, this replies to the sender of the message, *and* to all the recipients in a new email window, with the original message quoted in it. You can always add new recipients or delete existing ones. (If there's an attachment in the original email, it won't be included.)

- **Forward.** This opens a new email window with a blank To: field that you can fill in. The message includes the entire email that you had opened, including any attachments.

Understanding Gmail's Organization

Gmail has its own terminology and worldview when it comes to handling email, so you have new some terms and ideas to get used to. Here are the most common Gmail concepts:

- **Labels.** Think of these as email folders. Your regular email program has a folder called Inbox, for example, and lets you create other folders, such as Family, Work, and so on. Gmail calls these email containers *labels*.

That said, there's a slight underlying difference between the way you work with Gmail's labels and how you work with your email program's folders. In your typical email program, you might move mail between folders by dragging them. Not so in Gmail. In Gmail, you affix a label to an email message. When you do that, that email automatically appears when you sort for that label.

Labels actually give you more flexibility than folders, since you can attach multiple labels to a single email message to have it show up in multiple labels. For example, if you get an email from your brother about advice for your upcoming trip to France, you can add the labels Family and France to the email. That email then shows up in both your Family label and your France label.

- **Overall mail organization.** Because Gmail uses labels rather than folders, you may find mail in more than one location. Also, unlike some email software, Gmail gives you the option of viewing all mail in one single area titled "All mail," including mail you've archived and all other mail.

- **Archive.** In some instances, you'll get mail that you want to keep around but don't want showing up in your inbox, because your inbox would otherwise get too cluttered. So Gmail lets you *archive* messages. Archiving a message doesn't delete it, but it removes it from your inbox. You can still find the message listed in your "All mail" folder. You can also find it by searching.

Managing Incoming Mail in Gmail

ONCE YOU'VE READ A Gmail message, it's time to decide what to do with it. At the top of your screen when you're reading email, you'll find three buttons that can help:

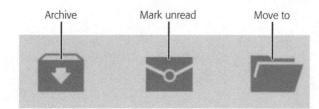

Archive   Mark unread   Move to

- **Archive.** This button appears if you haven't given the email a label. Tap the button to archive the message. It vanishes from your inbox, but still appears in "All mail."

- **Mark unread.** When new mail comes into your inbox, its background is highlighted in white, and its text is bold. After you read it, the background turns gray, which marks it as read. This shading makes it easy for you to see which messages you haven't yet read. If you want to keep the current email message looking like a new one (because you want to make sure you read it again later, for example), tap this button.

- **Move to.** Even if you haven't applied a label to a piece of mail in your inbox, it already has a label preapplied to it—Inbox. Tap this button to change the message's label. When you tap the button, a screen appears with all your labels on it. The labels for the mail you're reading have green checkmarks next to them. Add checkmarks for all the labels you want to add, and remove checks for labels you want to remove.

But wait, as they say in late-night commercials, there's more! Tap the Menu key and you get these options as well:

- **Delete.** Sends your email to the Gmail Trash. The mail is available in the Trash for 30 days, so you can always view it there if needed—but after 30 days it gets deleted forever. When you delete mail, you see a notification at the top of your inbox, telling you how much mail you've deleted, and giving you a chance to undo the deletion—in other words, take the message out of the Trash.

- **Change labels.** What gives? This sounds a lot like the "Move to" option—and it is. But there's a minor difference. With "Move to," you can move the mail to your Priority Inbox. With "Change labels" you can't.

- **Mark important.** If you get a very important message, tap this. The mail will appear with the Important label.

- **Mute.** Tap, and the email and all conversations related to it bypass your inbox and are automatically archived. When you mute a piece of mail, you're not just archiving that one piece of mail, but the entire "conversation" of which it's a part. Let's say, for example, you subscribe to a mailing list, and there is a long, ongoing series of back-and-forth emails about a topic in which you have no interest. (Justin Bieber, anyone?) You're tired of seeing emails in that conversation pop up in your inbox. Tap the Mute button, and you won't see it in your inbox anymore. It will, however, still appear in "All mail."

- **Report spam.** Tap the "Report spam" button, and a note goes to Google, saying you believe the email is spam. Google uses that information to determine which mail should be considered spam and be automatically rerouted into people's Spam label.

NOTE When you get a message that Gmail considers spam, it isn't automatically deleted. Instead, it shows up in your Spam label. It doesn't appear in "All mail," or anywhere else in Gmail. It also doesn't appear when you search through your email.

- **Report phishing.** Tap this, and a note goes to Google saying you believe the email is a nasty piece of work known as a *phishing attack.* In this kind of scam, you receive an email that *looks* legitimate—from your bank, for example—but in fact it's from someone who's trying to trick you into revealing personal information such as your bank login information. When you click a link in the email, you're sent to a site that looks like the real site, but in fact is one set up only to grab your information.

- **Settings.** Sends you to screen that lets you change your Gmail settings, including adding a new account.

TIP Mail stays in your inbox until you take away the Inbox label. So if you want to keep your inbox clean, remove the Inbox label from incoming email regularly. It's a good idea to add other labels to your messages, though, so you can easily find them later.

Managing Multiple Email Messages

You can also handle *groups* of messages rather than individual ones. To do that, first you need to group them all. Hold your finger in turn on each message that you want to take action on in a group. Each message gets highlighted, and the top of your screen shows how many you've put in the group. Now use the icons at the top of the screen for managing them all, such as moving them, archiving them, deleting them, changing their labels, and so on. To get to the full list of actions, tap the three stacked squares on the far right of the screen.

NOTE If you're viewing a different label than Inbox, not all these options may appear when you press the Menu key; the options that appear vary from label to label. To access all the options, just go back to your inbox.

Writing Messages in Gmail

WHEN YOU WANT TO create a new Gmail message, start from the inbox and then press the Compose button at the top of the screen—it's a plus sign on an envelope. A new, blank message form opens, and the keyboard appears so you can start typing.

NOTE If you want a larger keyboard, turn your Galaxy S4 90 degrees.

Write your message this way:

1. **Type the recipient's address in the To field.** As you type, Gmail looks through your Contacts list, as well as the list of people you've sent email to in the past, and displays any matches. (Gmail matches the first few letters of first names as well as last names as you type.) If you find a match, tap it instead of typing the rest of the address. You can add as many addresses as you wish.

2. **Send copies to other recipients.** Press the Menu, and tap Add Cc/Bcc from the menu that appears. Two new lines appear beneath the To field—Cc and Bcc.

   Anyone whose email address you put in the Cc and Bcc boxes gets a copy of the email message. The difference is that while everyone can see all the Cc recipients, the Bcc copy is sent in private. None of the other recipients can see the email addresses you enter in the Bcc field.

NOTE The term *carbon copy* comes from those long-gone days in the previous century when people typed mail, documents, and memos on an ancient device called a typewriter. To make multiple copies, typists added a sheet of carbon paper and another sheet of typing paper. The force of the keys striking the paper would imprint ink on the second sheet, using the ink in the carbon paper.

---

3. **Type the topic of the message into the Subject field.** A clear, concise subject line is a good thing for both you and your recipient, so you can immediately see what the message is about when you scan your inbox.

4. **Type your message into the Compose Mail box.** Type as you would in any other text field. You can also use copy and paste.

5. **Add an attachment.** To add an attachment, press the Menu key and then tap either "Attach picture" or "Attach video." Those menu choices don't really make any sense, because when you tap either, you can add any kind of file that you want, such as Office documents as well as photos, videos, and anything else. When you tap either choice, you come to another screen that doesn't make any sense. It reads "Choose type of attachment," but you don't, in fact, choose the type of attachment from that screen. Instead, you choose a location such as Drive

(Google Drive), your Gallery, and so on. Select the location of your attachment, then browse to select the attachment.

No matter what type of file you send, a paper clip icon appears beneath the subject line, and you see the file name and size. Tap the X button if you want to remove the attachment. You can keep adding attachments, if you want.

6. **Tap Send, Save draft, or Discard**. Tap the send icon at the top right of the screen, and the message gets sent immediately. If you instead want to save the message as a draft, tap the Menu key and select "Save draft." If you'd prefer to call the whole thing off and get rid of the draft, tap the Menu key and select Discard, which gets rid of the message for good.

Adding a Signature

The Gmail app can automatically add a signature—your contact information, for example—at the bottom of every outgoing message. To create a signature of your own, when you're in a label, press the Menu key and then select Settings and tap the Gmail account for which you want to add a label. (If you have only one account, only one will show up.) From the screen that appears, tap Signature. Type a signature, tap OK, and the signature will be appended to the bottom of all messages you send.

NOTE The signature will be appended to the bottom of outgoing Gmail, but not your other email accounts. You need to set up signatures separately for each email account.

Working with Labels and Search

LABELS ARE AN EXCELLENT way to organize your email in Gmail, because they're far more flexible than folders. A single message can appear in as many or as few labels as you want.

To go to a different label from the one you're currently in, tap the icon next to the label at top-left. You see a listing of every one of your labels. Scroll to see all of them. Gmail automatically creates the following labels for you:

- **Inbox** contains all your incoming messages.

- **Priority Inbox** contains messages that you've deemed to be of a high priority.

- **Starred** shows all the messages you've starred.

- **Important** shows all the messages you've tagged as being important

- **Chats** contains the contents of all chats done via Google Talk.

- **Sent** lists all messages you've sent.

- **Outbox** shows mail you've created and asked Gmail to send, but that has not yet been sent.

- **Drafts** contains mail you've created but not completed.

- **All mail** contains all mail and chats, except for Spam and Trash. It also includes mail that you've archived.

- **Spam** contains all mail marked as spam, either by you or by Google.

You can remove mail from Spam by going into the Spam label, reading a message, and tapping "Remove label" from the bottom of the screen.

- **Trash** contains mail you've deleted but hasn't been removed from the trash yet. Email is removed from the trash when it's more than 30 days old.

If you use Gmail's Priority Inbox on the Web, you'll also see a label here called Important, which shows all the messages that Gmail has flagged as being important to you. For details about how Priority Inbox works, and to set it up on the Web, go to *http://bit.ly/14GiCXL*.

If you've created any labels other than these, using Gmail on the Web, then you see them here as well. You can't create new labels in Gmail on the Galaxy S4. To create a new label, visit Gmail on the Web, using your phone's browser or a computer.

Searching Gmail

GOOGLE MAKES WHAT MANY consider the best search engine on the planet, so it's no surprise that it builds Google Search into Gmail on the Galaxy S4. Searching is straightforward. To search, press the Menu key, and then tap the Search button. As you type, Gmail displays previous searches you've done that match those letters and narrows the search as you type. If you see a search term you want to use, tap it. If not, type the entire search term, and then tap Search.

After you enter your search terms, you see a display of all matching email. Gmail searches through the To, From, and Subject fields, as well as the messages' text. In the upper-left corner, you see the search term you entered.

Advanced Gmail Searching

Gmail lets you do some pretty fancy searching—after all, Google is the search king. So you can search by To, From, Subject, specific labels, and a lot more. Say you want to search for all email with the word "Halloween" in the subject line. Type the following in the search box:

```
Subject:Halloween
```

You can search other Gmail fields, as shown on the following list (head to *http:// tinyurl.com/gmail-search* for a more complete list):

- **From.** Searches for mail from a specific sender.

- **To.** Searches mail for a specific recipient.

- **Subject.** Searches the subject line.

- **In <label>.** Searches in a specific label.

You can combine these search terms with one another, and with a search of the text of the message. So to search for all email in your Work label with the word "budget" in it, you'd do this search:

```
In:Work Budget
```

Setting Up Email Accounts

YOU'RE NOT CONFINED TO using Gmail on the Galaxy S4—you can use your other email accounts as well. How you set one up depends upon what kind of email account you want to add.

To get started, head to the App Drawer and tap Email. Fill in your email address and password, and then tap Next. If you're setting up a web-based mail account like Yahoo Mail or Microsoft's web-based mail (find it at Outlook.com or Hotmail.com), the S4 is smart enough to do all your setup for you, including your incoming and outgoing mail servers. After a moment or two, it makes sure everything is working properly, and then sends you to a page with your various account options, such as how you want to sync emails between the Web and your S4, whether to notify you when mail arrives, and so on. Most of the time, your best bet is to stick with the options the S4 picks for you—it's plenty smart about making the right choices.

POP3 and IMAP Accounts

If you instead want to set up a general email account, such as from your Internet service provider (ISP), after you fill in your email address and password and tap next, you'll come to a screen that asks what type of account you want to add—a POP account, an IMAP account, or a Microsoft Exchange ActiveSync account.

TIP If it's a Microsoft Exchange ActiveSync account, it's likely a work account. For details on how to set up ActiveSync and other corporate options, see Chapter 14.

As for POP and IMAP, that's techie talk for two different kinds of email services. Here's what you need to know about each before making your choice:

- With a **POP (Post Office Protocol)** account, the POP server delivers email to your inbox. From then on, the messages live on your Galaxy S4—or your home computer, or whichever machine you used to check email. You can't download another copy of that email, because POP servers only let you download a message once. So if you use your account on both a computer and your S4, you must be careful to set up the account properly, as described in the box on page 255, so you won't accidentally delete email. Despite this caveat, POP accounts remain the most popular type of email accounts, and are generally the easiest to set up and use.

- With an **IMAP (Internet Message Access Protocol)** account, the server doesn't send you the mail and force you to store it on your computer or phone. Instead, it keeps all your mail on the server, so you can access the exact same mail from your S4 and your computer—or even from multiple devices. The IMAP server always remembers what you've done with your mail—what messages you've read and sent, your folder organization, and so on. So if you read mail, send mail, and reorganize your folders on your S4, when you then check your mail on a computer, you'll see all those changes, and vice versa.

That's the good news. The bad news is that if you don't remember to regularly clean out your mail, your mailbox can overflow if your account doesn't have enough storage to hold it all. If your IMAP account gets full, then when people send you email, their messages bounce back to them.

NOTE With the exception of a Gmail account, you can add only email accounts that you've previously set up to your Galaxy S4. If you get a new email account at work or home, get it all set up before you add it to your phone.

Choose which type of account you want to use. In some cases, your ISP will let you use either IMAP or POP, but on other cases, it will require you to use one or the other. So check with your ISP. After you choose your account type, the S4 now attempts to automatically configure your email account for you. Most of the time it will be able to figure out your settings, but sometimes it fails. In that case, it shows you a screen where you need to fill in techie details, such as server names for the outgoing mail server (SMTP), whether you use POP3 or IMAP, the incoming mail server name, and so. If you don't have the information at hand (and face it, who does?), check with your ISP or your corporate tech support staff.

TIP If you're already using an email program on your computer, that means you've already set up the account there, and its settings are in the email program. So go to the account settings on your computer, and grab the settings from there.

Keeping Your POP Mailboxes in Sync

The difference between POP and IMAP accounts is that POP email only lives on whatever machine you download it to. With IMAP, a copy automatically remains on the server so you can download it again on another device. Say you read incoming email on your Galaxy S4, delete some of it, keep some of it, and write some new messages. Later that day, you go to your desktop computer and log into the same email account. You won't see those incoming messages you read on your phone, nor the ones you sent from it.

When you're using both your phone and home computer to work with the same POP account, how do you keep them in sync? By making your POP account act more like an IMAP account, so it leaves a copy of all messages on the server when you download them to your home computer. That way, you can delete messages on the Galaxy S4, and still see them in your inbox at home.

In Outlook 2013, choose File→Account Settings→Account Settings and then

double-click the account name. Select More Settings→Advanced. Turn on "Leave a copy of each message on the server." Also turn on "Remove from server when deleted from "Deleted items" so you won't fill up the server space allocated to your account. (In Outlook 2010, this setting is called "Delete messages from server after they are deleted from this computer.")

In Outlook 2011 for Mac, choose Tools→Accounts, choose the POP account in the left column, and then click Advanced at lower right. Turn on "Leave a copy of each message on the server," and also turn on "Delete copies from the server After Deleting From This Computer."

To get to these settings in earlier versions of Outlook, choose Tools→ E-mail Accounts→E-Mail→"View or Change Email Accounts"→*your account name*→Change→More Settings→Advanced.

Reading Mail

ON THE GALAXY S4, reading email on a non-Gmail account is much like reading Gmail. In the Apps Menu, tap Email to launch the Email app, and it sends you to your inbox immediately and downloads any waiting mail. As with Gmail, the Email app displays the subject line, time and date of delivery, and the sender of each message.

If you've organized your mail into folders on your computer, that organization won't be reflected on the Galaxy S4. You won't be able to see or use the folders from your computer's email software.

To read a message, tap it. At the bottom of the screen are icons that take you to the next and previous messages, for deleting mail, and for replying to or forwarding mail.

If the sender is a contact for whom you have a picture, the contact's picture will show up next to his name in the From area.

But there's a whole lot more you can do with your mail message than that. Tap the Menu key, and you'll get the following choices, which will vary according to whether you're checking mail from an ISP or web-based mail, and according to the web-based mail program you're using:

- **Mark as unread.** When you look in your inbox, the mail will appear bold-faced, as if you hadn't yet read it.

- **Add to spam.** Considers the mail as spam. The sender will be also be sent to your spam list, so all new mail coming from him will be considered spam.

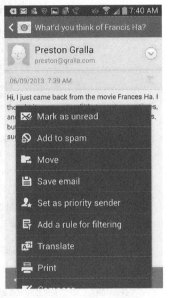

- **Move.** Lets you move the message to another folder.

- **Save email.** Lets you save the mail locally on your S4. It's saved in a file that ends in .eml. You'll be able to read the mail by using a file manager and browsing to the My Files folder (page 343).

- **Set as priority sender.** When you choose this, whenever mail shows up in your inbox from this sender, there's an orange icon next to his name, indicating his mail is important.

- **Remove from priority sender.** This option only appears on mail from priority senders. It removes the priority status of the sender.

- **Add rule for filtering.** Lets you create a rule that will look through incoming mail, and then manage the mail for you. For example, you can create rules that automatically move all mail from your mother to a Family folder, or from your boss to a Work folder (or to a Circular File folder, if you'd prefer to handle his email that way). When you tap this option, simply follow the instructions for creating a rule.

- **Translate.** Have a friend in Italy who's sending you mail in *italiano?* If you don't *parli italiano* tap here and Google Translate will do a translation for you.

- **Print.** As the option says, prints the mail to a wirelessly available printer.

- **Compose.** Lets you create a new email. For details, see page 264 later in this chapter.

- **Font size.** Lets you choose a larger or smaller font size, for easier reading.

- **Settings.** Brings you to the general setting screen for the mail account. From here, you can make many changes to things such as whether you want a confirmation screen flashed before you can delete an email, and so on.

- **Helps.** Gets you help.

Handling Attachments and Pictures in Email

MORE AND MORE EMAIL messages contain pictures. Sometimes, the picture is in the content of the message itself, such as a company logo. Other times, the picture is an attachment, like a family photo. Email handles the two types of graphics differently.

If the graphics are embedded in the content of the message, you'll see a "Show images" button at the top of the mail, and where the photos would normally be, you'll see text reading "Inline image." Tap "Show images," and the photos appear right in the mail, where they were placed.

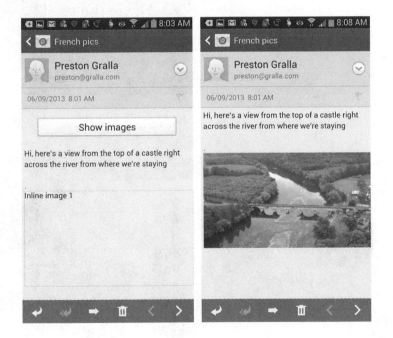

If someone has sent an email and attached a picture, you'll see an Attachments button near the top of the message. Tap it and two buttons appear—Preview and Save. Tap the Preview button, and the image gets downloaded so you can preview it. Depending on the size of the photo, it might take some time. You'll see the progress as it downloads. After it downloads, the photo opens in the Gallery, as any photo normally does. If it's a wide photo, you can rotate the phone 90 degrees, and see the full picture as the phone switches to its wider orientation.

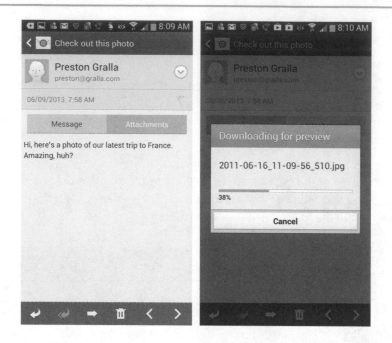

If you tap Save, the file is downloaded and saved in your Download folder.

Attachments in Email

When you receive an email attachment in Word, Excel, PowerPoint, or some other file types, you can preview and download them. You handle these attachments in the same way you handle pictures. The attachment button shows up in the email, and when you tap it you can preview it or save it in the same way you can a photo. If it's a Word, Excel, or PowerPoint file, the preview opens in an app called Polaris Office that's built into the Galaxy S4.

Adding the Sender to Your Contacts

If you get a message from someone and would like to add her to your Contacts list, open the email and then tap the small button to the left of the sender's name. A screen appears that lets you create a new contact with the sender's name and email address, or send email to that contact. If you tap the name of someone who is already a contact, you'll see a button that lets you view that contact's information, and take action on it, such as sending an email, making a phone call, and so on.

Managing Mail

WHEN YOU'RE IN YOUR inbox, you've got more options for managing your mail. Press the Menu key, and a menu appears with these options:

- **Sort by.** Lets you sort your email in several different ways: newest mail first, the oldest mail first, alphabetically by sender, by priority, and so on.

NOTE The options that appear here vary according to whether you're reading mail from an ISP or web-based mail, and according to what web-based mail service you use.

- **View mode.** Lets you choose the traditional way of viewing mail, by date, and so on, or else what's called by "Conversation view," which groups entire conversations together. Conversation view takes some getting used to, but it's the best way to track a message trail.

- **New meeting invitation.** If you use a mail service like Hotmail.com or Outlook.com that also includes a calendar, you can create meeting invitations by choosing this.

- **Documents.** If you use Hotmail.com or Outlook.com, this lets you view documents from a Microsoft file service such as Sharepoint Services. If you don't know what that is, you don't need to use this option.

- **Font size.** Changes the font size of your messages.

- **Delete all.** Think of this as a nuclear option. It deletes all your email. Don't do it.

- **Settings.** Brings you to a settings screen for the email account.

- **Help.** Need help with your email service? Here's where to get it.

You've got even more options than that. Look down at the bottom of the screen. You'll see a bar with four icons. The leftmost one lets you create a new mail message; the one to its right checks for new mail. The one in the shape of a magnifying glass lets you search mail. And the one on the far right that looks like a folder displays all your folders for the mail service you're currently using. Tap any folder to go to it.

Mail from Multiple Accounts

If you're like most people these days, you have more than one email account. It can be a pain to have to check every single one of them for new mail. Surprise—you don't have to. You can view mail from all of them at one time. When you're in any inbox, tap the icon to the left of the mail icon at the upper-left of the screen. (It looks like three stacked lines.) When you do that, you'll see a combined inbox that tells you how many emails you've received from all of your accounts. Tap it to see all the email in one place. You'll also see all the folders from all your email accounts.

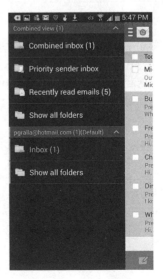

Note that on the S4 Gmail is its own universe, and so you won't see mail from it in the unified inbox, and vice versa.

Creating and Sending Mail

TO CREATE A NEW email message, when you're in the inbox or any folder, tap the pencil-and-paper icon on the lower-left of the screen. If you want to create a new message when you're reading an email message, tap the Menu key and then tap Compose.

You create a new email message in nearly the identical way in the Email app as you do in the Gmail app, so go to page 247 for details about filling in the To, Subject, and other fields.

Adding a Signature

When you send an email, the Galaxy S4 appends text to the bottom of it, but will read something like: "Sent from my Samsung smartphone on AT&T." That text is visible as you type, and you can delete it if you want. In fact, you may want to delete it from every message and use some text of your own there instead—your email signature.

To add a signature to all your outgoing mail or to delete the built-in text at the bottom of the screen from all outgoing mail from any email service, press the Menu key, then select Settings and tap the name of the account. Scroll down until you see Signature. To stop the built-in signature from being sent on all messages, switch the button from On to Off. To create a new signature, tap Signature, type the text you wish to use, and then tap Done.

The changes will affect all the email messages you send with the Email app. (The signature you make in Email doesn't apply to your Gmail account. For details about handling signatures in Gmail, see page 249.)

Using Web-Based Mail Programs

OUTLOOK.COM (AKA HOTMAIL) AND Yahoo Mail are both web-based mail programs, but the Galaxy S4 lets you read them, using its built-in email software. Just create new accounts for them, and you'll be able to use its email software to read them.

But if you'd like, you can read email from Hotmail and Yahoo, or any other web-based mail program. Simply visit the site with your phone's web browser and use the email site just as if you were using it on a computer. In some cases, when you visit the site, you're automatically routed to a site specifically built for smartphones, so all the features are formatted nicely for your phone.

In some instances, there might even be an app you can download from the Google Play Store, or from the Web, that you can use instead of a web browser. Search the Google Play Store to see.

NOTE In some cases the downloadable app may not be built by the company that owns the web-based email service, but instead by a third party. It's generally better to find an app built by the original developer.

You'll learn to:

- Use Facebook on the S4
- Use Twitter on the S4
- Use Google+ on the S4
- Chat and videochat on the S4

CHAPTER 11

Facebook, Twitter, Google+, Chat, and Videochat

THE GALAXY S4 HAS everything you need to keep in touch with friends, family, and associates throughout the world via social networking apps like Facebook, Twitter, Google+, and more. It connects to the Internet, has GPS capabilities (so you can let others know where you are), a big beautiful screen for displaying updates, and a camera so you can take photos and videos and share them. Because it's also got a front-facing camera, it's great for videochat as well. If you're a social butterfly, you've landed on the right phone.

In this chapter you'll find out how to get the most out of your S4 and social networking services, chat, and videochat.

NOTE At this writing, the S4 doesn't have social networking apps built into it. You have to download those apps from Play Store. But that may change, so check your App Drawer to see if any social networking ones are included. See Chapter 12 for the full details on installing and using apps.

Facebook

FACEBOOK IS NOT JUST popular, it's ubiquitous. Millions of people around the globe use it to keep in touch with friends, play games, and publicize their favorite causes. In fact, millions of businesses now have a Facebook page, showing how much social media has become integral to marketing and public relations.

To use Facebook on the S4, you can go to *www.facebook.com* in the Browser, but most Facebookers use an app that's specially designed for the phone. As mentioned earlier, the app doesn't come preinstalled on your S4, so you have to download it and install it yourself. Search for Facebook on Play Store, and then download the app. After a few minutes, when it completes downloading, tap the Open button to run the app.

TIP Make sure that you download Facebook, not Facebook Home. Facebook Home nearly takes over your entire S4. Many users have complained long and loud about Facebook Home— at this writing half the people who rated it gave it only one out of a possible five stars.

After you launch the app, sign in. If you don't yet have a Facebook account, tap "Sign up for Facebook" at the bottom of the screen and follow the directions. You'll be asked to enter a bunch of personal information to create your account.

Once you sign in, you get a chance to sync your Facebook pictures, contact information, and status updates with your existing contacts. You can choose to sync with your existing contacts, not to sync, or else have Facebook add its contacts to your own Contacts. The suggested choice is to sync with existing contacts, which ensures that you can interact with all your Facebook friends on your S4 without creating duplicates.

Tap Sync. In the background, your contacts sync. Meanwhile, you're taken to your Facebook news feed so you can start using Facebook right away.

TIP When you use Facebook and look at your contacts in the S4's contact app, any of them who are also Facebook friends will have a small Facebook icon next to them.

The first screen you come to is the main Facebook page—your news feed page. You'll see updates from all your Facebook friends, including their pictures, how long ago the update was posted...pretty much the same thing you see when you visit Facebook on the Web.

Scroll through the feed the same way you scroll through any other screen on your S4, by flicking and dragging. When you get to the bottom of the screen, there will be a delay as your phone contacts Facebook to load Older Posts. Keep scrolling to the bottom as many times as you want. If you've got a lot of friends, there may seem to be no end to the eternity of postings.

NOTE This chapter assumes that you already know the basics of using Facebook. If you don't, check out the Facebook website at *www.facebook.com*. Click the Help link down at the bottom of the page. On the Help Center page, click the "Get Started on Facebook" link. And if you want to become a real pro, check out *Facebook: The Missing Manual* by E. A. Vander Veer.

The Facebook app regularly checks for updates on its own. If you're like most Facebook denizens, though, you like can't wait. To make sure that you're seeing up-to-the-minute postings from every single one of your friends, tell the Facebook app to check Facebook for any new postings. The S4 gives you a quick way to do that: drag the top of your news feed down a bit, and then release it. The Facebook page appears to bounce and then refreshes itself. Use Facebook for a few minutes, and this gesture will become second nature.

As you scroll down the news feed, look at the bottom of each update. There are three buttons there: Like, Comment, and Share. Tap the appropriate button for what you want to do.

Tapping Like sends your friend a notification of your approval and adds your name to the list of people who also gave the post a thumbs-up. Tap Comment, and you'll see a list of all comments to the post and a box where you can add your own. Tap in the box, and the S4's keyboard appears. Type your comment, tap Comment, and off it goes. You can also add a picture to your comment by tapping the photo icon, and choosing a photo from the Gallery (page 119).

When you're on the screen for making a comment or adding a Like, you can view the profile of the person whose update you're reading. Tap the Menu key at the bottom of the page and select View Profile.

NOTE The official Facebook app that you use may look and work a bit different than what you see pictured here. That's because the app gets updated, so you may be using a different version of the app as the one in use when this book was published.

Writing Posts, Uploading Photos and Using Check In

Now that you've got Facebook on your S4, what should you do? Start posting, of course. What's the point of Facebook if you can't share your innermost secrets with the world?

To post an update, tap the Status button at the Facebook screen's upper left; the keyboard appears. Type what you want, tap Post at upper right, and you'll share with the world your all-important news about your cat's recently changing sleep patterns.

Ah, but what if you want to not just talk about his sleeping patterns, but also show a picture of him sleeping as part of the post? What if you want to share the post only with specific friends? What if you want people to know the exact location of your cat while he continues with his frustrating sleep habits?

That's where the icons just above the keyboard come in. Tap the leftmost one (the picture of a person), to send the post to a specific friend. Tap the location button just next to it, and then choose a location. Tap the photo icon to go to the Gallery to choose a photo to include in the post. And tap the icon all the way on the right to choose how private the post will be: For anyone to see, for friends only, friends of friends, and so on.

You can also just post a photo, without tying it to a post: back on the news feed page, tap the photo icon in the middle upper part of the screen, and then choose a photo from your Gallery to post. And if you want to choose a location for your postings, tap the Check In icon at upper right.

Navigating Facebook's World

Look at the very top of the Facebook app's screen—there are five icons there. They're there so that you can navigate Facebook's gigantic, ever-changing world. Here's what they do, from left to right:

- **The leftmost icon (a menu)** gives you access to countless Facebook features and settings. You'll learn more about them on page 268.

- **The second-from-left icon (two people)** shows you all the requests for people to friend you. Respond to any right on the screen.

- **The middle icon (a message balloon)** lets you see any messages sent to you. Tap any message to respond to it, Like it, and so on.

- **Tap the second-from-right icon (a globe)** to see notifications send to you. Likes and comments to your posts, messages from games you play, and so on.

- **Tap the rightmost icon** to see a list of your contacts, and to chat with them individually or collectively in a group.

Interacting with Friends and Finding New Ones

Facebook is all about keeping in touch with friends and making new ones. To do all that, tap the menu key (leftmost at the top of the screen), and then tap Friends in the menu that appears. A screen appears with a list of your friends.

If you've got a long list of friends, it can take a long time to scroll through them and find the specific one you're looking for. So a better idea is to tap the Find Friends button. From here, you can do several things, including, as the name says, find your friends. So tap the Search button, and search for the name.

How about if you want to add new friends? It's a snap. When you tap the Find Friends button, a screen appears with a list of people you might know. How is that list compiled? It's Facebook magic. But part of it comes down to mutual friends—if there's someone with whom you've got a lot of friends in common, they'll show up here.

TIP You can also unfriend friends from this menu. Tap the small icon to the right of any friend's name.

If you don't find the person you want, tap Search. You'll come to a list of people who match that name. Keep in mind that if you're looking for common name, like Joe Smith, there may be plenty of matches. Scroll through the list, and when you find someone you might be interested in, tap to go to a page with details like picture, location, hometown, activities, interests...the whole Facebook nine yards. Tap Add Friend, and your friend request goes off on its merry way. From this page you can also send a message, without having to request becoming friends.

Viewing Your Friends' Walls, Info, and More

When you first tapped the top-left menu button and tapped Friends, you saw a list of your friends. Tap any friend, and you'll get sent to her Timeline, where you can see her most recent updates and much more. Scroll down to see all her updates, tap the Message button to send a message, tap the Photos button to see photos, the Friends buttons to see her friends. You'll also be able to comment on any post...well, you get the idea. You can do anything with the Android app that you can do on the Web.

Facebook Notifications

Facebook uses your S4's Notification panel to let you know when something important has happened—someone responded to a friend request, wants to chat, and so on. You'll get a notification via the Notification panel. Tap it to open it and take any action needed.

Add a Facebook Widget

If you want to interact with Facebook updates at a glance, you don't need to run the Facebook app. Instead, add a Facebook widget or two to one of your Home screen panes. Adding a widget is a great way to use Facebook on your S4, because that way, you can get updates and interact with Facebook without having to run the app.

To add a widget, hold your finger on your Home screen or any pane. From the menu that appears, tap Apps and Widgets and then tap the Widgets button at the top of the page. Flick through them until you find the ones for Facebook. Widgets are in alphabetical order, so it shouldn't take you too long to get to the Facebook ones.

When you find the one you want to add, hold it and drag it to the highlighted area of the screen that appears above. There may be several widgets, so drag as many as you want. Facebook Status is a good one, since it shows you all your friends' updates at a glance. The widget constantly refreshes itself. From the widget, you can also post updates and see how many notifications you have. Tap it to go straight to Facebook.

> **NOTE** If you try to put a widget on a pane that is already full, the widget will refuse to be put there. For more details about handling widgets see page 33.

Twitter

ARE YOU ONE OF the vast army of tweeters? If so, you're not alone. Celebrities, politicians, pundits, and even the Pope now communicate with the world in 140-character messages called *tweets*. You'll be pleased to know that you can use Twitter right on your S4.

As with Facebook, you must first to download and install the Twitter app (page 268). Make sure it's the official one from Twitter; Twitter will be listed as the author on the app's description page.

> **NOTE** This section assumes you already know how to use Twitter on the Web (or have at least heard of it). If you're just getting started, go to *www.twitter.com* and click the Help link at the bottom of the page. The Help Center features a "Welcome to Twitter" link where you can learn more.

Once you install it, log into your existing Twitter account. (If you're one of the remaining people on earth without a Twitter account, you can click the Sign Up button to create a new account.) After a moment or two, you'll be logged in. Tap Finish. Voilá—you're there! You'll see updates of all the people you're following. Scroll through to read them.

> **NOTE** When you sign in, you'll be asked whether Twitter can use your location. If you're worried about your privacy, just say no.

When you come to the main Twitter screen, look across the top—that navigation bar is Twitter central for your interactions.

Home. Takes you to Twitter's home page, where you see tweets from all the people you follow.

Discover. Shows you recommendations for other people you might want to follow, suggests tweets for you, and more. You can also see which hashtags are trending.

Connect. Displays a screen of retweets by your followers.

Me. Takes you to your personal profile, including stats on your tweets, retweets, and followers.

The Home Screen

6:50 PM

Home

Right Now ow.ly/mB5g3

Why Microsoft @whymicrosoft 1h
Are you deciding between Microsoft Dynamics CRM and Salesforce.com? This comparison will help. ow.ly/mDcFk

Laughing Squid @LaughingSquid 1h
Glow-in-the-Dark T-Shirts You Can Draw on With Light by LUM Apparel squid.us/11etyxw

Mike Elgan 1h
Who says you can't take it with you? fplus.me/p/2fA0

Wall Street Journal @WSJ 1h
Breaking: Egypt's Morsi addresses nation on TV after rebuffing calls to step down. on.wsj.com/12BJYyk

The Connect Screen

12:53 PM

Connect

PCHelps @PCHelps 6m
MT @pgralla: While you weren't looking, #Windows8 & Windows Phone start to shine bit.ly/15YMtbM. Do you agree?

40m
Microsoft's not-so-secret plan to vault Bing over Google by @pgralla bit.ly/19R0AEd #Bing #Google #Microsoft

50m
Windows 8.1 deep-dive review: Well, it's a start @Computerworld @pgralla computerworld.com/s/article/9240...

50m
Windows 8.1 deep-dive review: Well, it's a start @Computerworld @pgralla computerworld.com/s/article/9240...

NOTE A retweet is when someone forwards your tweet to his own Twitter stream. Sort of like saying, "You've gotta see this tweet!" You can also retweet tweets of any of the people you follow (more on that in a moment).

The Discover Screen   The Me Screen

Just above those four buttons are several more buttons:

- **The bird button** takes you to Twitter's main screen.
- **The person button** lets you add people to Twitter in several ways, including importing them from your S4 contacts, browsing through categories or people, and more.
- **The magnifying glass button** lets you search for people's Twitter pages.
- **The quill button** is what you click to create and send a tweet.

Creating a tweet is straightforward. Tap the tweet button, type in your message, and then tap Tweet. Your message will be sent. As you type, you'll see an indication at the top of the screen about how many characters you have left, so you can stay within Twitter's 140-character limit.

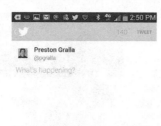

But there's more to it than that. At the bottom of the screen are three buttons that let you enhance your tweet in the following ways:

- **The arrow button** turns on location services, so that your location is shared along with your tweet.

- **The camera button** lets you take and send a photo as part of the tweet. It launches the Camera app (page 137), where you can snap a photo; that photo is then included in the tweet.

- **The picture button** launches the Gallery, where you can take an existing photo and attach it to the tweet.

Taking Action on Tweets

The Twitter home screen shows you all the tweets, retweets, and direct messages from the folks you follow. You see a list of tweets, along with the person's Twitter ID and photo, as well as how long ago the tweet was made. Small icons give more information about the tweet—for example, whether it's a retweet, a direct message between people, or if the tweet has a photo attached.

Press any tweet and hold it, and a bar appears with four icons on it:

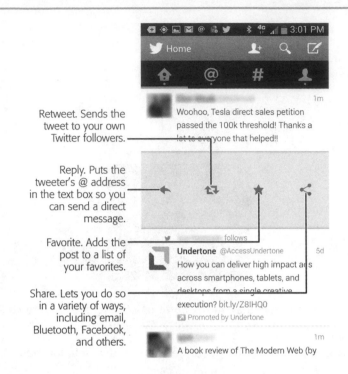

Retweet. Sends the tweet to your own Twitter followers.

Reply. Puts the tweeter's @ address in the text box so you can send a direct message.

Favorite. Adds the post to a list of your favorites.

Share. Lets you do so in a variety of ways, including email, Bluetooth, Facebook, and others.

Similarly if you tap the tweet, you'll come to a screen that shows the tweet and has four buttons across the bottom. They're the same buttons that appear if you press and hold on a tweet.

Twitter Notifications

Twitter uses your S4's Notification panel to let you know when something important has happened—you have a message sent to you, you've been retweeted, and so on. Tap the notification to open it, and take any action needed.

Google+

GOOGLE'S SOCIAL NETWORKING SERVICE, Google+, isn't as popular as Facebook or Twitter, but those in the know will tell you that it's a winner and a great way to extend your social circle. Google+ also has some capabilities that competing social networking services don't have, like the ability to organize your friends and family into *Circles*, which better lets you manage how you interact with them. Circles also integrates with Google Chat, YouTube, and Gmail. So when someone comments on a post on Google+, for example, it also shows up in Gmail.

Circles form the core of Google+, which makes it very different from Facebook and other social networks. When you add friends, family, and so on, you add them to a specific circle or circles, which you create according to your needs. That way, you can fine-tune posts so that only circles see them—for example, sending a post about your upcoming 35th birthday party to your Family circle, or about next year's soccer league schedule to your Soccer circle. Similarly, you can more easily follow posts based on interests as well, by looking at posts from specific circles.

No need to download it; it's built right into your S4. Tap the Google+ icon in the App Drawer, and you're ready to go. You may already have a Google+ account without knowing it, because it's tied to your regular Google account. That's another advantage of Google+ over other social networks: connecting to all your Gmail contacts in Google+ is a breeze.

NOTE This chapter assumes that you've already tried your hand at Google+ on the Web. If you need to learn more, check out the Google+ information page at *http://bit.ly/1a6DdXx*. And if you want to become a real pro, check out *Google+: The Missing Manual* by Kevin Purdy.

When you first launch the app, it asks whether to add your Google+ connections to the contacts on your phone. (It's nice to have it all on one place, no matter where you are.) Tap Next and you'll be asked whether to back up your photos from your phone to Google +, and if so, how to back them up, in other words, only when you're connected to a WiFi network, or when you're connected to a WiFi network or your mobile network. (If you've got a lot of photos uploaded to your Google+ account, it's better to only back up when you're connected to WiFi, to cut down on any potential charges for using too much data on the network.)

After that, you're logged into Google+ and ready to go. When you first launch it, you'll see the feed from all the people in your Google+ circles.

Tap to see Google+ notifications, such as messages to you

Tap to see a list of your Circles, and choose which one's posts you want to see

Tap to refresh and get new posts

Tap to display a menu of Google+ features, such as creating a Profile and seeing people in your Circle

Tap to make comments on a post

Tap to add a + to a post (the equivalent of a Facebook "like")

Tap to share your post with others

Tap to share your location

Tap to write a post

Tap to upload a photo

Tap to indicate your mood by selecting an emoticon

Scroll through the list to read them, and tap any to read the full post if it's too long to display on the initial screen. Beneath each post there are buttons for adding your +1 to it (the equivalent of a Like on Facebook), adding a comment to it, or sharing it.

Look at the top of the screen. Over on the top left tap the small triangle next to the G+ symbol and the word "All." A drop-down list appears, letting you see only a subset of all the Google+ posts from your Circles. Some subsets are auto-created, like "What's hot." But most of them allow you to see just posts from the various Google+ circles that you've created.

Over at the top right of the screen, tap the Refresh button to see the latest posts. And to see any notifications, tap the icon all the way on the top right. (It looks like a bell.) If there are any new notifications, you'll see a red number on the bell.

To write a new post, tap the icon of the green pen on the lower right, with the word "Write" underneath it. Type the text in the text area, and tap down arrow at the top right of the screen to select with whom you want to share the post.

When the keyboard appears it blocks out the bottom part of the screen, so make sure that you don't ignore it. Down at the bottom, tap Photo to choose a photo from the Gallery to include in the post, tap Link to include a link to a Web page, and tap Mood to choose an emoticon to indicate your mood. And if you want to share your location on the post, tap the Location button. When you're done, tap Share, and off your message goes.

Back on the Google+ main screen, you'll notice a few other icons down at the bottom of the screen. They mirror the icons at the bottom of the screen when you're creating a post. With them, you can upload a photo, share your location, and choose an emoticon to indicate your mood.

Chat and Videochat with Google Hangouts

SOCIAL NETWORKING APPS ARE great for keeping in touch with people by posting comments, reading people's posts, commenting on their posts, and so on. But if you want direct, live communication, there's something better—chat and videochat. With them, you establish a direction connection with one or more people simultaneously, and then communicate via the keyboard or video.

Many Galaxy S4 phones come with a feature called Hangouts. Hangouts replace a previous Google program called Google Talk, and they do much more than

Talk—like make it easier to videochat in groups. In that respect, they're similar to the Hangouts feature built into Google+ on the Web.

If you don't see the Hangouts app on your S4, download it from Play Store.

NOTE There's also a chance that your S4 has the old Google Talk program. If so, it's a good idea to replace Talk with the newer, spiffier Hangouts. You may even be prompted to download Hangouts if you try to run Google Talk.

You can use Hangouts on its own, or run it from within Google+. Either way, it works the same. To run it by itself, tap the Hangouts icon in the App Drawer. To run it from Google+, swipe in from the left-hand side to display a menu, and then select Hangouts. You'll come to the main screen, which shows you previous Hangout sessions, and lets you create new ones.

The app name "Hangouts" is a general broad term that describes any interaction in it between you and other people. So a Hangout can be as simple as a one-on-one text chat, or as complex as a group video chat.

NOTE Hangouts are often used by websites to broadcast video discussions. They set up a Hangout, invite specific people to participate, and then do a bit of magic to broadcast it from a website. For example, the Huffington Post has a site called HuffPostLive (*www.huffpostlive.com*) that frequently uses Google Hangouts to broadcast. This author has appeared on it for a panel discussion about Apple, Microsoft, and the power of branding.

On the main screen, tap any previous hangout to initiate a chat with the person listed.

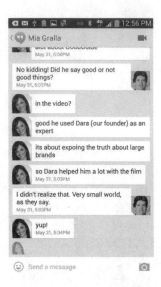

To start a new Hangout with someone else, tap the + sign, or else swipe in from the right side of the screen. Whichever you do, you come to a screen with lists of people, gathered from several places—Google+ and your normal contacts list. At the very top are big icons representing people with whom you communicate most frequently, not necessarily via Hangouts, but via email as well.

Either scroll through the list to find someone you want to chat with, or at the top of the screen, type a name, email address, or even a Google Circle that you've created. When you find someone you want to chat with, tap her name.

At this point, one of two things will happen. If the person uses Google+ or Hangouts already, you'll be able to initiate a Hangout with her. If not, you'll come to a screen that lets you contact the person via phone or email in order to invite her to a Hangout. In practical terms, this means she'll get a message, but will have to download Hangouts to her phone, or head to it on the Web if she wants to communicate with you.

You can create a Hangout and chat with a single person or multiple people. To create one with multiple people, just keep adding people until you've added everyone you want. Here's also where Google+'s Circles feature helps. You can initiate a Hangout with an entire Circle. In fact, if there are people you frequently videochat with—for example, a group of people at work with offices in different locations—you can create a Circle for just that purpose.

The next step is simple. To chat via the keyboard, tap Message at the bottom of the screen. Type in your message, tap the little Send icon to the right of the message, and off it goes.

You'll then see your message onscreen, next to your picture, or an icon representing your face. The person responds, and you see the reply onscreen. Keep chatting this way as long as you like.

You can send a photo as well. Tap the icon of the camera to the right of the text input box and a screen appears that lets you take a photo and send it, grab the photo from photos you've uploaded to Google+, or from your Gallery. To browse the gallery, tap Other photos and select the one you want to send.

If you want to switch to a videochat, tap the videocamera icon at the top right of the screen. The next section gives you the lowdown on how to videochat with Hangouts.

Videochat with Hangouts

When you videochat, your S4 uses the camera facing you as a videocam. When you speak, its microphone sends what you're saying, and when the other person speaks, the S4's speakers play his words.

The main part of the screen shows the person with whom you're videochatting, and you'll see a picture of yourself down towards the bottom. Normally during the chat the screen around all that is black. But if you tap the screen, two rows of icons appear, one at the top and one at the bottom. Here's what the top icons do, from left to right:

- **The red telephone icon** ends the videochat.
- **The paper icon** switches to a text chat.
- **The person icon** lets you add new people to the video call

Here's what the bottom icons do:

- **The microphone icon** turns off your microphone. If it's already off, it turns it back on.
- **The speaker icon** lets you turn off the speaker, or else switch to wired head-phones, a handset earpiece, or Bluetooth headphones.
- **The videocamera icon** turns off the video camera and sends your Google+ picture, or if you don't have one, a generic icon representing a person.
- **The video camera with arrow icon** switches your camera from the one facing you to the one facing away from you. If you're using the one facing away from you, tapping the icon switches to the camera facing you.

Hangout Options

When you're in the middle of a Hangout, if you tap the Menu key, you get these options:

- **People & Options** lets you do several things, including blocking the person or people with whom you're in a Hangout—you won't get notifications when they contact you.

- **New group Hangout** does what it says—lets you create a new Hangout with multiple people in it.

- **Turn history off**. Select this and from now on, whenever you use Hangouts, they won't show up as having happened.

- **Archive** lets you archive the Hangout so that later you can review it. (You'll see how to retrieve archived Hangouts in a bit.)

- **Delete** tosses out the current Hangout and all its content. Tap with caution; you can't retrieve a deleted Hangout.

Retrieving Archived Hangouts and More

If you tap the Menu key on a main Hangouts screen, you'll get these options:

- **Hangout requests** shows you the Hangout requests you've gotten but not yet responded to.

- **Snooze notifications** stop any notification requests for Hangouts. Tap this and you can turn them off for a variety of intervals ranging from an hour to 72 hours.

- **Archived Hangouts** lists all the Hangouts you've archived. Tap any to review it. If it was a text Hangout, you'll see the text. If it was a video Hangout, you'll see a summary of who was on the call and their pictures, but not the video itself.

- **Settings** gives you control over a variety of Hangout settings, such as changing your Google + profile picture, whether to be alerted via sounds and vibrations when you get requests for a Hangout, and so on.

Responding to a Hangouts Invitation

When you receive a message via Hangouts, it will appear in the status bar. Pull down the Notification panel, and then tap the message. You'll be sent to Hangouts, where you can chat or participate in a video call as outlined earlier in this section.

Chat and Videochat with ChatON

THERE'S ANOTHER WAY TO chat or videochat on your S4—Samsung's ChatON app. So far, very few people use the app, so it might be a lonely place to be until it catches on. Launch the app by tapping the ChatON icon in the App Drawer. The first time you launch it, it may take a few minutes to set itself up. When the registration screen appears, tap in your phone number and then tap Register. (Your number may already be filled in for you.) After you tap Register, you'll be asked whether you want to verify the phone number via text (SMS) or a voice call. Make your choice, then get verified via either voice or phone, and you're ready to go.

> **NOTE** In order to use ChatON, you'll first have to have a Samsung account. To find out how to set one up, turn to page 22.

After verification, contacts from your phone will be imported into ChatON. That means that you'll be able to contact them directly from the app, and they'll be able to contact you as well—as long as they use ChatON, that is. Not all your contacts will be imported, only those who also use ChatON. So you may only have a friend or two, or you have many available for videochats.

On the ChatON main screen you see all your contacts, and it's easy to add more. Tap the button to the right of the search box near the top of the screen. A screen appears with four tabs across the top: Suggestions, Tell friends, Phone number, and Search by ID. Tap the Suggestion tab to see if the ChatON app has uncovered any people who might be suitable for you as a friend. "Tell friends" lets you send a download link to any friends who you think might want to use ChatON. "Phone number" lets you type in the phone number of a friend who's on ChatON, and in that way add him to your contacts. And "Search by ID" lets you search for someone on ChatON by typing in his email address.

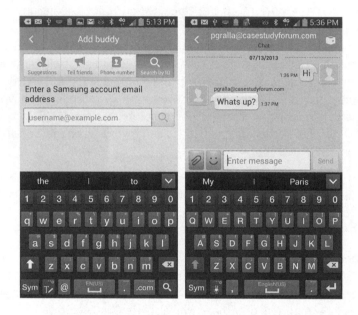

Once you've got your friends set up, chatting is simple: Tap the person with whom you want to chat, and from the screen that appears select the way in which you want to contact them. Tap the balloon to chat with them, the phone to call them, and the icon of the video camera for a videochat.

Other Social Networking Apps

Facebook, Google+, and Twitter are just three of the most popular social networking apps—there are plenty more out there, many of which have nifty Android apps for your S4. To find many of them head to Play Store, and go to the Social category.

Here are just a few you might want to try:

- **Snapchat.** This clever app lets you quickly take a photo and share it with others. But there's a catch—the photo vanishes after the amount of time you specify. After that, it's as if it never existed. It's become extremely popular.

- **Vine.** Create short, looping videos with your camera, and share them with friends, family, and anyone else you want.

- **Instagram.** This popular app lets you customize photos by adding filter effects, and then share them with others.

- **Foursquare.** This app is designed for mobility from the ground up. Share your location information, share pictures, get discounts, and so on.

- **Seesmic.** Technically, this isn't a social networking site. Instead, it's

a piece of software that works as a kind of front end to Facebook and Twitter, so you can use both from the same interface.

- **HootSuite.** A front end to multiple social networks, including Facebook, Twitter, LinkedIn, and others.

- **LinkedIn.** Think of LinkedIn as Facebook for business. It's buttoned-down, and mainly for work, although it has begun expanding beyond that as well.

You'll learn to:

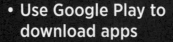

- Find and download apps
- Use Google Play to download apps
- Download apps from the Web and using a barcode scanner
- Update, manage, and uninstall apps
- Get 13 great apps

CHAPTER 12

Downloading and Using Apps

WHY DO YOU HAVE the Samsung Galaxy S4 rather than a plain-Jane cellphone? If you're like most people, it's for the phone's apps, which let you do remarkable things like using your phone as a bar code reader or guitar tuner.

The S4 features plenty of great built-in apps, which are covered throughout this book. In fact, you've been using apps and may not even know it. When you check your email on the S4, that's an app. When you shop at the Google Play Store, it's courtesy of an app. One of the phone's great features, though, is that it lets you download and use new apps as well—and those new apps do just about everything under the sun (and sometimes things that seem beyond the range of the solar system).

In this chapter, you'll find out how to get and use those apps, as well as how to uninstall and troubleshoot them. It'll also show you a few of the more amazing Android apps available online.

The Galaxy S4's Free and Easy Approach to Apps

THE SAMSUNG GALAXY S4 takes a different approach to the use of apps than some other devices in that there's absolutely no limitation on what you can download. Android's developer, Google, doesn't step in to say what you can and can't download, and neither do the phone's manufacturer, Samsung, or its carriers. If the app runs on Android, you can run it on your S4.

You're free to choose from hundreds of thousands of apps, with thousands more being written every month. There are apps for tracking expenses, playing music, chatting with people, playing games, using social networks like Facebook and Twitter, finding new friends, making your S4 work better, viewing maps of the night sky, and much more.

TIP Some Android apps cost money, but many more are free. So whenever you find a for-pay app, do a bit of searching to see if you can find a free one that does the same thing.

These apps tie into the Galaxy S4's unique hardware and software. One even automatically detects potholes as you drive, using the S4's various sensors to measure sudden movements. The app then uses the phone's positioning software to locate exactly where the pothole is, and creates a text file with all the relevant information so you can send it to your local Department of Public Works. (Unfortunately, no app has yet been developed that will get your local Department of Public Works to actually fix the pothole.)

Running apps is simple. Tap the icon of any on any Home screen or pane, or in the App Drawer.

Apps and Multitasking

THE GALAXY S4 IS great at multitasking—running more than one app at a time. For example, you can browse the Web while you listen to music, receive email, and have Facebook updates delivered to you, all without breaking a sweat.

You usually don't notice that Android is multitasking, though, because unlike in an operating system like Windows or Mac OS X, you don't see all running apps simultaneously in their own separate windows at once.

When you're in an app and want to do something else on the S4, you typically press the Home key. From there, you can tap to run an app such as the web browser, or open the App Drawer to run more apps. When you do that, though, that first app is still running in the background. If it's a music-playing app or a radio app, it keeps playing until you close it. With many other apps, though, at some point the phone will notice that you haven't used it in a while and close it down. You won't even notice that the S4 has closed it.

NOTE You can find apps called *task killers* that claim to speed up your Galaxy S4 by automatically closing apps when they're no longer needed, or by letting you manually close those apps. However, the era of task killers is drawing to a close, now that the S4 has built-in features that do the same thing. For details, see page 313.

There is a way to make sure that an app closes when you switch away from it, though. Rather than pressing the Home key to run another app, press the Menu key and look for a menu choice that closes the app. Not all apps offer this choice, but that's OK; the S4 will close the app when it's no longer needed. If for some reason, though, you want to close an app and it doesn't have a menu choice for that, you can still do it—flip to page 313.

Seeing Your Most Recently Run Apps

There's a quick way to see the most recent apps you've run or that are still running. Hold down the Home key and a screen appears that shows them. Tap any app in the list to run it.

Where to Get Apps

THE GALAXY S4 OFFERS you not just one, not just two, but three different ways to download and install apps:

- **Google Play Store.** Here's the primary way that most people download and find apps. It's right on your Home screen. Tap the Play Store button and it launches. From here you can search for apps, find information about apps, and pay for them.

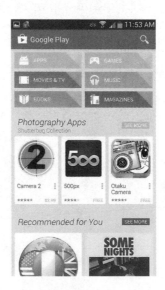

- **The Web.** You can download and install apps from websites. Visit the site on your phone's browser, and download from there.

In a few cases, you can download an app to your PC or Mac, and it will then be installed on your Galaxy S4 when you connect your computer. Generally, this happens if you've downloaded an app that works with your PC or Mac as well as with Android.

- **Using a bar code scanner.** Of all the amazing tricks the Galaxy S4 can do, this one may just be the coolest. A free app gives you S4 the ability to scan bar codes and QR codes. (*QR codes* are a special kind of bar code used by smartphones, cameras, and other devices.) After you've installed  this app, you can scan a QR code to download other apps. When you're browsing the Web with your PC or Mac, and you come across a bar or QR code for downloading, just point your phone at it, click a button, and the magic begins. The phone grabs and installs the software from the website. For more on bar code scanning, see page 311.

QR stands for *quick response.* QR codes are designed to be scanned at high speeds. They were initially created by a subsidiary of Toyota as a way to track the auto manufacturing process, but are now used for many other purposes. Nowadays, you see them on TV, book covers, and even bus ads. Grab your S4 and shoot.

Using Google Play Store

TAP THE PLAY STORE icon, and you get sent to Google Play, which has hundreds of thousands of apps you can download, with more added every month. The apps are either free or very low cost—typically under $4, although some business-related apps can cost up to $30:

- **Major library divisions** are at the top—Apps, Games, Movies & TV, Music, Books, and Magazines.

- **Featured apps, games, movies, and more** take up most of the screen and scroll off the bottom. Flick to see them; tap any one for more details.

NOTE Google sometimes reorganizes the Google Play store, so it may look different from what you see here.

At the very top of the screen, at upper right, is a search button. Tap it to search for an app.

Browsing by Library Divisions and Categories

Tap one of the major library divisions at the top of Google Play— Apps, Games, Movies & TV, Music, Books, and Magazines—and you come to a screen that lets you explore the category. In Apps, for example, you'll find photos and icons representing individual apps, as well as a Games area and a Staff Picks area. Flick to find more off the bottom of the screen.

Notice across the top of the screen that there are buttons for Top Paid, Top Free, and others. You can't see them all onscreen, so swipe to the right to see them in turn. Tap any category, and you come to a list of all the apps in that category. Each listing shows the name of the app, its maker, its price, and an average user rating.

Searching Google Play for Apps

Browsing is all well and good when you've got the time and want to scroll leisurely through lists looking for an app. But often you're on a mission: You know the type of app you want, and you want to find it fast.

In that case, you want to search. You can search by the type of app, the name of the program, or the name of the software company that created it. Tap the Search button, and a keyboard and a search box appear. Type in your search term or select a term from the list that appears when you begin typing. You'll see a list of programs, books, and movies that match what you're looking for, sorted into their categories.

NOTE When you view a list of apps, you may notice that some of them, instead of showing a price, will show the word "Installed." Yup, it means what you think it means—you've already installed the app on your Galaxy S4.

Getting Info About an App

No matter what type of list you look through—whether as a result of a search or by browsing—you'll eventually want to get more details about an app and possibly download it. In that case, tap the name of the app, and you come to a page with a great deal of information about it, including the number of downloads, the total number of ratings on which the star rating is based, the price, a description of the app, screenshots, and individual user reviews.

TIP Be careful when using the star ratings as a guide to download and pay for an app. In some instances, that star rating may be based on just a rating or two. Any star rating based on a few ratings may not be particularly accurate, especially because the ratings may come from the developer and the developer's friends. If there are a dozen or more user ratings, they're more trustworthy. So read the actual reviews, and see how *many* ratings each app has gotten.

Scroll down, and you'll find a great deal of information about the app, including any videos showing it in action, individual user reviews, and a particularly useful section that's often overlooked—information about the developer. It lists other apps the developer has written, links to the developer's home page, and lets you send email to the developer.

NOTE If you come across an app that you believe has inappropriate content, such as pornography or gratuitous violence, scroll to the bottom of the page and tap "Flag as inappropriate."

Downloading and Installing Apps

Say you've read all about an app, and you've decided to take the plunge. You're ready to download. What's next? Depending on whether the app is free or paid, you do things slightly differently.

If the app is free, you see an Install button. Tap it. A screen appears, telling you what kind of information and features the application has access to, such as your location, your Galaxy S4's storage, and so on. Typically, the application needs this kind of access—a GPS app can't do its job without access to your phone's GPS features, after all. Still, it's a good idea to take a look, and if you're concerned about anything, don't download. (See the box on page 308 for more information.)

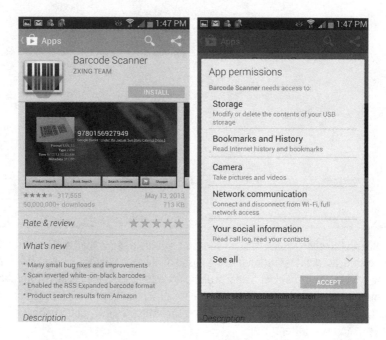

To download it, tap Accept. The app immediately starts downloading in the background. A small green arrow appears in the status bar, showing you that the application is downloading. While the download goes on, you can use your phone in any way you want; the download won't interfere. Soon a checkbox appears, indicating that the download is complete. Pull down the Notification panel, and you see that the app has downloaded and been installed. Tap the notification to run the app. You can also run the app by heading to the App Drawer and tapping the icon there.

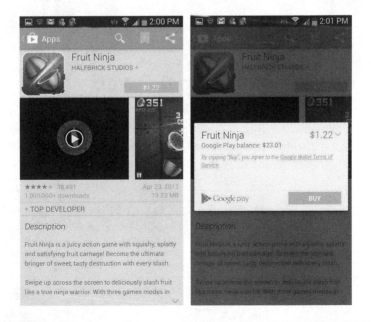

If the app is a for-pay one, you need a Google Checkout account, so set one up ahead of time on the Web at *https://checkout.google.com* It's simple and free.

With that done, you can buy the app. Instead of an Install button, a Buy button appears. Tap it. As when you're downloading a free app, a screen tells you what kind of features and information the app will use. Tap Accept. Now it's time to pay. On the next screen, you see how much the app costs. Tap Buy, and follow any onscreen instructions that appear. After you've paid, the download proceeds in the exactly same way as for free ones.

Download with Caution

Your Galaxy S4 is a computer, and just like any computer, it can be targeted by malware or by hackers trying to steal personal data, or track your online behavior. There's software—like Lookout Security (*www.lookout.com*)—you can use to keep yourself safe. But software by itself isn't enough—you also need to be smart about what to download.

One of the biggest dangers comes from apps that invade your privacy by sending out information about you, or that dial your phone without your knowledge to call for-pay services, or send text messages to for-pay services. There's a way to see what kind of information apps will grab, and what kinds of access they have to your computer—and you can see that before you download. When you tap to download, you see a list of the features and information the app can access. Look closely at those features and informa-

tion. If an app is asking for access to information or features that don't seem related to the app, it could spell trouble. For example, if you're downloading a simple, single-player game and it says that it uses your GPS to determine your location, that might be a red flag, because there's generally no need for a game of that kind to have that information. The app may attempt to track your location and send information about it to advertisers.

On the other hand, a social networking app that connects you to friends nearby will certainly need access to your GPS location. So the key is to see whether the information and features seem to match the purpose of the app.

For more details and more advice, see this Computerworld article on privacy with smart-phone apps: *http://bit.ly/q4bRyG*.

Downloading from the Web

YOU'RE NOT LIMITED TO getting apps from the Google Play Store—you can download them from the Web as well. You can either visit the app developer's website to download the app, or instead head to one of the many web libraries that house thousands of apps.

NOTE Be aware that when you install apps from the Web, they don't go through the same kind of vetting procedure that they do in Google Play. So be careful about what you download. It's a good idea to download apps only from well-known developers or well-known, trusted download libraries.

Downloading from the Web takes a bit more work than from Google Play. It's a several-step process, rather than a simple all-in-one:

1. Go to a website using your phone's browser and search for an app, or go directly to a developer's site.

2. Download a file to your S4.

3. Install the app using the downloaded file.

NOTE You can also download the file to your PC or Mac and then transfer it to your S4. For details about transferring files between computers and your phone, see page 332.

Unless you know a specific app you want to download and the URL of the developer's website, your best place to start is one of the many Android download libraries. The Android Freeware site—*www.freewarelovers.com/android*—is one good place. The download library *www.download.com* also has an Android area, and *www.appbrain.com* is good, too.

Once you find a file you want to download, tap the link to download it. A file will then be downloaded, and you'll see the progress on a download screen. You'll notice an odd file name—*Ghost_Commander_1.50b2.apk*, for example. (Android apps end in the extension *.apk*.)

NOTE In some instances when you go to a website to download the file, when you click to download, you'll be sent to Google Play and can then download it from there in the usual way.

After the file downloads, tap the notification. Either the file will install, or else you'll come to a screen asking you whether you first want to scan the file with an anti-malware program, if you've got one on your S4. (Your S4 probably comes with the anti-malware program Lookout.) It's a good idea to scan first, so go ahead and do that for safety's sake. If it passes muster, continue the installation. If it doesn't pass, then don't install the software.

Don't worry if for some reason you miss the notification after the download. You can still easily find the file. In the App Drawer, tap Downloads, and you'll see it.

Depending on how your S4 is set up, you may next come to a screen saying that for security purposes, you can't install any software outside the Google Play Store. Tap Settings. From the screen that appears, scroll down to Unknown Sources and turn on the checkbox next to it. A screen appears warning you that if you do this, you may be vulnerable to attack. Tap OK.

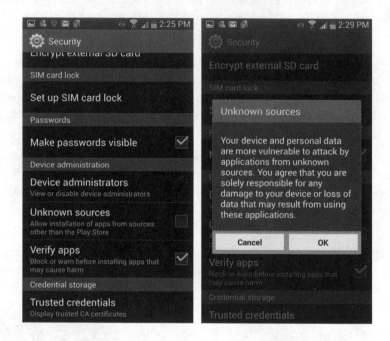

A screen similar to the one you've seen in the Google Play Store appears, which tells you what kinds of features and information the app will need access to. Tap Install to install the app, or Cancel to cancel the installation. When the app is installed, you can immediately run it by tapping Open, or tap Done and run it later. You'll be able to run the app anytime from the App Drawer.

When you're done installing the app, you won't need the original download file any longer, so you can delete it.

Downloading and Using a Bar Code Scanner

HERE'S AN EVEN NIFTIER way to download apps—use a bar code scanner. You browse the Web by using your PC or Mac, and when you come across a file you want to download, install a free app for scanning bar codes, point your S4's camera at the onscreen bar code, and the app downloads to your PC. In fact, you don't even need to browse the Web to download apps in this way. The bar code can be somewhere in the physical world, for example in a magazine.

First you need to get one of the many bar code scanner apps. One highly rated, popular app is called Barcode Scanner, from Zxing Team. And it's free, as well.

NOTE Barcode Scanner does a lot more than just let you download apps. It can also scan a bar code on a products, identify the product, and send you to web pages with more information about it, including reviews and places to buy.

After you install the scanner app on your Galaxy S4, you're ready to go. Many web-based Android libraries and developer websites have bar codes next to the app descriptions, so you can easily download them.

Place a barcode inside the viewfinder rectangle to scan it.

When you come across a bar code for downloading an app, run Barcode Scanner, and then point the phone's camera at the bar code just as if you were snapping a photo, centering it in the window in the middle of the viewfinder. The app quickly recognizes the bar code and shows you information about it, including the web page's URL. At the bottom of the screen, tap "Open browser," and the file downloads just as if you had tapped a download link. You can then install the app in the usual way. For details, see page 306.

NOTE You can also share the link to the app with others by tapping either "Share via email," or "Share via SMS." If you do that, you won't send the app or the bar code, but instead a link to the page, using either email or text messaging.

Updating Apps

APPS ARE OFTEN UPDATED, and the nice thing about the Galaxy S4 is that it tells you when any of your apps are ready for updating—and then updates them with a single tap. When an update is available, you get a notification in the status bar. Drag down the bar, tap the notification icon, and you see a list of all the apps that have updates available, as well as all your downloaded apps. Even better, many apps automatically update themselves, so you don't need to update them.

Tap any update you want to download, and you see the description page you normally see before downloading an app, except that the buttons at the bottom have changed. Tap Update to update the app or Uninstall to remove it from your phone. You can also update all your out-of-date apps in a single swoop by tapping "Update all." When you tap Update, you'll get the same note about the features and information the app will use. Tap to install it, and the S4 downloads the app in the background. You see its progress as it downloads, but you don't have to watch it unless you really want to.

TIP If you want the app to update itself automatically, instead of you having to update it, turn on the checkbox next to "Allow automatic updating" on the Update screen.

Managing, Sharing, and Uninstalling Apps

AFTER AWHILE, YOU MAY suffer from app overload: You've downloaded so many apps you don't know what to do with them. It's time to get them under control.

There's a single app for doing that, the Application Manager. Pull down the Notification panel, tap the Settting button and select More→Application Manager. (You can also tap the App Drawer, then tap Settings and select More→Application Manager.)

You'll see a list of your apps, including their names and file sizes, categorized in four tabs. It's tough to tell at first that there are four of them, because there's not enough screen real estate to show them all But they're there. To see each tab, swipe to the right. Here's what each tab shows:

- **Downloaded.** These are apps that weren't on the Galaxy S4 when you started using it, but that you've downloaded and installed.

NOTE Some apps show up on the Downloaded tab even if they were preinstalled, such as those you've updated. But even some you didn't update show up there...go figure!

- **All.** This is the mega-list of your apps—every single one on the phone, including those built into it and those you've downloaded.

- **On SD card.** Normally, apps install to your Galaxy S4's main memory, not to its SD card. But as you'll see in a bit, there's a way to move some of them from the phone's memory to its SD card.

- **Running.** These are apps that are currently running on your S4.

TIP The list of apps is arranged alphabetically. You can instead view them by their size (biggest first). Press the Menu key, and then choose "Sort by size" to list them by size order.

Tap any app, and you come to a screen chock-full of information about it—its version number, its total size, the size of any data associated with it, the size of the program itself, and toward the bottom of the screen, information about what kinds of features and data the app uses.

You can uninstall the app—tap the Uninstall button. If you see that an app is running and you want to close it, tap the "Force stop" button. That button is grayed out if the app isn't currently running.

From this screen, you can also move an app from the Galaxy S4's main memory to its SD card. Tap "Move to SD card," and the Galaxy S4 moves it. If an app is already on the SD card, tap a button to move it back. (Not all apps can be moved to the SD card—its developer must have programmed that capability into it.)

Using the Task Manager for Managing Apps

The Galaxy S4 also has a handy built-in task manager that shows information about your apps, and lets you control them in some very useful ways. To
launch it, hold down the Home button, then tap the far-left button—it looks like
a pie graph. You'll see a screen that looks a little bit like the one covered in the
previous section. There are some big differences, though. The Task Manager is
designed for closing down apps and managing memory and storage, and more
as well. It's a great app, organized in four tabs:

- **Active Applications.** Shows all the applications that are currently running.
  It also shows how much RAM (memory) each uses, and how much of your
  smartphones CPU it uses. (The CPU is your phone's brains.) If any app is
  problematic (for example, using too much battery, too much RAM or too
  much CPU), it shows up red. This information is helpful if you find your S4
  running sluggishly, because it may be that your apps are taking up too much
  memory or too much of your CPU. To free up memory or the CPU, you can
  force some apps to close. Tap the End button next to any you want to close.

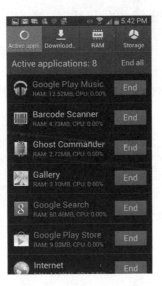

- **Downloaded.** Shows all your downloaded apps, including how much storage
  each uses. Tap uninstall to uninstall any you no longer want.

- **RAM.** Shows you how much RAM your S4 is currently using. It also offers
  a very nice way to free up memory the phone is using but may no longer
  need. To do it, tap "Clear memory." When you do that, it cleans out any apps
  or pieces of apps you're not using and don't need any more, and frees up
  memory. Keep in mind, though, that it might kill some apps, so make sure
  that you've saved data in any running apps before doing this.

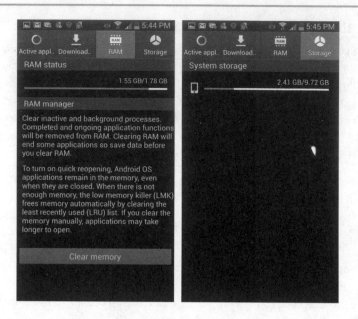

- **Storage.** Shows how much storage you have on your main system and SD card, and how much you've got left.

Putting an App on the Home Screen or Panes

THERE MAY BE AN app you use frequently, and so you get tired of the constant dance of having to open the App Drawer, scroll down to the app's icon, and then tap it. There's a much easier way: You can put its icon right on your Home screen or any pane, so it's always there at your command:

1. While you're on the Home screen or any pane, press the Menu key.

2. From the menu that appears, select "Add apps and widgets."

3. App icons appear. Scroll through the list and find the app you want to add, and then drag it to the Home screen or pane where you want it to appear.

4. The icon is added to the Home screen or pane.

The Home screen or a pane may have too many app icons on them to have any new ones added. In that instance, you'll have to first remove an icon from the screen or pane before you can add a new app.

What if you want to delete the icon but still keep the app? Put your finger on the app and hold it there until a Trash can appears at the bottom of the screen. Drag the icon to the Trash. The icon disappears, but the app remains, and is accessible from the App Drawer.

Troubleshooting Apps

IN A PERFECT WORLD, apps would never misbehave. Unfortunately, it's not a perfect world. So an app may quit the moment you launch it, or cause your Galaxy S4 to restart, or do any number of odd things. If that happens, try these steps:

- **Launch the app again.** There's no particular reason why this should work, but it often does. When you launch the app again, it just may work properly.

- **Uninstall and reinstall.** There may have been an oddball installation problem. So uninstall the app and then reinstall it. That sometimes fixes the problem.

- **Restart your Galaxy S4.** Just as restarting a computer sometimes fixes problems for no known reason, restarting the S4 may have the same effect. Power it down by pressing and holding the Power/Lock key, and then press and hold the Power/Lock key again to restart.

- **Reset the Galaxy S4.** If an app causes the phone to stop responding, you'll have to reset the phone. See page 432 for details.

If none of this works, it's time to uninstall the app. Don't fret; there are plenty more where it came from.

Thirteen Great Apps

THERE ARE TENS OF thousands of great apps, and a whole world of them to discover. To give you a head start, here are 13 favorites—and they're all free. You can find each of them in the Google Play Store, although in the instance of S Health, it's already right on your S4.

S Health

This very useful Samsung app helps you manage your health, including setting and keeping to fitness goals, and keeping track of your health in general. To run it, tap S Health in the App Drawer.

After you agree to the terms of use, you fill out a basic profile about yourself, including your name, age, gender, height and weight, and your activity level. Based on that, S Health calculates how many calories you should consume a day, and how many calories you likely burn a day. When you're done, tap the Start button.

NOTE Keep in mind one thing about S Health: It can be a guilt-inducing little app, tracking every part of your health. The truth is, though, that it's unlikely you'll use every part of it. So pick and choose what you want to use, and it'll be your friend instead of a nag.

The Health Board is S Health's main screen, and it shows you the current state of your health, including the calories you've burned today, and how many calories you've eaten. But it can only do this and keep track of other parts of your health if you tell the program to start tracking you.

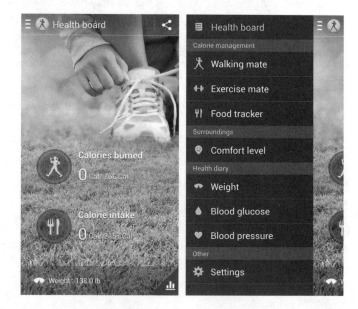

To do that, tap the icon of three horizontal lines at the top left of your screen. You'll come to a screen with various modules for tracking your health, including for walking, exercising, blood pressure, blood glucose, and others.

It's all self explanatory, so there's no need to go into details. Tap the module you want to use, and fill in the information (such as how much you exercise in a day). S Health then totes up everything you've done, reports on it, and tells you how you're doing.

But there are some truly great features worth mentioning that take advantage of the S4's built-in magic:

- **Walking mate** uses the S4's sensors to track how much you've walked in a day. Just turn it on and forget it, and carry your S4 with you. At the end of the day, it tells you how much you've walked, and how many calories you've burned. It tracks this over time, so you can see graphs.

- **Comfort level** measures the temperature and humidity to let you know whether your environment is comfortable or not. Time to turn on (or off) the air conditioner!

Make sure to check in regularly to the Health board to see how you're doing, and adjust your meals, exercise level and so on to keep on track. And tap the small chart icon at the bottom right of the screen to see graphs that display how you're doing over time.

Endomondo

If you're serious about running, cycling, hiking, mountain biking, and other sports, you should give Endomondo a try. It's a combination training tracker and analyzer combined with social media and networking. The app uses the S4's sensors, notably its GPS, to automatically track your workout. So you can use it while running, for example, to see your progress—running distance and time elapsed, and current and average speeds. After your run or workout, you upload the information results so that friends can see them, and either sneer at your measly results or go green with envy over your athletic prowess. There's plenty more here as well, such as automatically created maps of your workouts, and linking to music apps so you can listen to music while you jog and sweat.

Pulse News

Are you a news junkie? Then you'll want the great, free news app Pulse. It grabs articles from newspapers, magazines, and websites. Using Pulse, you grab articles and information from all over the Web and display them in a big tablet-friendly format with lots of photos and graphics. You customize exactly what kinds of stories and publications you want to show. It's easy to use, beautiful to look at, and keeps you up to the minute on everything.

Tap any story to read it. To share the story, tap the share button at the bottom of the screen and you'll be able to share via Facebook, Twitter, LinkedIn, or Google+. You can also share via other apps by tapping the "Share to other apps" button. At the top right of the screen, tap the settings icon for more features as well, like changing the text size, style and brightness, opening the page in the browser, and more.

Pulse is already set up to grab a variety of news feeds from around the Web, but it's easy to change that to your own selections. When you're at the app's main page, tap the settings icon at upper right to add or remove news sources.

There's a lot more to Pulse as well. It's free and it gives you great sources of information, so if you're a news junkie, or even if you're not, give it a try.

Google Currents

Here's another excellent free app for news and information junkies. It grabs stories from many resources, publications, and sites, ranging from print newspapers and magazines to blogs, websites, television channels and more. You can follow constantly changing sections, such as Business, Science & Tech, Entertainment, Sports, and so on, or you can instead follow just a single publication, such as The Daily Beast. It's also easy to share stories with other people. And a particularly useful feature is Save, which lets you download articles to your S4 in a single location for later reading.

Evernote

If you suffer from information overload, here's your remedy. Evernote does a great job of capturing information from multiple sources, putting them in one location, and then letting you easily find them—whether you're using your computer, your tablet, or another Android device.

Not only that, it's free.

You organize all your information into separate notebooks, and can then browse each notebook, search through it, search through all notebooks, and so on.

No matter where you capture or input information, it's available on every device on which you install Evernote. So if you grab a web page from your PC and put it into a notebook, that information is available on your S4, and vice versa.

You can capture information from the Web, by taking photos, by speaking, and by pasting in existing documents. And you can also type notes as well.

The upshot of all this? Evernote is the best app you'll find for capturing information and making sense of it all.

Aldiko Book Reader

That big 5-inch, high-resolution S4 screen is crying out for you to use it for something other than making phone calls or sending and receiving texts. And with the free app, you can do just that—read books, and plenty of them. It's a very good ereader that gives you access to reading (for free or pay, depending on the book) thousands of book. There's plenty of nice options, such as changing the reading settings between day and night mode (black text on white background for day; white text on black background for night). There are also bookmarking features, a nice search feature, and plenty more. There's also an excellent selection of O'Reilly books for download.

Candy Crush Saga

This free puzzle adventure game, is so addicting you should only start playing when you know you won't have something that needs doing for the next twenty minutes...or hour...or two. You touch and swipe candies around on a grid in order to put three of them in a row. When you do, they're crushed, and more candies slide in. Match even more candies and you create special candies which can be used for more power. They can also be combined for even more power.

Simple, yes? Well, not quite so much, as you'll find out as you make your way through this increasingly complicated game.

Google Goggles

This may well be the most amazing app you'll ever see. Run Google Goggles, and then point it at an object, a sign, a piece of artwork, a logo, the label on a bottle of wine, and so on. It will identify what you're looking at (or translate the sign if it's in a foreign language), and provide more information about it. Point it at a menu in a foreign country to translate the menu, identify landmarks...there's a lot more here as well. It doesn't always work, but when it does, it's mind boggling.

TedAIR

If you're a Ted fan, you'll want this app. And if you're not one, you should download it just to see what the fuss is about.

Ted stands for Technology, Entertainment, and Design, and it's the name of a conference that has been held every year since 1984. The conference's motto is "Ideas Worth Spreading" and it's a perfect description of the talks held there—in fact, it's even understated, because they're some of the most fascinating talks you'll ever see. And seeing them is where this app comes in. You'll be able to choose from thousands of talks from the well-known, the little-known, and the just plain brilliant in almost every walk of life. Bill Clinton, Bill Gates, Jamie Oliver, Amy Tan, Ben Katchor...the list is long, and gets longer all the time.

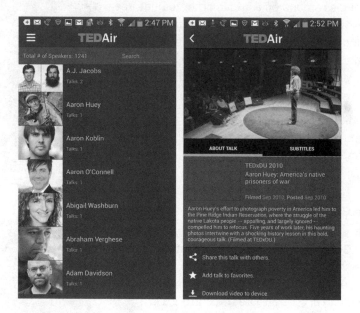

You can browse the speakers and get their bios, search for talks, view the talks, download talks for later viewing, tag talks, comment on them, and more.

Vine

This Twitter-created app does for videos what Instagram does for photo-sharing—lets you create simple, six-second looping videos, then post them and share them with others. And it lets you check out looping videos that others create as well.

Creating a looping video is simple. Launch the app, tell it to create a video, and it switches to your camera. Hold your finger on the screen to record; lift your finger from the screen to stop recording. A bar across the top shows you how much you've already recorded of your six seconds of fame, and how many seconds are left. After you've created it, it's ready to go, and can be shared via Twitter and Facebook. There's also a Vine feed, so that people can subscribe to your feed, and you to theirs. That means you'll be able to see a constantly changing feed of these little videos. There's also all the usual associated social media features, such as comments and so on.

Instagram

This popular app combines excellent photo filtering tools with photo sharing, and is a great way to play with photos and share them with friends and family, especially via Facebook. And it's also great for seeing photos that others take, and not just friends and family, but the famous as well, many of whom seem to be Instagram junkies.

Load Instagram, use its tools to snap a photo, and then use its magic. You can add a frame and select a specific focus point, but that's just the beginning. It's the filters that you'll care about, well over a dozen. Retro, black and white, Nashville, Hefe, Kelvin...you'll find anything you need to indulge your inner photographer.

After you're done, it's time to share, and Instagram makes it easy. You can share via Twitter, Facebook, Flickr, Tumblr, and Foursquare without any heavy lifting, because they're all built into the app. And you can use the app to follow others' photos as well.

New to Instangram is a Vine-like capability for creating and sharing videos as well. Oh, and by the way, one last thing: If you're looking to take a selfie, this is a great app to do it with.

Snapchat

This app is the latest and greatest mashup of chat, social media, and photos, and it's been spreading like wildfire. You take a photo or video, add text and drawings, and then send it to a friend or friends. Those friends can be ones gathered from your social networks, your contacts, and so on, or new ones you make on Snapchat. When you send it, it ends up on your friend or friends Snapchat mailbox.

Sounds straightforward, and it is. But here's the twist: The photo or video is perishable, and lasts between one second and ten seconds after it's opened. After that, it gets deleted from the user's phone and the snapchat servers. It's a great app for taking selfies and annotating them so your friends can see exactly what you're up to at exactly that instant.

Minecraft Pocket Edition Demo

This Android version of a popular PC and console game takes some getting used to, but once you do, you'll likely be hooked. Begin an a peaceful landscape, then start mining it with a variety of tools to find cubes in the ground. Use those cubes to build castles, bridges, and more. But be smart about it, and be fast about it, because when night arrives, creatures come out and start destroying them—and chomping you if you didn't protect yourself well enough with the structures you created. If you die (and you will), you start all over.

There's a lot more to this game, including being able to fight back against the monsters with strafe buttons, and plenty more. And if you like multi-player games, you'll be happy, because when multiple people are on the same WiFi network, they can all play together.

Note that this is a demo version of the game, and so is limited. If you want the full version, you'll have to fork over $6.99. If you like the demo version, you'll be more than happy to pay full freight for the whole thing.

Advanced Features

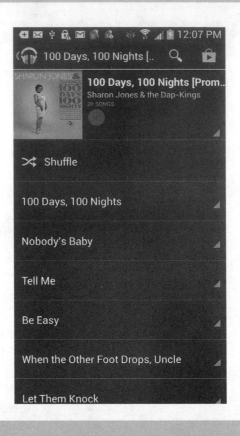

You'll learn to:

- Transfer files to your PC or Mac
- Use Windows Media Player to transfer and sync music, photos, and videos
- Use the S4's My Files app
- Beam files and use WiFi to transfer them
- Use Group Play to share screens and files, and play games

CHAPTER 13

Transferring Music, Videos, Pictures, and Other Files, and Using Group Play

YOUR GALAXY S4 IS not an island—it's built to work with your computer as well. So if you've got a music collection on your PC, for example, you can copy that collection to your phone and listen to music there. You can also transfer pictures and videos between your S4 and PC or Mac. In fact, you can transfer any file between your S4 and your computer. And you can synchronize the files as well.

When you transfer files between your Galaxy S4 and your computer, the S4 looks to your computer just like a USB storage device, and in many ways, you transfer files the same way as you do between your computer and any USB device. In fact, you have a few more options, with the help of software like Windows Media Player, My Files, and Kies via WiFi. This chapter covers them all. You can even *beam* files back and forth with other S4 owners—like magic!

Another sharing option on the S4 is Group Play—a Samsung innovation that lets you share files by WiFi with nearby Galaxy phone fans. You can even use Group Play to...well, play group games by WiFi.

Connecting Your Galaxy S4 to Your Computer

TO TRANSFER FILES BETWEEN your Galaxy S4 and your computer, first connect your S4 to either your Mac or PC by using the phone's data cable. Connect the micro USB plug into your S4 and the normal-sized USB plug into your computer's USB port.

A USB icon ( ) appears in the status bar. That means that your S4 is ready to start receiving files.

NOTE When you connect your Galaxy S4 to your Windows PC for the first time, the PC may not recognize it. It may need a special *driver*—a small piece of helper software—in order to see the S4 and communicate with it. Your PC will look for and install the drivers automatically, assuming it's connected to the Internet.

If you pull down the notification, you will see that the notification reads "Connected as a media device." Tap the notification, and you come to a screen that tells you that you've connected your phone to your PC as a media device— in other words, you can transfer media files between it and a PC or Mac. To do so, make sure the "Media Device (MTP)" checkbox is turned on. Underneath that setting, there's another one, "Camera (PTP)." Turn on this box if you have a camera and want to transfer files between the camera and your phone.

TIP If you're having trouble transferring files between the phone and a PC or Mac, not a camera, it's a good idea to turn on the "Camera (PTP)" checkbox anyway, because in some magical way, it can sometimes make sure you can transfer files.

Transferring Files by Using Your PC

AFTER THE DRIVERS HAVE been installed on your PC, when you connect your Galaxy S4 to it, the AutoPlay screen may appear, as it sometimes does when you connect a USB device to your PC. However, don't be concerned if it doesn't, because it doesn't show up on every PC; that depends on your operating system and computer setup (and maybe even the phase of the moon).

After you've connected it to your PC, launch Windows Explorer. Your S4 now shows up as a removable disk, just like any USB drive.

You can now use your phone as if it were any USB flash device—copying files to and from it, creating folders, and so on. That's fine in theory, but in practice what can you actually do? You'll find a number of folders on the S4, some of which have names that make no sense—like DCIM.

There are several important folders that contain information you might want to transfer from your S4 to your PC, or vice versa. You'll see a lot more folders, but these are the important ones:

- **Download.** If you've downloaded content to your Galaxy S4 from the Internet, such as pictures or web pages, you see them in here.

- **DCIM.** Here's where the Galaxy S4 stores all the photos and videos you've taken. Drag photos from this folder to your PC to copy them, or drag photos from your PC to here to put them into the Galaxy S4 Gallery (page 119).

- **Movies.** As the name says, here's where you'll find movies and videos you've watched or transferred to your S4.

- **Music.** The Galaxy S4 stores music here, although it might also store music in other places as well. If you download music files by using the Amazon music app, for example, there will be an Amazonmp3 folder where your music is stored.

- **Pictures.** Here's where your photos are stored. There may be subfolders underneath this as well.

- **Ringtones.** Downloaded ringtones to your phone? Here's where to find them.

- **Samsung.** Samsung uses this folder for a variety of different reasons. For example, in addition to the primary music player built into the phone and other Android phones, Samsung has its own music player, and music for it is found in a subfolder underneath this folder.

If you're transferring music from your PC to your Galaxy S4, first create a new folder on the phone using Windows Explorer, as you would create any other folder. Then transfer the music to that folder, using subfolders if you want. When you do this, your S4's music player will automatically recognize the music you've transferred. (For details about using the music player, see Chapter 4.)

Transferring Files by Using Your Mac

TO TRANSFER FILES BETWEEN your Mac and Galaxy S4, you must first download the free Android File Transfer tool. Go to *www.android.con/filetransfer* and follow the instructions for downloading and installing it.

Once you do that, connect the S4 to your Mac with the USB cable. Then run the Android File Transfer app. After you run it for the first time, it should automatically start after that whenever you connect your S4 to your Mac.

You can then transfer files back and forth between your Mac and your S4 using Android File Transfer. It works just like Finder or any other file management app.

If you specifically want to transfer photos between your Mac and S4, first change the S4's USB mode to tell it you're going to transfer photos. Connect your S4 to your Mac via USB; the USB notification appears in the status bar. Pull down the Notification panel, tap the USB notification, and on the screen that appears, select "Camera (PTP)." You can then use iPhoto to transfer photos between the Mac and your S4.

Transferring Music, Videos, and Pictures by Using Windows Media Player

THERE'S ANOTHER WAY TO transfer media files from your PC to your Galaxy S4 than using Windows Explorer—Windows Media Player. Not only is Windows Media Player more automated, it also lets you preview and play the files before syncing them over. (If you use a Mac, you must use the Finder to move files, as described in the previous section; Windows Media Player won't work for you.)

NOTE If you transfer music that's DRM-protected from your PC, the Galaxy S4 won't be able to play it. DRM stands for *digital rights management,* and it limits the distribution of music files that have been paid for, making it difficult for them to be played on devices other than the one the music was purchased on.

Connect your Galaxy S4 to your PC, and then run Windows Media Player. On the left side of the WMP screen, in the library and navigation area, you'll see a new listing for your Galaxy S4. The icon looks like a phone, but it may have an odd title, like SGH-M9. When you first run Windows Media Player, you may also be prompted to rename the S4 to whatever name you want.

1. **At the top of Windows Media Player, click Sync.** Select the name of your device, and then click Advanced Options.

2. **Click the Sync tab.** You'll see two important options here:

   - **Create folder hierarchy on device.** This way, when you sync your music files to your S4, WMP creates folders on the S4's SD card that are the same as on your PC. Make sure you leave this turned on.

   - **Start Sync when device connects.** If you select this option, it means that as soon as you connect your S4 to your PC, the sync starts, without you having to take any action. Select this only if you're absolutely sure that you want all music on your PC to be transferred to your phone, and vice versa. If you don't want all your music transferred, make sure this box is unchecked. To be on the safe side, turn off this option, at least the first several times you sync your Galaxy S4 and PC. You can always turn it back on later.

3. **Click the Quality tab.** Here you select the quality level of the music and video you'll transfer to the phone. This determines whether and how Windows Media Player converts the quality of the media files on your PC when it transfers them; for example, decreasing the quality of the media by shrinking its size in order to save space on the S4. If you leave the default settings as they are, Windows Media Player determines the best balance between media quality and saving space. However, you can instead specify the maximum size of files to be transferred.

Preston Gralla (SGH-M9 Properties

Sync | Quality

Specify conversion and quality settings for files on this device.

Music

⦿ Select quality level automatically (recommended)

○ Select maximum quality level

Smallest Size — Best Quality

Uses about 27 MB per hour (64 kbps)

Videos and TV shows

⦿ Select quality level automatically (recommended)

○ Select maximum quality level

Smallest Size — Best Quality

Uses about 450 MB per hour (1.04 Mbps)

OK | Cancel | Apply | Help

4. **When you're done making your choices, click OK.** You're back on the main Windows Media Player screen.

5. **At the top of Windows Media Player, click Sync.** Select the name of your device and then click Set Up Sync.

6. **The Device Setup screen appears.** Make sure that the "Sync this device automatically" checkbox is turned off if you don't want the Galaxy S4 to always automatically sync whenever you connect it to your PC and run Windows Media Player. If you want to customize the general types of music to sync—such as only five stars, only music played in the past month, and so on, make your selection here. You can also have your playlists (page 112) synced to your phone.

Windows Media Player - Device Setup

Device Setup

Preston Gralla (SGH-M9 (9.5 GB)

Select Playlists to Sync

Sync this device automatically

Available playlists:

Personal Playlists

All playlists in this category are already selected, or no playlists of this type are in your library.

Add >

< Remove

Playlists to sync:

Calculating

Music auto rated at 5 stars
Music added in the last month
Music rated at 4 or 5 stars
Music played in the last month
Pictures taken in the last month
Pictures rated 4 or 5 stars
TV recorded in the last week
Video rated at 4 or 5 stars
Music played the most
All Music
All Pictures
All Video

New Auto Playlist...

Shuffle what syncs   Priority:

Finish   Cancel

7. **When you're done making your choices, click Finish to go back to the main Windows Media Player window.** You don't have to make any choices here if you don't want. As you'll see in the next step, you can also drag individual tracks to be synced to your S4.

At top right, there's an icon representing your phone, listing it as a removable drive, showing its drive letter, and showing you how much storage space is available on its SD card.

8. **Drag all the albums and tracks you want to synchronize to your S4 from the list of music on your PC on the left side to the Sync List area.**

After you drag each album or track, it appears on the Sync List. Review the list, and remove any files you don't want to sync. At the top of the screen (just underneath the Galaxy S4 icon), you'll see the amount of space you'll have left on your phone after you sync, so make sure you don't take up too much space with your music.

NOTE When you drag music to be synced, the music will still stay on your PC and in Windows Media Player—it doesn't get deleted.

If you have other media, such as pictures, video, or recorded TV shows that you want to sync to your S4, go to those areas in the Windows Media Player.

9. **Drag the files you want to sync to the Sync List area, just as you did for music.**

10. **Click Start Sync.** A screen appears showing you the full list of files that are syncing. You see the progress of each file as it syncs. After each file syncs, the file turns gray, and the status line next to it reads "Synchronized to device." When all the files have synced, on the right side of the screen you see a notification saying that you can now disconnect your S4.

![Windows Media Player sync screen showing music files being synchronized to device]

Windows Media Player

Now Playing | Library | Rip | Burn | Sync | Media Guide

♫ ▸ Music ▸ Preston Gralla (SGH-M9) ▸ Sync Results

Title	Status	Playlist	Album	Album Artist	Rating
Files You Added					
...And the Gods Made Lo...	Synchronized to device	Files You Added	Electric Ladyland	The Jimi Hendrix Experie...	☆☆☆☆☆
Have You Ever Been (To ...	Synchronized to device	Files You Added	Electric Ladyland	The Jimi Hendrix Experie...	☆☆☆☆☆
Crosstown Traffic	Synchronized to device	Files You Added	Electric Ladyland	The Jimi Hendrix Experie...	☆☆☆☆☆
Voodoo Chile	Synchronizing (57%)	Files You Added	Electric Ladyland	The Jimi Hendrix Experie...	☆☆☆☆☆
Little Miss Strange		Files You Added	Electric Ladyland	The Jimi Hendrix Experie...	☆☆☆☆☆
Long Hot Summer Night		Files You Added	Electric Ladyland	The Jimi Hendrix Experie...	☆☆☆☆☆
Come On, Pt. 1		Files You Added	Electric Ladyland	The Jimi Hendrix Experie...	☆☆☆☆☆
Gypsy Eyes		Files You Added	Electric Ladyland	The Jimi Hendrix Experie...	☆☆☆☆☆
Burning of the Midnight...		Files You Added	Electric Ladyland	The Jimi Hendrix Experie...	☆☆☆☆☆
Rainy Day, Dream Away		Files You Added	Electric Ladyland	The Jimi Hendrix Experie...	☆☆☆☆☆
1983... (A Merman I Sho...		Files You Added	Electric Ladyland	The Jimi Hendrix Experie...	☆☆☆☆☆
Moon, Turn the Tides......		Files You Added	Electric Ladyland	The Jimi Hendrix Experie...	☆☆☆☆☆
Still Raining, Still Dreami...		Files You Added	Electric Ladyland	The Jimi Hendrix Experie...	☆☆☆☆☆
House Burning Down		Files You Added	Electric Ladyland	The Jimi Hendrix Experie...	☆☆☆☆☆
All Along the Watchtower		Files You Added	Electric Ladyland	The Jimi Hendrix Experie...	☆☆☆☆☆
Voodoo Child (Slight Ret...		Files You Added	Electric Ladyland	The Jimi Hendrix Experie...	☆☆☆☆☆
100 Days, 100 Nights		Files You Added	100 Days, 100 Nights [Pr...	Sharon Jones & the Dap...	☆☆☆☆☆
Nobody's Baby		Files You Added	100 Days, 100 Nights [Pr...	Sharon Jones & the Dap...	☆☆☆☆☆
Tell Me		Files You Added	100 Days, 100 Nights [Pr...	Sharon Jones & the Dap...	☆☆☆☆☆
Be Easy		Files You Added	100 Days, 100 Nights [Pr...	Sharon Jones & the Dap...	☆☆☆☆☆
When the Other Foot Dr...		Files You Added	100 Days, 100 Nights [Pr...	Sharon Jones & the Dap...	☆☆☆☆☆
Let Them Knock		Files You Added	100 Days, 100 Nights [Pr...	Sharon Jones & the Dap...	☆☆☆☆☆
Something's Changed		Files You Added	100 Days, 100 Nights [Pr...	Sharon Jones & the Dap...	☆☆☆☆☆
Humble Me		Files You Added	100 Days, 100 Nights [Pr...	Sharon Jones & the Dap...	☆☆☆☆☆
Keep on Looking		Files You Added	100 Days, 100 Nights [Pr...	Sharon Jones & the Dap...	☆☆☆☆☆
Answer Me		Files You Added	100 Days, 100 Nights [Pr...	Sharon Jones & the Dap...	☆☆☆☆☆

Stop Sync

Synchronizing

NOTE If you want all your files to be synced every time automatically, and you made the "Start sync when device connects" choice, you won't have to drag files to the Sync List area, or click Start Sync. Synchronization begins automatically.

Your music, video, and pictures will now be available on your S4. Tap the Play Music app in the Application Tray, and you'll be able to play and manage your music. (For more information about playing music, see Chapter 4.)

Transferring Music, Videos, and Pictures to Your PC

Windows media player does double-duty and works in both directions—you can use it to transfer music, videos, and pictures from your Galaxy S4 to your PC as well. First, follow the instructions in "Transferring Music, Videos, and Pictures from a PC by Using

Windows Media Player" to connect your phone to your PC, and set up sync options. Then do the following:

1. **On the left-side navigation panel of Windows Media Player, you see the S4 listed.** Click it to display the categories of media it holds: Recently Added, Artist, Album, and so on.

2. **Drag the media you want to transfer from your S4 to your PC to the Sync area on the right side of the screen,** just as you did when transferring music to your Galaxy S4 (except you're dragging in the opposite direction).

The button at the bottom right of your screen changes from Start Sync to "Copy from Device."

3. **Click the "Copy from Device" button to transfer the files.**

TIP When you're in Windows Media Player browsing through the S4, you can delete S4 files right from that screen. Highlight the file you want to delete and press Delete. A warning will appear asking whether you're sure you want to delete the file. Click OK.

Using the Galaxy S4 My Files App

TO BROWSE THROUGH THE files of your Galaxy S4, you don't need to rely on your PC or Mac—you can use the S4's My Files app. From the App Drawer, tap My Files to launch it.

The app opens to browse the files on your S4, in much the same way that you can browse remotely using Windows Explorer or the Mac Finder.

You see the name of each folder. Tap any folder to open it, and then tap any file to open it—view a photo, play a piece of music, and so on, using the Galaxy S4's various built-in apps.

Hold your finger on a folder, and you get a menu of options for file and folder management:

- **Open, Delete, and Rename** are self-explanatory.

- **Move** lets you change the folder's location.

- **Copy** puts the folder on the Galaxy S4's Clipboard.

- **Rename** lets you rename the folder.

- **Details** gives you more information about the folder, including its name, number of folders and files it contains, and its size, as well as when it was last modified.

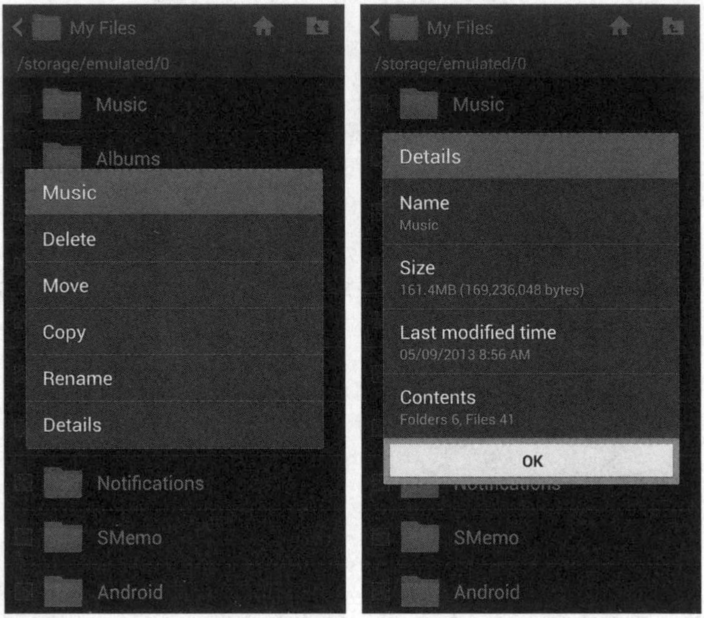

To create a new folder, when you're viewing a list of folders, tap the Menu key, select "Create folder," type its name, and then tap OK. To select multiple folders and move or delete them all, tap the Menu key; checkboxes appear next to all folders. Tap any folders you want to select for moving or deleting, and then tap Move or Delete from the menu.

When you hold your finger on a file, you get the same options as for a folder, plus "Share via," which lets you share the file in multiple ways, including via email, directly over WiFi, via Bluetooth, and several other options, depending on the apps you have installed on your S4.

To select multiple files to move or delete, when you're in a folder viewing a file list, press the Menu key. Empty checkboxes appear next to all files in the list. Tap any files you want to select for moving or deleting, and then tap Move or Delete on the menu.

Using the Kies via Wi-Fi App

THE GALAXY S4 GIVES you another way to transfer files between your S4 and PC or Mac—Kies via Wi-Fi. Using this built-in app, you can connect to another device and then transfer files wirelessly. To be sure, connecting via USB is much faster—and usually easier. But if you insist on living cable-free, you may want to give it a try.

First, you have to download and install the Kies software to your PC or Mac; get it at *http://www.samsung.com/us/kies/*. Then, run the software on your computer and make sure you're connected to your wireless network. Once the software is running on the PC or Mac, go to your S4, make sure it's connected to your wireless network, and run the Kies via Wi-Fi app by going to the Home screen, pressing the Menu key and tapping Connections→"Kies via Wi-Fi." Kies via Wi-Fi will scan for any PCs or Macs running the software. After it finds your computer, simply follow the prompts for connecting and sharing files.

Sharing Files by Beaming

THE GALAXY S4 CAN share files with other phones without the help of cable or WiFi or even Bluetooth. These awesome powers are new, and hidden so well, that you likely don't know about them. So here's your secret decoder ring.

> **NOTE** Beaming files works only between your S4 and other mobile devices, not Macs or PCs.

Beaming is made possible by a relatively new technology called NFC, which stands for Near Field Communications. Depending on your point of view, NFC is either the future of mobile computing, or else a dead-end that few people will ever use. At the moment it's a dead-end, but who knows what the future holds? And the point is, you've got it baked right into the guts of your S4, so there's no reason not to give it a try.

NFC

NFC is a way to get mobile devices to talk to one another or transferring files by touching the devices to each other. You may have seen it in Samsung's ads.

You can only use the S4's NFC with another device that uses NFC. At this point not many do. But S4s do, so you can always start there. To turn on NFC, pull down the notification panel, tap the Settings icon and, from the screen that appears, tap Connections. Go to the "Connect and share" section, and switch NFC on.

You can then transfer files to another device using NFC, just by tapping the devices together. First open the file you want to transfer, such as a photo, video, song, or other file. Then tap the phones together. Screens appear on both devices with the words "Touch to beam" on them. Touch the screen, and the file gets transferred.

S Beam

You can also transfer files using a related service called S Beam, which uses NFC along with a wireless technology called Wi-Fi Direct, which makes it easy to connect directly to other WiFi devices without having to use a WiFi network. Instead of connecting to a network, you connect directly to a device. For details about Wi-Fi Direct, see page 202. You turn on S Beam from the "Connect and share" settings, just like NFC. Then to transfer files to another device that has NFC, Wi-Fi Direct, and S Beam turned on, put the devices next to each other and you'll be able to start transferring files.

Checking Space on Your Galaxy S4

IF YOU TRANSFER LOTS of music and files from your PC or Mac to your Galaxy S4, you may eventually run out of storage space. It's a good idea to regularly check how much space you've got left on it. To do so, from the Home screen, press the Menu key and tap Settings→More→Storage. You see the total amount of capacity on your SD card and phone's USB storage.

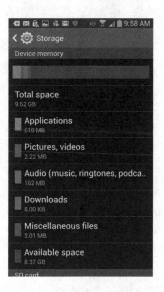

If you're running out of space, you can delete files (page 343).

WARNING If you're deleting music, use the Music app rather than the Files app, because if you delete the files using the Files app, the Music app may still show the music as being present, even after the files are gone.

Using Group Play

GROUP PLAY—A SHARING FEATURE introduced on the Galaxy S III—has been considerably beefed up in the S4. As with the previous version, it lets you share documents and photos with others nearby. But now it lets you participate in multi-player games as well.

With Group Play, a leader sets up a group, and then others join it via WiFi. At that point, they can share files, play games, and so on.

Say you're the leader. To set up a group, first tap the Group Play icon in the App Drawer. From the screen that appears, tap "Join group." If you want to make sure the group is password-protected, turn on the "Set group password" checkbox at the bottom of the screen. Give that password to other group members.

At that point, you've set up Group Play. Now other people can join the group. They tap the Group Play icons in their App Drawers, and when they come to the main screen, tap Join Group. They'll see the name of your device and can connect to it by using the password you've provided.

Once you're all connected, tap what you want to do: share music, pictures, or documents; or play games. Choose what you want to share by tapping the category. You're then prompted to choose what you want to share—for example, a specific photo or song. After you do that, if others in the group want to have it shared with them, they also tap that category. So, for example, if you want to share music, you'll tap "Share music," then browse to the music you want to share. Everyone else then taps "Share music," and the music plays on all your devices—in surround sound.

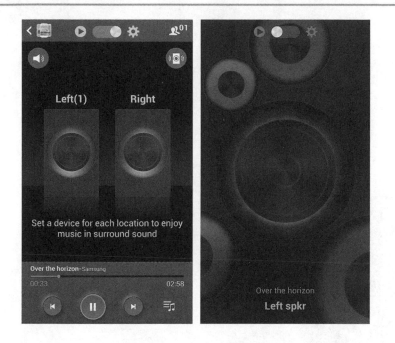

Depending on what you choose to share, you may have sharing options. With music, for example, you can set with device plays which stereo channel. To set the sharing options, tap the Settings button (it looks like a gear).

You can do the same thing with pictures and documents, and whatever is on your screen will be visible to everyone in the group. If you use this feature, make sure to explore the various sharing options for each category you're sharing. For example, with pictures, there's a drawing mode so you can draw on the slide, and everyone can see what you're doing.

Dropbox

If you've ever have had to transfer work files or family pictures that were a *little* too big for email, you've probably already heard of Dropbox. It's a website that lets you easily drag files into an online storage unit. Anyone can then download them onto any computer as long as you share the link.

You can access this service from your S4 as well—just get the Dropbox for Android app from *www.dropbox.com/android* or Google Play (page 301).

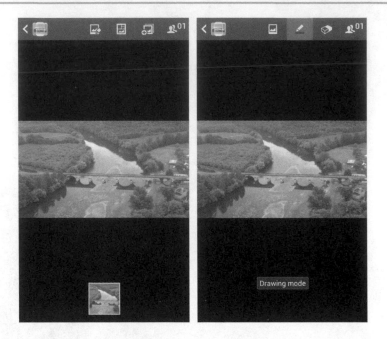

When you choose games, you can play head-to-head. Note that you'll only be able to play games that have been specifically designed to be multi-player games. Several come preinstalled on the S4; head to Google Play to find others.

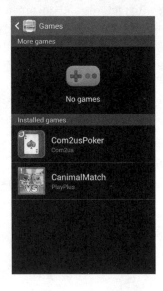

You'll learn to:

- Set the S4 to work with your company email account
- Connect to your company's Virtual Private Network (VPN)
- Use Microsoft's Mobile Office for Android
- Use Polaris Office for office files
- Use Google Docs

CHAPTER 14

Taking the Galaxy S4 to Work

YOUR GALAXY S4 MAY not wear a pinstriped suit and a rep tie, but that doesn't mean it can't be a good corporate citizen. In fact, the S4 can easily hook into enterprise-wide resources like your corporate email account and calendar.

A big reason is the Galaxy S4's ability to work with Microsoft Exchange ActiveSync servers. These systems are the backbone of many corporations, and they can automatically and wirelessly keep smartphones updated with email, calendar information, and contacts. So when you're hundreds or thousands of miles away from the office, you can still be in touch as if you were there in person.

Setting Up Your Galaxy S4 with Your Company Account

FIRST, LET THE IT department know that you'd like to use your Galaxy S4 to work with the company's network and computers. They'll set up the network to let your phone connect. Then all you have to do is add the company account to your phone, which works much the same way as adding any other new email account.

To get started, on the Home screen, tap the Email icon. If you haven't set up an email account yet, you'll come to the usual screen for setting up an email account (page 252). If you've already set up an email account, you'll go to the email account you've already set up, so you'll need to set up a new account. Press the Menu key and select Settings→Add account.

Which ever way you get there, type the user name and password that you usually use to log into your work email, and then tap "Manual setup" at the bottom of the screen. On the screen that appears, tap "Microsoft Exchange ActiveSync."

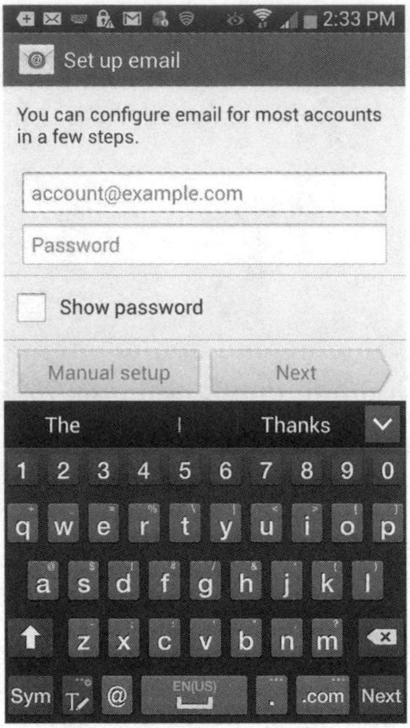

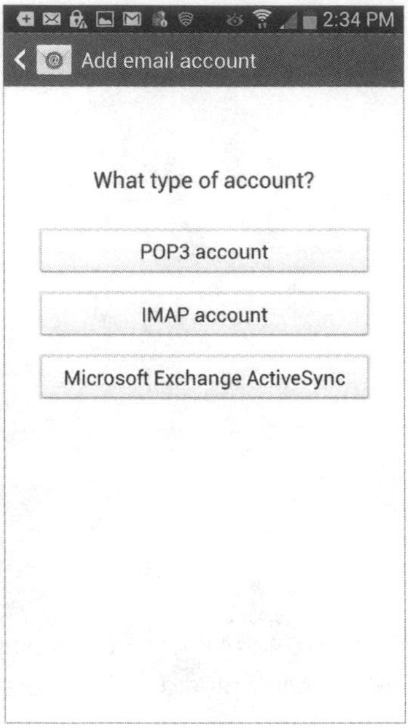

On the next screen, enter all the information that your IT folks supplied you—the domain name and user name, password, and email address. You'll see that the user name and password you supplied on the first screen area already filled in.

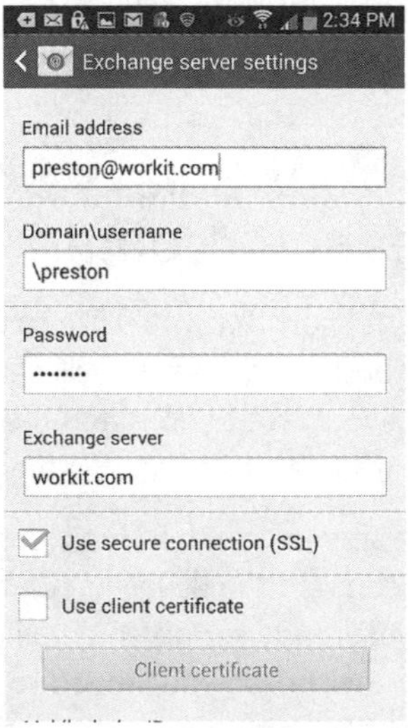

Make sure to enter the information in exactly the same way the IT staff gave it to you, including whether letters are capitalized. If you make even a single mistake, you may not be able to connect.

Ask the IT department exactly what you should use as your user name. If no one's around, here are some things you can try:

- The first part of your work email address. If your email address is *goodguy@ bighonkingcompany.com*, your user name may be *goodguy*.

- The first part of your work email address, plus the company's *Windows domain*. For example, *honkingserver\goodguy*. If this looks familiar, it may be what you use to log into the company network.

When you type your domain name and user name together, make sure you use the *backslash* key, not the regular slash. On the Galaxy S4, it's not easy to get to. Tap the Sym key at lower left, and on the screen that appears, tap the 1/2 key. The backslash is in the second row from the top.

After you input all the information, there's a chance that you won't be able to connect, and you'll get an error message that the Galaxy S4 was unable to find the right server. If that happens, another screen appears, asking you to input all the previous information, plus the server name. You should then be able to connect. If not, check with your IT folks.

When you're done, tap Next, and you're set up and ready to go. If you run into any problems, check with the IT staff.

As with your Gmail account, you can choose whether to have your Galaxy S4 sync your mail, calendar, and contacts. When your new corporate account shows up in My Accounts, tap it and you'll be able to turn each of those on or off. You may now use your corporate account the same way you use your other accounts for email, contacts, and your calendar.

Virtual Private Networking (VPN)

IF YOUR COMPANY HAS a VPN, you may need to connect to it in order to do things like check your email. Check with the IT staff. If your company has a VPN, and if you're permitted to use it, they'll give you the information that lets your Galaxy S4 connect to the corporate network over the VPN. They'll also set up an account for you.

Here's what you'll need to set up your S4 to access the VPN:

- **The type of technology it uses.** The S4 can work with pretty much any kind of VPN technology out there. Ask whether yours uses PPTP (Point-to-Point Tunneling Protocol), L2TP (Layer 2 Tunneling Protocol), L2TP/IPSec PSK (pre-shared, key-based Layer 2 Tunneling Protocol over the IP Security Protocol), or L2TP/IPSec CRT (certificate-based Layer 2 Tunneling Protocol over the IP Security Protocol). (You don't have to memorize these terms. There's no quiz later.)

- **Address of the VPN server.** The Internet address of the server to which you need to connect, such as vpn.bigsecurehoncho.com.

- **Name of the VPN server.** The name isn't always needed, but check, just in case.

- **Account name and password.** The IT folks will supply you with this.

- **Secret.** When it comes to VPNs, there are secrets within secrets. If you use a L2TP connection, you'll need a password called a Shared Secret in addition to your own password in order to connect.

- **Other special keys.** Depending on which VPN protocol you use, you may require additional *keys*, which are essentially passwords. Again, the IT folks will know this.

- **DNS search domains.** These servers essentially do the magic of letting you browse the Internet and do searches.

Once you've got all that, you're ready to set up the VPN. There are two—count 'em, two!— VPN apps (called VPN clients) on your S4. Which should you use? That's something the Gods of your IT department will tell you, so ask before launching one. Either way, here's where to find them:

- **VPN Client.** In the App Drawer, tap the VPN Client icon to launch the app.

- **VPN.** Press the Menu key, tap Settings, and then choose Connections→More Networks→VPN.

Both apps work much the same general way; the same general rules and instructions apply to both. As an example, this chapter uses the VPN app in Settings (Connections→More Networks→VPN).

Before you can set up the VPN, you must first create a screen unlock pattern, PIN, or password (page 394). After you've done that, tap the + sign at the top of the screen, and an "Add VPN" screen appears. Name the VPN, and then type the server address that IT gave you. Tap Save.

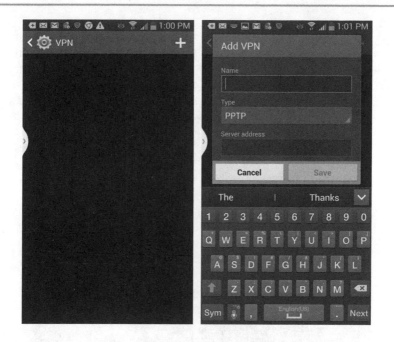

The VPN connection you've just set up uses the PPTP protocol. You'll see it on the VPN screen. To connect to it, simply type your VPN user name and password.

What if your VPN uses a different protocol than PPTP? Hold your finger on the name of the VPN you just created and select "Edit network"; the "Edit VPN network" screen appears. In the Type box, tap the small drop-down triangle, and a list of other protocols appears. Select the protocol your network uses.

From now on, when you want to connect to the VPN, go to Settings and then choose Connections→More Networks→VPN. Tap the VPN network to which you want to connect, enter your user name and password as described in this chapter, and tap Connect. The status bar shows you that you've got a VPN connection—or displays a notification if you've been disconnected, so you can reconnect.

To disconnect, open the Notification panel, touch the notification for the VPN, and then touch it again to disconnect.

Using Microsoft's Office Mobile for Android

THE GOLD STANDARD FOR creating and editing documents is Microsoft Office, and although your Galaxy S4 can't rival a computer when it comes to editing, it does give you several ways to work with Microsoft office documents, notably Microsoft's Mobile Office for Android. It's the mobile version of Microsoft's best-selling Office suite, although it's not nearly as powerful or as useful as the big-boy version of the software.

You can only use Mobile Office for Android if you subscribe to Microsoft's Office 365. That's the version of Office which requires that you pay a $100 annual subscription, and return lets you install it on five computers and five smartphones and tablets. It's a great deal for anyone who uses Office on multiple computers and mobile devices, but not so great if you only use it on one or two.

If you're not a subscriber and don't plan to subscribe, you can stop reading now, because you can't use Mobile Office for Android. If you are a subscriber or plan to become one, read on.

You've got two different ways to install the software. One is to head to your Office account on the Web and follow instructions for installing it. You'll end up sending a text to your S4 which will include a link, and then following the link to do the install. Or you can download Mobile Office for Android from Google Play, and then type in the user name and password of your Office subscription. Either way, you'll soon have the software up and running.

The app is designed to work with your SkyDrive. So when you run the app, it opens to a list of your most recently used SkyDrive files. Tap any to open it. The file downloads from SkyDrive, and you'll then be able to view it or edit it on your S4. The app does a great job of keeping fonts, graphics, and so on intact, although it may look somewhat different than it does on your computer, because Office Mobile reformats it for the smaller screen of the S4.

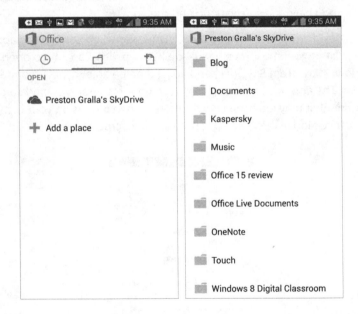

The table in the spreadsheet image:

	B	C	D	E	F	G	H
25	**100% Inspection**						
26							Alternate Option = Lab Analysis
					Assumptions	TruScan	Analysis
27	ientation)	5.6			raw materials	30	30
28	tion Time	3.4			#units purchased	2	1
29	Total	9.0			Samples / mo	1,000	1,000
30							
31							
32							
33							

To view all the files on your entire SkyDrive, tap the folder icon at the top of the screen, then tap your SkyDrive. From there you can browse all of your files, not just the newest. And from there you can also add new locations for browsing files, such as Team Site and Sharepoint.

Viewing and Editing Files

When you open a file, you'll see it with all of its fonts and graphics in place. But you can do more than scroll through it. Tap the screen and a row of icons appear across the top . The left-most one lets you see what is essentially an auto-generated table of contents of the document, which lets you jump to any section. The middle one lets you search for text in the document. The right-most, which looks like a pencil, opens the document for editing.

NOTE The capabilities for browsing, searching, editing and so on vary from app to app, so they'll be slightly different for Word, Excel, and PowerPoint.)

Tap the pencil to edit your document, and document editing tools appear. Don't expect full-blown Office editing tools, because you won't find them. They vary from app to app, and some are quite rudimentary. In Word, for example, you can't choose a specific font or font size, but you can change font attributes like bold and italic. And you can make text larger or smaller but can't set a specific font size. Excel lets you add formulas, and it's easy to navigate to different pages of a spreadsheet, but otherwise you'll find limited tools. And PowerPoint is the least powerful of all. You can rearrange slides and do basic things such as edit text, but not much else.

NOTE Office Mobile lets you edit only files in the newest Office formats—.docx, .xlsx, and .pptx—not older ones. So you can't edit files in the .doc, .xls, or .ppt formats.

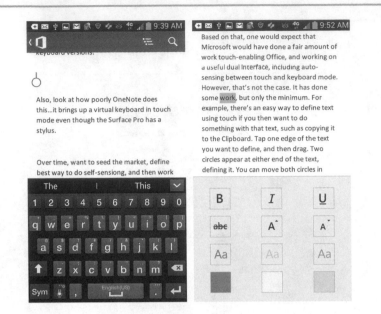

To create new files, head back to the main Office Mobile page, tap the icon at top right, tap the kind of document you want to create, and get to work. Especially useful is that there are pre-created templates for you, for example, a budget or mileage tracker for Excel, or an outline or report for Word.

Although Office Mobile is far from a powerhouse for editing files, you'll find its tools somewhat useful. But its ability to display Office files is superb, and particularly useful for reading Office files sent to you via email. So if you already have an Office 365 subscription you'll want to download it. But it's not a powerful enough tool to get you to pay $100 for a new subscription.

Using Polaris Office

IF YOU'RE NOT AN Office 365 subscriber, fear not, you've still got ways to create and edit Office documents. A very good app that does that is Polaris, which depending on your carrier, may come for free on your S4. If not, you can pay for it in Google Play for around $15. It lets you read, create, and edit Word files, Excel files, PowerPoint files, and PDFs.

To create a new document from the main screen tap + and select the type of file you want to create. From there, you can create a text document, spreadsheet, or presentation in the usual way; the screen and keyboard are just a little smaller than what you're used to. To open a file, tap either File Browser or "Form type" at the bottom of the screen, and then browse to the file you want to open. (The "Form type" option is a little cooler, since it lets you browse quickly to a specific type of file.)

Using Google Docs

AN INCREASING NUMBER OF companies and government agencies use Google Docs for creating and sharing documents, including word processing files, spreadsheets, presentations, and more. Google Docs works much like Microsoft Office, but the software and all the documents live on the Web, where you can share them with others. The basic service is free for individuals, although companies of all sizes can pay for pumped-up corporate features.

With the Galaxy S4's browser, you can view all the documents you have access to on Google Docs. You can't edit them in the browser, but you can create new documents. Launch your browser and visit Google Docs on the Web at *http://docs.google.com*. (If that doesn't get you to the right location, check with your IT department.)

NOTE If your Google Docs account is associated with a different account from the main one on your Galaxy S4, you may have to sign in. Otherwise, you may be automatically signed in when you visit Google Docs. For example, some people maintain separate Google accounts for their personal and work email addresses.

You come to a page that shows you all the documents you have access to in Google Docs. You have plenty of different ways to filter and sort the documents, so it'll be easy to find the one you want. Tap Sort and you can sort them by name, when they were last opened, or when they were last modified. Tap "Narrow by," and you can view only documents that you created, that are starred, that are a specific document type, and so on.

When you first use Google Docs on the Web, you may be asked to download the Google Drive app—an app that makes it easy to use Google's cloud-based storage service and easier to use Google Docs as well.

To view any document, tap it. The document opens in a built-in Google document viewer. You can scroll through the document and zoom in and out using the usual finger gestures. You can also use the controls in Google Docs for zooming in and out, and moving forward or backward in a document.

You can also create new Word documents and spreadsheets. Tap the icon just below the "more" icon, and select the type of document you want to create.

If you have PDF files in Google Docs, you'll be able to read those as well.

When you log into Google Docs, across the top of the screen you'll see navigation buttons for other Google services, such as Gmail, your calendar, and more. When you tap, you'll go to those services on the Web, not in any app you may have downloaded to your Galaxy S4. To see even more services than those shown, tap the "more" down-arrow at upper right.

Google Drive

There's another way to use Google Docs on the Web—the Google Drive app. Download it from Google Play (page 301). When you launch it, you see all your Google Doc files and any other files you've stored on your Google Drive. Simply navigate to the file you want to open and tap it to open it.

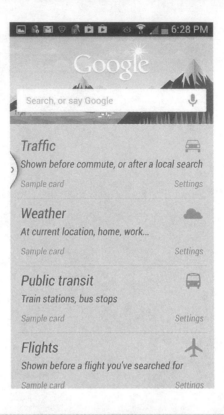

You'll learn to:

- Use Google Now to make your life easier

- Search your S4 by speaking

- Control your S4 with the magic of your voice

- Set Google Now and voice options

CHAPTER 15

Google Now and Voice Search and Control

YOUR GALAXY S4 HAS a lot more tricks up its sleeve than you can imagine. Any smartphone will do what it's supposed to do if you press the right buttons and use the right screen gestures—but the S4 is a whole lot smarter than you think. It doesn't just respond to your commands; it can learn from your behavior and adjust itself to what you want. For example, it knows that you're headed out on vacation, and so suggests a faster way to get to the airport to bypass a traffic jam.

You spend a lot of time talking into your phone when you make phone calls: that much is obvious. But you can do a lot more with your voice as well. Want to send a text messages, get directions to a city or street address, and visit a website? Rather than let your fingers do the walking, let your voice do the talking, and you can do all that and more.

In this chapter, you learn to do all this by using built-in voice search and control on the S4, plus an amazing app called Google Now.

Using Google Now

IMAGINE HAVING A NEARLY omniscient invisible assistant at your side all day long, giving advice when you need it—"avoid the Mass Pike driving home; there's been an accident"—telling you when packages you've ordered online have shipped, warning you that your flight has been delayed...pretty much helping you take care of the normal business of life.

That's what Google Now is like. Throughout the day, it displays helpful cards on your S4 that give you the information you need and want without you having to ask for it. When you wake up in the morning, it can pop up the current weather or the weather at your destination if you're headed on a trip. It can tell you about flight delays, traffic on your daily commute, birthday reminders, and a lot more. It does all this through the magic of knowing your patterns of behavior, such as buying airline tickets, using your S4 for mapping and navigation, and doing Web searches for particular items.

NOTE Some people feel that Google Now has a built-in "creepiness factor"; that it's too intrusive and invades your privacy far too much. Fear not: Google Now only springs into action after you've told it to. So if you don't want it hanging around, it won't.

To turn on Google Now for the first time, tap the Google search box right in the center of the S4 Home screen. A screen pops up telling you that you're about to use Google Now. To learn more, tap Next. Keep tapping Next through a series of screen describing Google Now's capabilities. Finally, you get to a screen that asks whether you want to turn on Google Now. Tap "Yes, I'm in." to turn it on, or "No, maybe later" to keep it dormant.

If you've turned Google Now on and want to turn it off, or if you declined to turn it on, don't worry—it's easy to switch. If you're turned on Google Now and want to turn it off, tap the Google search box on the Home screen (or anywhere else), then press the Menu key and select Settings. At the top of the screen, move the slider from On to Off.

To turn Google Now on at any time, repeat the steps: Tap the Google search box on the Home screen (or anywhere else) and then press the Menu key and select Settings. At the top of the screen, move the slider from Off to On,

When you do that, you come to a screen that has some introductory text at the top. Scroll down a bit. You'll may find that Google Now has already been thinking about you. For example, if you've searched for information about your favorite sports team—not just on the S4, but using Google on your computer or other devices—it shows you news about it. It displays the current weather where you live. It may have even recipes for you, news likely to interest you...and so on.

It knows all this because it uses your Google Search history, Google Map history, and other services you've used to do things like make restaurant reservations, purchase items online, and so on. It then delivers information relevant to what you tend to do.

At this point, all you really need to do to use Google Now is to tap the Google search box. Read on to see how to use it.

Using Cards in Google Now

After you've turned on Google Now by tapping into the Search box, it's easy to see your cards. Whenever you want to see them, tap the Search box, and they appear. If you only see a few and want to see more, tap "Show more Cards" at the bottom of the screen.

What's nifty about Google Now is that once you turn it on, you don't really need to do anything to have it display cards for you. Just go about daily life...and at least, use a variety of services and your S4. To understand how Google Now works, you need to understand how it interacts with these services.

For example, Google Now typically displays cards that are related to various confirmation messages sent to your Gmail account. Say you use OpenTable to make a reservation at a restaurant. OpenTable sends a confirmation email to your Gmail account, and it includes the location of the restaurant and the time of reservation. That means that before your restaurant reservation comes around, you'll see a card reminding you about it in Google Now. Similarly, if you use a package delivery service that sends email updates to your Gmail account, that information is displayed in a card as well. Have you searched online for a recipe recently? Expect there to be a card waiting for you with search results.

At times, Google also takes a more proactive approach. For example, say that you can't remember the date of Father's Day this year. Do a search asking Google when it is. You'll find right at the top of the search results a link that reads "Remind me on Google Now." Click it to get a reminder card.

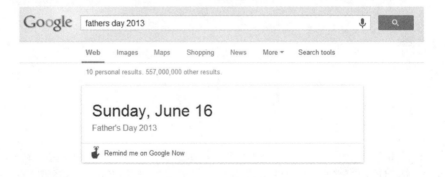

Depending on your searches, online habits, map navigation, and other activities—who knows, maybe even the phase of the moon—the exact cards you see may vary. The following are a sample of some common types of cards you'll come across.

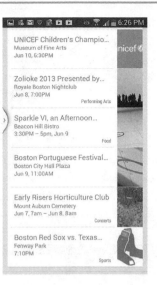

- **Commuting.** Probably at the top of the list of new cards will be one with a map, and with text about the kind of traffic on the map. Google asks whether it's the place you normally commute to every day. How does it do this? By tracking your location as you go about the day, as you drive, and as you use Google Maps. (Yes, it's creepy.) If it's the place you normally commute to, tap "Set as work." Otherwise, tap Edit and type your workplace's location; tap OK. From then on, you get a commuting card showing you the traffic en route to work. You can also ask for navigational directions if you suddenly suffer from amnesia and can't remember how to get there.

- **Nearby events.** Want to know about many different types of events near where you are? Tap the "View nearby events" card. What you'll see is exceedingly varied. For one example, this author found everything from a Portuguese Festival to the "Early Risers Horticultural Club" to a UNICEF fund-raiser to a dance club event to a Red Sox game. Tap any event for more information about it.

- **Weather.** Want to see the weather? This card grabs it for you.

- **Stocks.** Feel like gambling? Why go to Las Vegas when you can do it on the stock market? The Stock card shows you the current state of the stock market. To track specific stocks, tap the small information button (it looks like an "I" inside a circle), and add the stocks you'd like to track.

- **Next appointment.** Tells you when and where your next appointment is. So you have no excuse to miss it (even if it's the dentist).

- **Flights.** Have you searched for a flight and looked at information about it? Then expect a Flight card in your future, showing you when it leaves, when it arrives, whether it's on time or not, what the traffic is like from your current location to the airport, and for driving directions. With certain airlines, you'll even be able to get a boarding pass right on your S4.

- **Last transit home.** This card is for those who use public transportation and can't seem to drag themselves away from work. It detects whether you're still at work, and the last bus, train, subway, or other means of public transportation is going to leave soon. If you don't want to spend the night sleeping in your office, get a move on. (OK, like all of Google Now, this one is a bit creepy and intrusive, considering how much it knows about your life. But it sure is trying to be helpful.)

- **Movies.** Gives information about movies playing nearby.

You get the idea. You can see a list of available cards by tapping "Show sample cards." And for more details and to see a more complete list, go to *www.google. com/now* and click Learn More.

Using the Magic of Voice Search and Voice Control

THE WHOLE WORLD, IT seems, knows about Siri, the iPhone's search assistant. But the S4 also includes voice-powered search and assistance, the one built into Android, and there are a lot of people who believe it beats Siri hands-down...or is that hands-off?

The best part of Galaxy S4's Voice Search feature is this: The only thing you really need to know is how to talk. Your voice is its command. Launching it is a breeze. Simply tap the microphone button to the far right of the Google search box. You can do this anywhere you find the Google search box on the S4.

NOTE The microphone icon shows up wherever the Google Search box does, either when you're visiting Google on the Web, or in the Google Search Box, everywhere you find it on the S4.

One of the many amazing things about using voice search that it seamlessly uses two different speech technologies to do what you tell it to: voice recognition and speech-to-text. With voice recognition, it recognizes the action you want to take and then accomplishes the action: "Send text" or "Navigate to," for example.

With speech-to-text, it translates your words into written text and, for example, embeds that text in an email or text message. Say you tell your Galaxy S4: "Send text to Ernest Hemingway. Consider using young woman and the sea as title because demographics are better." Your Galaxy S4 will find Ernest Hemingway's contact information and then send him the text message "Consider using young woman and the sea as title because demographics are better."

When you tap the microphone button, all you need to do next is to tell the S4 what you want it to do, for example, "Find a Japanese restaurant near me." As you speak, the S4 displays onscreen what you've told it. Then it goes about and does what you've told it to do, sending the request to Google, and displaying the results.

You can also launch voice search by saying "Google" to your phone...or at least, you're supposed to be able to do that. That's more of a hit-and-miss affair, so the most sure-fire way is to tap the microphone button.

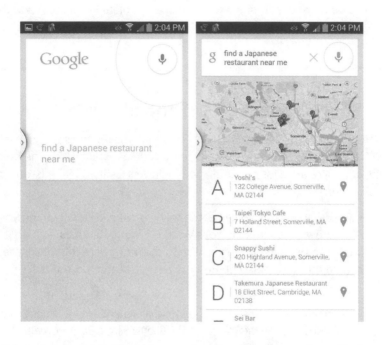

If the S4 can't connect to Google properly, after a few seconds you'll see a cryptic message—"Can't reach Google at the moment. Resend audio." It's actually asking, in its own confusing way, whether you want to send your request again to Google. To do it, tap "Resend audio." The odds are that this time around, your request will get through.

One thing to keep in mind is that you can use your voice to do much more than search the Web or find a nearby restaurant. You can also use it to control the S4 and its apps—compose an email or text message, for example.

What You Can Do with Voice Search

Here are the commands you can issue with Voice Search, along with how to use them:

- **Send text to [recipient] [message].** Composes a text message to the recipient with the message that you dictate. If there's confusion about the recipient, Voice Search displays potential matches. Choose the one you want.

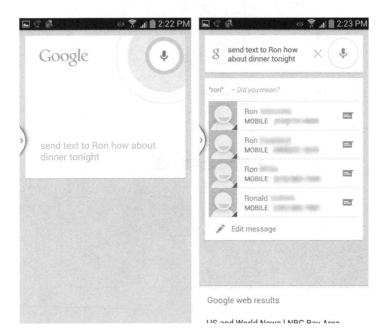

- **Send email to [recipient] [subject] [message].** Composes an email message to the recipient with the subject and message that you dictate. As with sending a text message, if there's confusion about a recipient, Voice Search shows you possible matches, and you choose the one you want.

- **Navigate to [address/city/business name].** Launches the Galaxy S4 Navigation app to guide you with turn-by-turn directions to the address, city, or even a specific business.

- **Call [contact name] [phone type/phone number].** Calls the contact. If the contact has more than one phone number, say the type of phone number to call—for example, home, work, or mobile. Alternatively, you can dictate a phone number, and the Galaxy S4 will call that number.

NOTE In addition to looking through your contacts, the Galaxy S4 also searches contacts in social networking services such as Facebook that you have installed on your phone.

- **Map of [address] [city].** Launches Google Maps and opens it to the address or city you named.

- **Directions to [address] [city].** Launches Google Maps and shows directions for how to get to the address or city you named. If the S4 knows your location, it uses that as the starting point. If it doesn't know your location, you must type it when Google Maps launches.

- **Listen to [artist/song/album].** Don't expect this to launch the Music app and play music—that's not what it does. Instead, it works in concert with a radio app, similar to Pandora, which you can download from the Google Play Store. When you speak the instruction, it plays the radio station that you've already created for the artist, song, or album. If you haven't created one, it creates it for you.

- **Call [business name] [location].** Calls the business you named. If there's more than one location, say the location. If the Galaxy S4 finds more than one phone number for the business, it lists all of them. Just tap the number you want to call. It will even list associated businesses. For example, if a café is located inside a bookstore, and you dictate the name of the bookstore, it may also list the café's phone number.

- **Play music [song name] [artist name].** Launches your default music-playing app. If it recognizes the artist or song you want to play, it will play them as well. If not, it simply launches the app, and you can then choose what music to play.

Google web results

Jimi Hendrix — Free listening, concerts

- **Go to [website].** Launches your browser to the website you dictated. Often, rather than going straight to the website, it displays a list of sites or searches that matches what you dictated. Tap the one you want to visit.

- **[Search term].** Simply say your search term, and the S4 searches the Web, using Google.

- **[Contact name].** Say the name of a contact you want to open, and your Galaxy S4 displays it, along with a list of possible actions, like calling her by phone, sending her an email, sending her a text message to her, and so on. The list of actions will vary according to what information you have about that contact.

> **NOTE** If you say a search term that is also the name of a contact, the Galaxy S4 opens the contact, rather than searching the Web.

All this is just a start. In essence, just about anything you can do on the S4 with your fingers, you can do with your voice as well.

Editing Text Messages and Email with Voice Search

Voice Search does a great job of converting your speech into text when you dictate an email or text message. But it's not perfect. So you might be leery of using Voice Search to dictate a message, worrying that when you dictate, "I love you, too," the message sent will be, "I move YouTube."

Not to worry. Before you send a text message or email, you get a chance to edit the text. When you speak the text message or email, you see the text you're going to send. To send it, tap "Send message" or "Send email," respectively. But if you want to edit the text, simply tap the text itself, and from the screen that appears, edit the text. You'll come to the usual text app or Gmail or email program, depending on what you're setting.

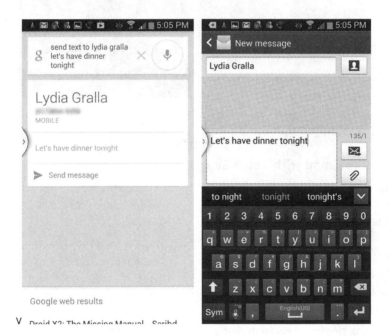

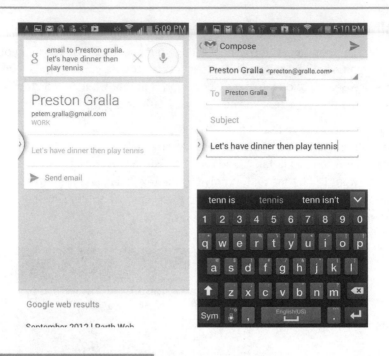

Google web results

September 2012 | Parth Web

Sending Email with Voice Search

If you don't use the S4's voice capabilities carefully when you're sending an email or text, you may find that it's more trouble than it's worth because you end up spending so much time editing. So take these steps, and you'll find sending email with voice can be faster than a speeding bullet:

- **Speak slowly and distinctly**. Think of the S4's voice capabilities as someone who speaks English as a second language and still has some learning to do. Speak slowly and distinctly, pronouncing each word carefully. (But don't speak too slowly and take long pauses between words—if you do, Voice Search will think you're done and will compose the message before you've finished dictating it.)

- **Speak the words "subject" and "message"** to fill in those email fields. After you say the name of the person to whom you want to send an email, say the word "subject" and then say the subject of the email. Then say the word "message" and dictate the message you want sent. If you don't do that, your Galaxy S4 will become confused. It may interpret what you want to be the subject line as several email addresses, for example, and will put in addresses you don't want.

Setting Google Now and Voice Options

Right out of the box, Google Now and its voice capabilities work just fine. But if you like to fiddle around with customizing things, you'll be pleased to know that you can while away many hours changing the way it works.

First, you can easily customize the way any of your Google cards work. Tap the small "i" on any card, and that brings up your options. The options you can change vary according to the card. You can add stocks to a stock card, for example, or change from Fahrenheit to Celsius in a weather card. On a commuting card, you can change your commuting method—from automobile to public transportation, for example—or where you work. Each type of card gives you different ways to customize.

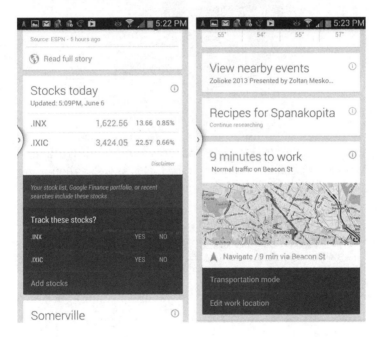

There's a lot more you can do as well. When you're viewing Google Now cards, press the Menu key and select Settings. From here, you can make changes like turning Google Now off (and on), and customizing how voice and phone search work.

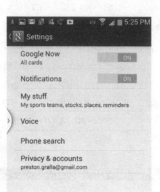

Particularly useful is the "My stuff" settings. This puts, in one location, various things you track, like your sports teams and stocks, as well as home and work locations, and what kinds of reminders you've set.

If you instead tap Voice, you get countless options: straightforward things like which language to use, whether saying "Google" launches voice search, whether to block offensive words, and so on.

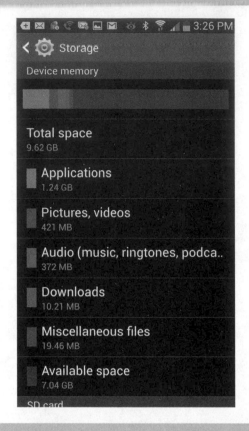

You'll learn to:

- Change your connection and wireless settings

- Change your Device settings

- Change your device and keyboard settings

- Change your account settings

- Change your email and related settings

CHAPTER 16

Settings

RIGHT OUT OF THE box, the Samsung Galaxy S4 is set up for you and ready to go. But what if you want to change the way it notifies you when there's a call, fine-tune the way its location services work, or alter its music setup? You turn to this chapter, which describes all its settings and explains what they do for you. To get to the Settings screen, press the Menu key when you're on the Home screen or a pane, and then tap Settings. You'll find four tabs across the top, Connections, My Device, Accounts, and More. Tap the appropriate tab, scroll to the setting you want to change, and tap it. Then head to the appropriate section of this chapter for the full description and advice.

Connections

THIS TAB CONTROLS THE many various ways you can connect your S4 with other devices, including WiFi, Bluetooth, via your carrier's network, and beyond.

Wireless and Network

Here's where you'll find all the settings for how the Galaxy S4 handles WiFi, wireless, and network access.

Wi-Fi

Tap On to turn on WiFi; if it's on, tap Off to turn it off. To connect to a WiFi network, tap the WiFi icon. For details on connecting to WiFi and other networks, turn to Chapter 8. You can also turn on WiFi by pulling down the Notification panel and using the WiFi widget there.

Bluetooth

Tap On to turn on Bluetooth (page 93); if it's on, tap Off to turn it off. As with WiFi, there's a Bluetooth widget on the Notification panel.

Data Usage

If your data plan charges you for data use above a certain limit, make this setting your friend. Tap it, and you'll come to a screen that shows you your data use for the month. That way, you can see whether you're on track to stay under your limit. Tap "Limit data usage," and after a limit that you set, your data connection will be turned off.

> **TIP** Your carrier may calculate data usage differently than your S4 does, so to be on the safe side, set the limit at less than your actual limit.

More Networks

This setting is a bit of a misnomer, since it's not really about other networks. Instead, it's a grab bag of other wireless and network settings.

Airplane Mode

When Airplane mode is turned on, all your wireless radios are turned off, as airlines require during parts of the flight. But you can still use all your Galaxy S4 apps in this mode.

> **NOTE** Increasingly, airplanes offer WiFi access, so you may not need to use Airplane mode during the entire flight. You can turn off all your radios by using Airplane mode, but then turn on only WiFi, so you can connect to the airplane's WiFi hotspot while you're in the air (usually at a price).

Mobile Networks

Here's where to configure a variety of options related to your wireless provider, such as whether to use the data network, and how to handle roaming when you're outside the provider's network and can connect to another carrier. (Depending on your plan, you may be charged for roaming.)

Tethering and Mobile Hotspot

This section covers settings related to using your Galaxy S4 to give Internet access to a computer or other device, either via WiFi or over a direct USB connection. Tap it for these settings:

- **Mobile Hotspot**. Turn this on to turn your phone into a mobile hotspot to which other devices can connect via WiFi. See page 198 for details.

- **USB tethering**. Lets you give a computer Internet access when it's plugged in via a USB cable.

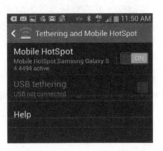

NOTE You may need to pay an extra monthly fee if you want to use your Galaxy S4 as a mobile hotspot or to use USB tethering. Check with your wireless provider for details.

VPN Settings

Here's where you can set up a virtual private network (VPN) connection (page 355) with your workplace and—once you've set it up—change settings like its URL, password, means of authentication, and so on. You'll need to get information from your company's IT gurus to make the connection, so check with them for details.

WiFi Calling

This is a great feature if you're ever out of range of your carrier's signal, but you're within range of a WiFi network. When it's turned on, you'll be able to make phone calls via a WiFi network, even when you're not connected to your carrier's phone signal.

NOTE The availability of WiFi calling varies according to your carrier, so you may or may not see the setting, and if you see it, you may or may not be able to use it.

The next settings are all related to ways you can connect to other devices and share files and other information. For details, see Chapter 13.

NFC

Tap this to turn on NFC (near field communications), which lets you share files with other nearby devices that use NFC. Not many other devices use NFC, so you may be waiting a long time to use this, unless you come across another S4 owner.

S Beam

A nifty way to send files to other people using NFC, and another wireless technology called WiFi Direct. It's easier than NFC, so worth using—that is, if you can find someone who has a phone that takes advantage of both NFC and S Beam. (For more details on these two new S4 features, see page 347.)

Nearby devices

Tap this, and you'll come to page that lets you share files with other devices on a WiFi network. You can also configure the way you share by choosing which devices are allowed to share, which files you want to share, and so on.

Screen Mirroring

This nifty feature lets you share what's on your screen with nearby devices.

Kies via Wi-Fi

Samsung's Kies software (page 345) gives you yet one more way to share files via WiFi. It even lets you share files with a Windows or Mac computer if you don't have a USB cable handy. Tap here and follow the instructions for sharing.

My Device

THIS TAB HAS EVERYTHING you want to know—and fiddle with—about your Galaxy S4.

Lock Screen

Worried about someone unauthorized using your S4? No problem. Tap here and you'll come to all the ways you can control the way your device locks:

Screen lock

When your screen is locked, all you normally need to do is swipe the lock to the right to unlock it. Trouble is, that's all anyone needs to do to gain access to your phone. Select this option, and you'll be able to set a PIN that must be typed in—by you, since you're the only one who knows it—to unlock your S4.

To create a PIN, first tap "Screen lock." From here you can set several methods for securing your S4, including via a PIN or by a pattern lock. Select PIN, type in the PIN, confirm it, and you're ready to go. If you instead select a pattern lock, follow the instructions for drawing a pattern, and then confirm it. It's important that you remember the PIN or pattern to unlock your phone, because if you forget, you'll have to reset your phone to its factory settings to get into it (page 435).

Lock screen widgets

Here's where to go if you want to lock access to your favorite apps, such as the camera and clock. You set up a PIN to do it.

Lock automatically

Tap this and you can set how long it takes for your S4 to go into screen lock. You can set it for anywhere from immediately to 30 minutes.

Lock instantly with power key

Want to be able to lock the phone instantly? Check the box next to this setting and you'll be able to lock your phone using the power key.

Display

Change your display options here. Tap this listing and you get more options than you can imagine. This section focuses on the most important ones:

Wallpaper

You can change the wallpaper background of your Home screen and lock screen (page 31). Tap here, select which you want to change, and follow the prompts.

Notification panel

Want to customize which widgets show up when you pull down the Notification panel? This does it. You get plenty to choose from. You can also choose whether you can adjust screen brightness from the panel.

Multi window

Do you want to be able to use more than one app at a time? Of course you do. So make sure this box is turned on. (Page 41 has the full story on how it works.)

Screen mode

Your *screen mode* is essentially the way the phone displays everything. So, for example, choose Professional photo if you want pictures to show off best. "Adapt display" (which it's normally set to) means the S4 adjusts itself to the task at hand, which is usually what you want.

Brightness

Normally, the Galaxy S4 chooses a screen brightness appropriate for that level of lighting—less light in the dark, and more in sunlight, for example. If you'd prefer to set it at a specific brightness level, and have it stay at that level until you change it, tap this option. From the screen that appears, turn off the "Automatic brightness" checkbox. A slider appears that lets you manually set the brightness level.

Auto-rotate screen

With this setting turned on, whenever you turn your phone from vertical to horizontal, the screen rotates as well. Unless you've got a good reason to change that behavior (or a really flexible neck), it's a good idea to leave this on.

Screen timeout

In order to save battery life, the Galaxy S4's screen goes blank after 1 minute. You can change that to as little as 15 seconds, or as much as 10 minutes. Tap this option and then choose the interval you want.

Here are a couple other settings to pay attention to:

Touch key light duration

When you press one of the hard keys at the bottom of your Galaxy S4, the keys light up and stay lit for a few seconds. This setting lets you change the setting to 1.5 seconds, six seconds, always off, always on, or on only in the dark.

Auto adjust screen tone

If you'd like to get every bit of use out of your battery, turn on this setting. It saves power by analyzing the image on your screen and adjusting the LCD brightness accordingly.

LED Indicator

Your S4's LED is your friend. It lights up red when it's charging and your screen is off, notifies you when your battery level is low, and lights up with various notifications—like missed calls and messages. Tap here to edit all that.

Sound

Here's where to go to change just about everything about the way that the Galaxy S4 handles sounds, like playing music, your ringtone, and even the display. Tap Sound to get to these options:

Volume

Tap to set the volume for media, notifications, system sounds, and your ringtone. A slider appears that lets you set the volume for each individually. The Galaxy S4 plays the new volume level when you move the slider, so if you're not satisfied with what you hear, change it until you reach the level you want.

NOTE To set the *overall* sound volume for your Galaxy S4, use the volume buttons along its left-hand side, near the top.

Vibration intensity

Tap to control the intensity of vibration for calls, notifications, and feedback from the phone when you tap certain keys or take certain actions—for example, when you unlock the phone, press a key on the dialer or keyboard, or add a widget. (It's called *haptic feedback*).

Ringtones

Tap this to change your ringtone. When you tap it, a list of available ringtones appears, including the one you're currently using. Browse the list, tap the new one you're considering, and you hear a preview. Select the one you want, and then tap OK to make it your ringtone.

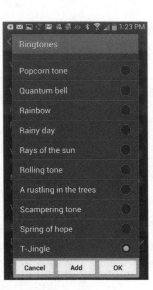

Vibrations

Yes, you can even customize the type of vibration the phone makes when you get a phone call. Tap here to do it. Choose from Basic call, Heartbeat, Jinglebell, Ticktock, Waltz, and Zig-zig-zig.

Notifications

This customizes the sound that notifications make.

Vibrate when ringing

Want your phone to vibrate when it rings? Check this box. Otherwise leave it unchecked.

System

These settings control things like whether to play a tone when you tap the keypad, whether the screen lock makes a sound, and so on.

Adapt Sound

Everyone has different levels of hearing acuity—some people can hear the smallest sounds, while others may be a bit hard of hearing. Tap this, and you'll teach your S4 your level of hearing so that it can make sure its sounds are just right for you.

Home Screen Mode

Whether you're a smartphone pro or just getting started, you can choose the Home screen that works best for you. Tap here and you can choose between Standard and Easy modes. With Standard mode, you see the normal Home screen layout, bristling with widgets and apps. Easy mode strips out much of that, and has a much simpler layout and larger, easier-to-see icons.

Call

You have plenty of ways to customize the way you make and receive calls on your Galaxy S4, like accessing voicemail, using call forwarding, and more. Tap Call and here's what you can do:

Call rejection

Here you can create and manage lists of phone numbers that your phone will automatically ignore and not answer.

Set up call rejection messages

Lets you create and manage messages that rejected callers receive when they call you.

Answering/ending calls

Controls the way you answer and end calls—for example, answering calls by pressing the Home key and ending calls by pressing the power key.

Turn off screen during calls

Turns on (or off) the proximity sensor so you don't accidentally interact with it during calls.

Call alerts

Lets you set how your phone acts when you receive or make calls—for example, playing a tone when a call connects, and whether your phone should play alarm and message notifications when you're on a call.

Call accessories

Do you use a regular headset or Bluetooth headset? If so, use this setting to customize how they work, like letting you make calls even when the S4 is locked when you've connected a Bluetooth headset.

WiFi calling

You already learned about this setting on page 392. (Why is this feature available in two places? That's anybody's guess.)

Additional settings

This leads you to a whole grab bag of settings, including ones for caller ID, call
waiting, auto-redial, and more.

Ringtone and sound settings

Here you'll find plenty of settings for customizing your ringtones, keypad tones,
and more. Pay attention to the "Noise reduction" setting. Turning it on sup-
presses background noises when you make phone calls, making it easier for
people to hear you when you're talking. (That's probably why, out of the box,
this setting is turned on.)

Voicemail

Here's the place to go to customize some basic things about your voicemail.
Don't expect a whole lot, because in many cases there's little you can do. These
settings also let you turn on what's called TTY mode (Teletype mode), which
lets the Galaxy S4 communicate with a teletypewriter, a machine that lets deaf
people make phone calls by reading and typing text.

Blocking Mode

Tired of getting so many notifications? Tap here, turn on Blocking mode, and
you can decide which notifications to turn off.

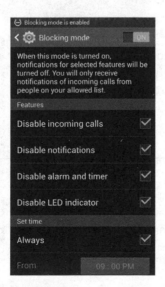

Power Saving Mode

Galaxy S4 owners, like most people who use power-ful smart-phones, tend to be obsessive about bat-tery life, and want to wring every last minute out of their batteries without giving up any of the phone's considerable power. This section helps you save bat-tery life by controlling its power saving mode.

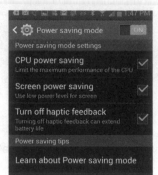

Power saving mode

With this setting turned on, your Galaxy S4 will switch to power saving mode when your battery gets low.

- **CPU power savings.** This helps save power by having your CPU—the brains of your phone—operate at less than its top level. Don't worry, it'll still be very, very smart, and very, very fast.

- **Screen power savings.** Tunes down the intensity of the screen to save power.

- **Turn off haptic feedback.** Stops the phone from vibrating when you perform certain actions (page 400).

Accessory

This section controls a grab bag of ways that the S4 works with accessories like a docks. Unless you have a dock, use HDMI (page 145), or have an S View flip cover, you don't need to go here.

Language and Keyboard

This section lets you change the language you use, as well as various keyboard options, including whether to use the Galaxy S4's built-in keyboard or Swype.

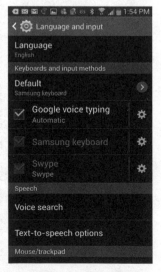

Select input method

You have three choices: The Samsung keyboard, Swype, or Google voice typing. Note that if you select Google voice typing, a keyboard will still pop up when you tap a box that requires text input. But selecting this option essentially let you input text by speaking. (See page 53 for details.)

Swype

If you turn on Swype, tap this icon to change a variety of Swype settings, such as whether to automatically capitalize the first letter of words that begin sentences, how long Swype shows its line "trace" on the keyboard, how quickly Swype responds to your input, and so on.

Samsung keyboard

If you turn on the Samsung keyboard, tap to change the Samsung keypad settings, such as whether to use the predictive text feature, whether to auto-capitalize, and so on.

The next section, **Speech**, covers how voice search and text-to-speech works on your S4. Tap Voice Search, and you'll get to choose these options, among others.

Language

Tap to choose your language.

Block offensive words

Blocks the results of a voice search using offensive words. Uncheck it if you don't want those results blocked.

Personalized recognition

Tap here, and Google attempts to improve voice recognition by using past words and phrases you've spoken into the Galaxy S4 and comparing them to what you're currently saying. To do that, it needs to tie recordings of those words and phrases to your Google account—normally they're kept anonymous. But if you worry about the privacy implications of this, don't turn this option on.

Google Account dashboard

Launches a web page that lets you manage all your Google account settings (page 408). This group has nothing to do with voice recognition, so it's not clear why it's here. But here it is.

Tap the Text-to-Speech Settings option, and you'll come to a screen with these options:

- **Samsung text-to-speech engine.** Select this to use the Samsung engine. If you choose it, tap the settings icon to change how it works.

- **Google text-to-speech engine.** Select this to use the Google engine. If you choose it, tap the settings icon to change how it works.

- **Speech rate.** Tap to select how fast the text should be read to you. There are
five choices, ranging from "Very slow" to "Very fast."

- **Listen to an example.** Tap to hear a voice read text to you. Yes, it's robotic-
sounding—that's the nature of text-to-speech.

Pointer speed

Can you guess what this does? That's right, you win! It controls how fast your
pointer responds to you. Tap it and move the slider to adjust the speed of the
pointer.

Motion and Gestures

Here's where you control all the Galaxy S4's nifty motion features:

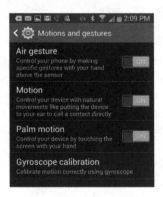

Air gesture

There's only one way to describe this feature—magic. With it turned on, you
don't even need to touch your S4 (page 40). Just make specific gestures above
the screen and your wish is the S4's command. When it's turned on, tap it and
you can customize which gestures to have on, and which to have off.

Motion

Magic, part 2: This turns on (or off) your phone's motion features, such as putting it next to your ear to make a phone call. Once it's turned on, tap it to turn
various motions control features on or off.

Smart screen

Magic, part 3: Your S4's screen is smart. Very smart. It does things like pause a video when you look away from the screen, and keep the screen on if you're looking at it, even if you don't touch the phone. Tap here to customize which smart screen features to turn on and off.

Air view

Magic, part 4: with air view, when you hover you finger above the screen when it's doing something, your screen will show certain information or perform a certain task, like use speed dial, preview a video, and more. Once it's turned on, tap it to turn features on or off.

Voice control

This one isn't magic. It's been superseded by some nifty new Google voice technology (page 375). Out of the box, this old voice control feature is turned off. Since it's not nearly as good as the newer voice technology, you may want to keep it that way.

Accounts

This tab controls all the accounts that you have on your S4. Depending on how you've set it up and what apps you've got installed, there may be many of them, or only a few. So what you see on your S4 may vary from what you see here.

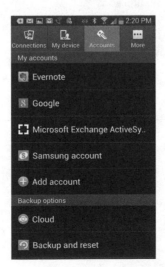

Google

This section handles everything about your Google account, including how it syncs and your privacy settings. Tap the "Sync all" button at the bottom of the screen if you want to sync the whole kit and caboodle.

At the top of the screen, tap your account name to set how to synchronize data between your phone and various Google services such as Google Docs, Gmail, Google Calendar, and so on. Check the boxes next to any Google services you want to sync, and uncheck the box next to those you don't want to sync. To sync all you see listed, tap "Sync now." To remove your Google and Gmail account from your Galaxy S4, tap "Remove account."

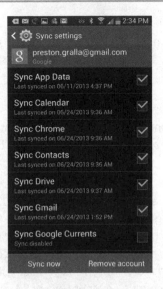

The next section, Privacy, puts you in control of how Google uses data it compiles about you for its various services. Tap each to customize your privacy settings. Here's what you need to know about the most important aspects of each.

Maps & Latitude

From here, you can control privacy-related aspects of these services, like whether to share your location with your friends automatically, whether Google should constantly keep track of your S4's location, and so on.

Search

Do you want Google to keep a history of your searches? Personalize search results based on your past searches? You can do all that and more from here. You may also want to pay attention to the SafeSearch filter settings, which filters search results based on whether they might contain pornography and other objectionable content. You get three choices: Strict, Moderate, and No filtering.

Location Settings

Lets various Google apps access your location—or not. It's up to you. Tap it, then tap "Location access" to turn it on and off. You'll also get to control other settings. There are a few notable ones. With "Use wireless networks" turned on, your phone determines your location by using WiFi or mobile networks, via techniques such as triangulation. With "Use GPS satellites" turned on, the Galaxy S4 will determine your location via GPS satellites, which are a more precise means of locating you than wireless networks (page 156). GPS uses a good deal of battery power, so turn it on only when you need GPS services.

Google+

If you use Google's social networking Google+ service (page 283), go here to customize various privacy settings. However, you'll first have to sign into the service on your browser.

Ads

Do you want to see personalized ads based on your interests or not? If not, tap here and turn it off. You'll still see them, but they won't be customized.

Samsung account

If you've chosen to set up a Samsung Account (page 22), here's where you customize it. As with Google, tap "Sync all" to sync all the data between the account and your S4. Tap the name of your account to set how to synchronize data between your phone and various Samsung services such as Calendar, Contacts, bookmarks, and more. To sync all you see listed, tap "Sync now." To remove your Samsung account from your Galaxy S4, tap "Remove account."

Under the **General Settings** section, you'll find these settings:

Account settings

Tap here to read the terms of service and change your profile.

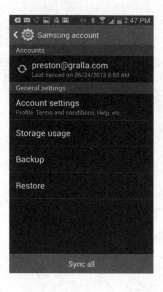

Storage usage

Tap here to see how much data you're using in various categories, including contacts, calendar, and others.

Backup

Tap here to set what kind of data should automatically back up, including you text and multimedia messages and more

Restore

If you've lost data on your phone for some reason, tap this to get it back from what's been backed up to your Samsung account.

Add Account

If you want to set up a new social networking account, or similar type of account, tap this button. You come to a page with a list of account types, such as email, Facebook, MySpace, and so on. Tap the account you want to set up, and follow the instructions (which vary for each type of account).

Backup Options

This final section of the tab has two settings:

Cloud

Shows whatever cloud-based backup services you have installed and lets you customize how each works.

Backup and reset

Backs up your data and account. Also lets you choose the nuclear option of restoring your S4 of the way it was before you opened it—factory pristine with no data or accounts on it. Following are the important settings you'll see here.

- **Backup account data.** Backs up your Galaxy S4 settings and data to Google's servers so if you later have a problem with your Galaxy S4, you can restore the settings and data. Obviously, if you don't feel safe with your data riding on an anonymous server somewhere, turn this option off.

- **Automatic restore.** With this turned on, if you uninstall an app, and then later decide that you want to install it again, the Galaxy S4 automatically grabs the relevant data you've backed up using the "Back up my data" option and puts it back on your Galaxy S4.

- **Factory data reset.** When you're ready to get rid of your phone, you won't want anyone else to get all your data. Tap this button and then follow the onscreen instructions for setting the Galaxy S4 back to the way it was before you began using it. It deletes all your data, eliminates any changes you made to the phone, deletes any apps you've installed, and makes the phone look and work exactly the way it did when it was shipped from the factory.

More

THERE ARE PLENTY OF miscellaneous settings here. Read on to learn them all.

Location Services

For the full story, head to "Location Settings," on page 409.

Security

Worried about someone getting access to your phone and all its data? This section lets you lock them out...or not, depending on how you like to balance security with ease of use.

Encrypt device

If you turn this on, your phone will be encrypted; that is its contents will be scrambled so no one who happens to break into your information will be able to read it. To unscramble them, you'll need a password in addition to any screen lock.

Encrypt external SD card

Turning this on encrypts your SD card, so that a password will be required to access its data.

Set up SIM card lock

Select this option, and you can set a PIN that anyone who wants to use your phone has to type in. It only applies to the specific SIM card currently in the phone.

Visible Passwords

With this option turned on, you can see passwords as you type them. This setup makes it easier to ensure that you're typing in passwords correctly, but it could theoretically be a security risk if someone looks over your shoulder as you type.

Device Administration

Unless you're an IT god, you don't need to know all these settings. However, two are important. If you turn on "Unknown sources," you can download apps outside of Google Play. And if "Verify apps" is turned on, you'll get a warning if you try to install an app that the S4 thinks might be dangerous.

Credential Storage

Your IT gods need to know about this section, not you, so skip it.

Application Manager

Tap to launch the nifty Application Manager, which lets you control how your apps work. Page 313 has the details.

Battery

This launches a screen that shows you what has been using your battery. It's very useful if you want to figure out how to extend your battery life, because it tells you what's been drinking juice.

Development

Are you an Android developer? If not, don't bother with this setting. If you are, it lets you set options such as for USB debugging and whether the screen should stay awake when the Galaxy S4 is charging.

Storage

Here's where to get details about the storage on your phone and SD card (page 21). It shows you how much total space you have, how much has been used, and how much is used by various content types, such as applications, pictures and videos, and so on.

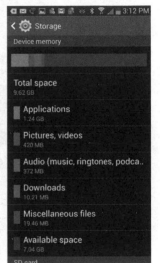

At the bottom of the screen, in the SD card section, tap "Mount SD card" if you haven't yet installed an SD card. Put the card in the phone, get here, and tap this so you can use the card. If you've already installed an SD card and need to remove your SD card for any reason, tap "Unmount SD Card" before removing the card. If you're installing a new SD card, or if your existing one gets corrupted for some reason, tap "Format SD card" to format it. Keep in mind that when you format an SD card, you erase all its contents.

If you've got an SD card installed, you'll get details about the storage on the SD card, including the total and available space.

Date and Time

Choose from these settings for the date and time:

Automatic date and time

As long as this checkbox is turned on, you won't have to worry about setting the date and time—the Galaxy S4 automatically gets it from your wireless provider's network, including your location (to set your time zone).

Set date

If you haven't turned on the Automatic setting, and want to set the date yourself, tap here to do so.

Set time

If you're not on Automatic, tap here and choose your time zone.

Automatic time zone

With this turned on, your S4 automatically adjusts its time to the current time zone.

Use 24-hour format

Tap if you prefer the 24-hour format—14:00 instead of 2 p.m., for example.

Select date format

You've got other options here if you don't like the U.S. standard (09/22/2014), including 22/09/2014, and 2014/09/22.

About device

Go here for more information than you can ever imagine about your phone, including the version of the Android software you're running, your current signal strength, whether you're roaming, and much more. Much of what you find here is informational only.

Software update

Tap here to check whether you need to update your S4's software. It checks to see whether if an update is needed. If there is, follow the instructions for installing it.

NOTE Technically, you don't need to update your phone's software manually by tapping "Check for updates." Updates are automatically delivered to you over the your wireless provider's network, via what's called an over the air (OTA) update (page 431).

Status

Tap for a mind-boggling amount of detail about your phone's status, including its signal strength, whether it's roaming, the battery level, your phone numbers, the phone's WiFi MAC address (a unique number that identifies your Galaxy S4), the network you're using, and a barrage of techie details that only a full-time geek could love.

Legal information

Here's where you can while away the hours reading Google's terms of service, and the licenses that govern the use of Android. If you're not a lawyer, you don't want to read this. In fact, even if you are a lawyer, you don't want to read this.

Device name

Shows you the name of your S4. Tap it to change it.

Model number

Gives you the official Samsung model number of your phone, such as SGH-M919-SGH-I777.

Android version

Lists the current version number of your phone's Android operating system.

Other Information

The rest of the screen gives you a variety of very technical information that you most likely will never need to know, such as the kernel version and the Baseband version. However, if you ever need tech support, you may need to read the information to a techie

Appendixes

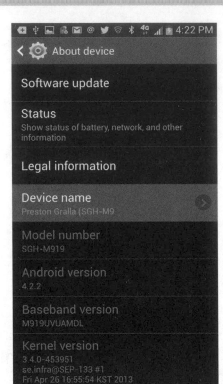

You'll learn to:
- Select a service plan
- Set up the S4
- Make service plan changes on the Web
- Upgrade the S4's software

Setup and Signup

SETTING UP YOUR SAMSUNG Galaxy S 4 is easy, especially if you buy it at a your wireless carrier's store. There, the sales folk will walk you through the process of activating your phone and signing up for a plan. If you buy your Galaxy S 4 over the Web, you set everything up either on the Web or over the phone. This appendix tells you everything you need to know.

Choosing a Plan

WHEN YOU BUY A Samsung Galaxy S4, you'll usually get it in conjunction with a one- or two-year service plan in addition to the cost of the phone. When you buy a plan, your provider knocks a few hundred dollars off the list price that runs usually between $600 and $700. The cost of the plan varies according to how many minutes of talk you want each month, and whether you want text messaging as well. Your carrier offers enough permutations to meet almost any need imaginable.

For the most recent rates, visit your wireless carrier's website. You'll have to buy a data plan, and you may also have a data cap, which means that if you use more than a certain amount of data in any given month, you'll pay extra. You can buy texting on a per-text or unlimited basis. Heavy texters will find the unlimited plan is cheaper in the long run, while occasional texters will do better paying on a per-text basis.

Your Phone Number

The phone number you use on your Galaxy S4 depends on whether you already have an account with your existing provider:

- **Keeping your old number.** If you already have an account with your provider, you can have an old cellphone number transferred to your new Galaxy S4. Transferring the number to your new phone usually takes an hour or less. During that transition time, you can make calls with your Galaxy S4, but you can't receive them.

- **Getting a new number.** If you don't already have an account with your provider, the company will assign you a new phone number. They'll try to give you one within your area code, and they may have several numbers you can choose from. Once you get the new phone number, you can start making and receiving calls.

TIP If you already have an account with your provider, you may not be able to get the reduced price when you switch to a Galaxy S4. Providers usually require you to have your current phone for a certain amount of time—usually a year or more—before you can get a reduced price for buying a new phone. However, if you have a family phone plan, there may be a workaround. If one of your family members' lines is eligible, you may be able to get the reduced price. Just make sure that your provider connects your Galaxy S4 to your phone number and not the family member's.

Making Account Changes on the Web

YOU CAN CHANGE THE details of your plan anytime—for example, adding new services, or taking away old ones—via the Web. Sure, you can do the same thing by showing up at one of your carrier's stores, but it's much easier on the Web. Head to your provider's website.

Upgrading to the Newest Software

YOUR SAMSUNG GALAXY S4 uses the Android operating system, built by Google. The S4 also includes some tweaks and changes that Samsung made to Android, so your phone's software will look a bit different from other phones running Android.

Google regularly upgrades the Android operating system, but unlike with a computer, you won't need to buy the upgraded software, or even download it. Instead, it comes automatically to your phone, by an over the air (OTA) upgrade. You don't need to do anything about it; it happens automatically.

TIP Wondering which version of Android you're running? The Galaxy S4 will be happy to tell you. From the Home screen or any pane, press the Menu key and then select Settings→More→"About device." Look at the Android version number for the version of Android you've got on your phone.

To check whether your phone has the latest and greatest software from Google and Samsung, from the Home screen or any pane, press the Menu key and then select Settings→More→"About device"→"Software update." The phone will let you know whether your system is up-to-date. If an upgrade is available, the phone will ask if you want to install the new software, and then do so over the air. You can also tap "Check for updates" to see if any are available, and then install them.

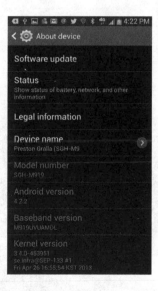

NOTE After Google releases a new version of Android, it takes at least a month—maybe even several months or more—before your Galaxy S4 gets its OTA update. That's because Samsung has to add its tweaks to the new version of Android and make sure everything works properly on the Galaxy S4.

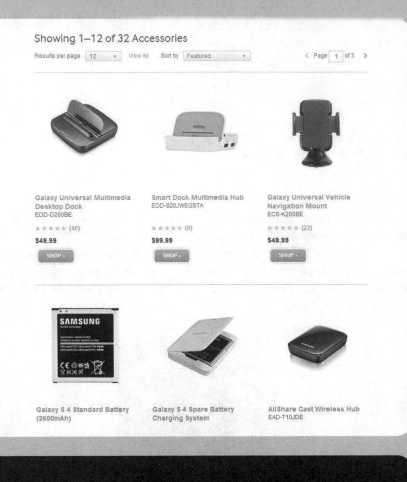

Showing 1–12 of 32 Accessories

Results per page 12 ▼   View All   Sort by Featured ▼   ‹ Page 1 of 3 ›

Galaxy Universal Multimedia Desktop Dock
EDD-D200BE
★★★★★ (46)
$49.99
SHOP ›

Smart Dock Multimedia Hub
EDD-S20JWEGSTA
★★★★★ (9)
$99.99
SHOP ›

Galaxy Universal Vehicle Navigation Mount
ECS-K200BE
★★★★★ (23)
$49.99
SHOP ›

Galaxy S 4 Standard Battery (2600mAh)

Galaxy S 4 Spare Battery Charging System

AllShare Cast Wireless Hub
EAD-T10JDE

You'll learn to: • Buy useful accessories
• Find the best places to get accessories

Accessories

THERE ARE PLENTY OF accessories you can buy to get more out of your Samsung Galaxy S4—for example, to protect its case or screen, connect it to a car charger, and more. In this appendix, you'll get the rundown on what types of accessories are available, and a sampling of where to buy.

Useful Accessories

IF YOU ENJOY TRICKING out your car or accessorizing your outfits to the max, there's plenty of Galaxy S4 bling out there for you to find. If, however, you're in the market for something useful, consider the following:

- **Cases.** Cases protect the Galaxy S4 against damage—when you drop it, for example. You'll find plenty of kinds of cases to choose from, depending on your style preferences, budget, and needs. You'll find hard protective cases, rubberized protective cases, holsters with belt clips, and more.

- **Screen protectors.** These thin sheets of plastic safeguard your S4's glass screen, greatly reducing the risk of scratches. They're thin enough so that you won't notice they're there.

- **Car chargers.** Plug one end into your S4, and the other into your 12-volt power outlet, and you can charge your phone while you're on the go.

- **HDMI adapter.** This adapter lets you connect your S4 to a TV, and watch HD video from your phone on the TV's big screen.

- **Multimedia docking station.** Put your S4 into the docking station, and you can watch video, use it as a digital picture frame, and so on. You can also connect an HDMI cable from it to a TV.

- **Chargers and cables.** There are plenty of battery chargers and USB cables you can buy to supplement or replace the ones that came with your Galaxy S4, including portable chargers.

- **Bluetooth headset.** With one of these, you can talk on your Galaxy S4 by speaking into the wireless headset.

- **Headphones.** You'll want these to listen to your music collection. Headphones can be as cheap as $30 or less for basic one without great sound, or up to $300 or more for high-end noise-canceling ones. It's a good idea to try them out, or at least read reviews before buying.

- **External and Bluetooth speakers.** Want to share your music with others? Get external speakers to plug into the Galaxy S4. There are plenty made for portability, with surprisingly good sound. Increasingly popular are Bluetooth speakers, so that you don't need to physically connect your S4 to them. Merely make a Bluetooth connection.

- **Replacement batteries.** Not happy with how long your battery lasts on a single charge? You can buy a more powerful replacement battery that lasts longer, for example, the Mugen Power 5500mAh Extended Battery (*http://bit.ly/15Dr4rX*), which the company claims lasts more than twice as long as the one included with the S4.

- **MicroSD cards.** These cards give you plenty of extra storage. The S4 can handle ones with up to 64GB of additional memory. The higher the storage capacity, the more you'll pay. For example, you can generally get a 64GB card for about $55 to $60, and a 32GB one for $20 to $25.

Places to Shop

There are countless places online where you can buy Galaxy S4 accessories, but you want to make sure to order from someplace reputable, and where they know what works with your phone. Here are a few of the best:

- **Samsung** (*http://store.androidcentral.com*)**.** You can buy accessories straight from Samsung, which makes the Galaxy S4. Head to *http://bit.ly/19T9tgH* and shop to your heart's content. Prices here tend to be higher than elsewhere, and there's less of a selection. However, what you buy here is guaranteed to work with the Galaxy S4!

- **Best Buy (***www.bestbuy.com***).** Both the physical stores and the website are well worth checking out for a wide range of products. You can even order online, choose a nearby store where you'll pick up what you're ordering, and it will be waiting for you when you get there.

- **Your carrier.** The place that sells the Galaxy S4 also sells accessories. As with Samsung, prices tend to be high and selection low. Go to your carrier's website and search for accessories. There may be some available at their brick-and-mortar store as well.

- **Amazon (***www.amazon.com***).** This shopping site has a good selection of accessories. Search for *Samsung Galaxy S4*.

- **Android Central (***www.androidcentral.com***).** Sells accessories for many types of Android phones, including the Galaxy S4.

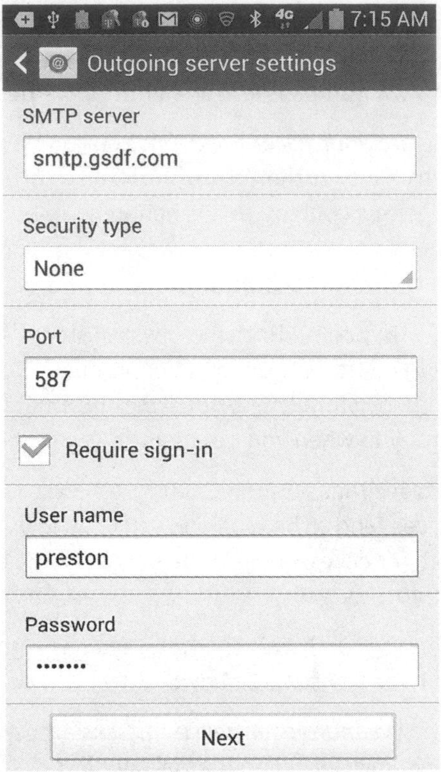

⊕ ⋃ ▤ ❈ ❈ M ◉ ❤ ✳ 4G ⬟ ▋ 7:15 AM

‹ ◎ Outgoing server settings

SMTP server

smtp.gsdf.com

Security type

None ◢

Port

587

☑ Require sign-in

User name

preston

Password

•••••••

Next

You'll learn to:
- Make sure your software is up to date
- Fix a frozen phone
- Troubleshoot email settings
- Troubleshoot an SD card
- Reset your phone
- Find where to go for free help

Troubleshooting and Maintenance

THE SAMSUNG GALAXY S4 runs on the Android operating system (page 27), so it's vulnerable to the same kinds of problems that can occur in any computer operating system. Like any electronic device, the Galaxy S4 can be temperamental at times. This appendix gives you the steps to follow when your phone is having...issues.

Make Sure Your Software Is Up-to-Date

NO COMPUTER OR PHONE is ever perfect; neither is any operating system. So phone makers and software companies constantly track down and fix bugs. They then send those fixes to you via software updates delivered wirelessly—called over the air (OTA) updates (page 417).

So if you have a bug or other nagging problem with your phone, there may already be a fix for it via one of these updates. You shouldn't have to do anything to install these updates, because they're delivered to you automatically. On the off chance that you didn't get your update, you can check and download it manually. To do it, from the Home screen or any pane, press the Menu key and then select Settings→More→"About device"→"Software update." The phone will let you know whether your system is up-to-date. If an upgrade is available, the phone will ask if you want to install the new software, and then do so over the air. You can also tap "Check for updates" to see if any are available, and then install them.

Fixing a Frozen Phone

IT'S EVERY PHONE OWNER'S nightmare: Your phone won't respond to any of your taps, or even when you press any of its hard keys. There's seemingly nothing you can do.

Often, your best bet is to try a quick reset by removing and replacing the battery, and then turning on your phone again. First turn off the phone. Then, to remove the battery, flip the Galaxy S4 over, and you see the battery cover (page 18). Put your fingernail underneath the small slot on the upper right and remove the cover. You'll see the battery. Slip your finger into the small slot at the top of the battery and gently remove the battery.

After you've taken it out, put the battery back into place, and replace the battery door. Now turn on the Galaxy S4. In many cases, this thaws your frozen phone.

Correcting Email Settings

THE GALAXY S4 EASILY syncs with your Gmail or Yahoo account, but when you add other email accounts—like your work email or home ISP account—you have to enter all the account and server information yourself. And that's where errors can creep in despite your best efforts. Even if you set the account up successfully at first, you may encounter problems later, like being unable to send email.

If Email Doesn't Work at All

If you're having trouble getting email to work for the first time, the most likely problem is that you've got a setting wrong, like your incoming or outgoing server. To check these settings, on the Home screen, tap the Menu key and select Settings. Go to the Accounts tab and then tap Email→Settings and tap the name of the account you're having problems with. Then tap More Settings and scroll to the bottom of the screen. Tap the Incoming settings, and the Outgoing settings, and make sure you've entered everything correctly. Even a single misplaced letter or number will cause a problem. Check your ISP's website, or call your ISP to confirm the settings. You may have copied down the settings wrong, or your ISP has different settings for accessing email on a mobile phone. If it's a work email account, call your company's IT department for assistance:

- Make sure you actually have a WiFi or cellular signal. You can't send or receive email if you don't have a connection.

- If you're connected via WiFi, try turning it off, to see if that solves the problem—just make sure you have a cellular signal.

If You Can't Send Email

Any computer—including your Galaxy S4, which is, after all, a computer—uses *ports* to communicate with the Internet. They're not physical things; think of them as different channels. So one port is used for web traffic, another for sending email, another for receiving email, and so on. To cut down on spam-sending, some ISPs curtail the use of the standard port for sending mail—port 25. When you send mail using port 25 via these ISPs, they let your mail go to your ISP's mail servers, but not get sent anywhere from there. So your message never gets delivered to the recipient. To get around the problem, you have a couple of alternatives.

Try using a different port

On the Home screen, tap the Menu key and select Settings. Go to the Accounts tab, tap Email→Settings, and then tap the name of the account you're having problems with. Then tap More Settings and scroll to the bottom of the screen. On the Outgoing Server listing, tap the Outgoing settings, and then, in the Port box, delete 25 and type *587*.

Use Gmail's outgoing mail server

You can use Gmail's server to send email from another account. On the Outgoing Server screen, use the following settings:

- For SMTP, enter *smtp.gmail.com*.

- For Port, enter *465*.

- For username and password, use your Gmail user name (your full Gmail address) and password.

- Turn on the checkboxes next to "Use secure connection" and Verify Certificate.

Troubleshooting the SD Card

HAVING PROBLEMS WITH YOUR SD card? There's plenty that can go wrong, so try following this advice:

- First, make sure that the SD card is the right type. It has to be a MicroSD card, and can only be up to 64 GB.

- Make sure the card is *mounted*—that it's showing up in Windows Explorer or the Finder. If it's not mounted, the Galaxy S 4 won't recognize it, and you can't access files from it, or store files on it. To mount your SD card, press the Menu key (while you're at the Home screen or a pane), select Settings→More→Storage, and then make sure that "Unmount SD card" is highlighted. If it isn't, that's your problem. Turn off your Galaxy S4 and restart it. If it's mounted and you're still having problems, turn off both your computer and your Galaxy S4 and restart them—that should remount the SD card.

- Try removing the SD card and putting it back in or replacing it with a new one. From the Home screen or a pane, press the Menu key, and then choose Settings→More→Storage→"Unmount SD card." After several minutes, the card will be unmounted—the Galaxy S4 reports you have no SD storage available.

- Next, turn off the phone's power and remove the battery cover, as described earlier in this chapter. Then slide out the MicroSD card. (It's located just above the battery. Make sure that you're not sliding out the SIM card, which is more prominent.) Examine it to make sure it's not damaged. If it's not damaged, slide it back into the empty space, replace the battery cover, and turn on your Galaxy S4. That may fix the problem. If the card is damaged, put in a new one.

- If all else fails, try reformatting your SD card. This option *erases all its data*, so do it as a last resort. From the Home screen or a panel, press the Menu key, and then choose Settings→More→Storage→"Format SD card," and then tap "Format SD card" from the screen that appears, to confirm that's what you want to do. After the card is formatted, either turn off your Galaxy S4 and turn it on again, or connect it to a PC or Mac via the USB connection, and after the computer recognizes the phone, unplug the USB cord. In both cases, the Galaxy S4 should recognize the card.

Resetting the Galaxy S4

IF ALL ELSE FAILS, you may need to reset your Galaxy S4—that is, delete all its data, and return it to the state it was in before you bought it, with all the factory settings replacing your own. Your contacts, social networking accounts, email and Gmail accounts, and so on all get deleted, so save this step for a last resort.

NOTE A factory data reset doesn't delete files you have on your SD card, which means that your photos, videos, and any other files stored there will stay intact after the reset.

From the Home screen or a pane, tap the Menu key and select Settings→ Accounts→Backup and Reset. Make sure that the box next to "Back up my data" and "Automatic Restore" are both checked. That means your settings and other application data are backed up to Google's servers, and after you reset and log back in, the Galaxy S 4 will automatically restore the data and settings. To perform a reset, tap "Factory data reset." That erases all the data on your phone. (Now you see why it was so important to back up first.)

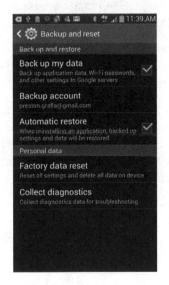

Warranty and Repair

THE GALAXY S4 COMES with a one-year warranty from Samsung. If you bought your Galaxy S4 from someone else, or someone gave it to you, the warranty doesn't transfer to you; it covers only the person who originally bought it.

The usual types of caveats apply to the warranty—if you've misused the phone, dropped it into water, and so on, the warranty gets voided.

For more details about your warranty, read the warranty guide that came with your phone.

Where to Go for Help

IF YOU'RE LOOKING FOR more information or help, there are plenty of places to go:

- **Samsung's official Samsung Galaxy S4 support.** This web page has plenty of helpful information, tutorials, tips and tricks, and a searchable database of help. It's well worth the visit. Head to *www.samsung.com/us/support/* and search for Samsung Galaxy S4.

- **Google's Android forum.** If you've got questions about Android, the Galaxy S4's operating system, this forum might help. Keep in mind, though, that Samsung has customized Android for the Galaxy S4, so what you read here may or may not apply. Still it's a good place to try. Go to *https://support. google.com/android/.*

- **AndroidForums.com.** Here's another very useful forum where Galaxy S4 users congregate, which covers many Android phones. The one for Galaxy S4 is *http://androidforums.com/samsung-galaxy-s4/* .

- **Android Guys.** If you're interested in news and rumors about Android in general, this site is an excellent place to start. It's not specific to the Galaxy S4, but if you're an Android fan, it's worth checking out—*www.androidguys.com.*

Index

ringtones, 400, 403

  contact specific, 82

  folder, 334

Roaming icon, 9

Rotate right/left command (Gallery app), 131

Rotation tool, 128

RSS, 321

S

S4. *See* Galaxy S4

SafeSearch filter settings, 409

Samsung

  account, 22

    settings, 410

  Calendar vs. Google Calendar, 169

  Galaxy S4 support, 436

  purchasing accessories, 429

  text-to-speech engine, 405

Samsung folder, 334

Samsung keyboard, 46

  accented and special characters, 50–51

  auto-suggestions, 48–49

  dictionary, 48–49

  entering apostrophes, 49

  five special keys, 48

  insertion point, 49

  overview, 47–53

  punctuation marks, 51–52

  setting, 405

  swiping text, 52–53

S Beam, xvii, 347, 392

Scan for nearby devices command (Gallery app), 131

"scanning" for text with the camera, 45

screen

  locking, 5

  overview, 6–18

  sensors, 6–18

Screen lock setting, 394

Screen Mirroring setting, 393

Screen mode setting, 396

screen protectors, 427

Screen timeout setting, 397

SD cards, 21, 428

  Application Manager and, 314

  Encrypt external SD card setting, 413

  moving apps from Galaxy S4's main memory to, 314

  SD card is full icon, 10

  troubleshooting, 434

Search command, 14

searching, 68–70

  address bar as search box, 214–215

  bookmarks and web history, 68

  contacts, 68

  contacts on social media sites, 69

  controlling searches, 70

  finding text on web page, 226, 228

  Gmail, 251–252

  Google search, 68

  Kindle, 68

  music, 68

  titles of installed apps, 68

  voice search, 70–71

Search settings, 409

Galaxy S4

THE MISSING CD

There's no
CD with this book;
you just saved $5.00.

Instead, every single Web address, practice file, and piece of downloadable software mentioned in this book is available at *missingmanuals.com* (click the Missing CD icon). There you'll find a tidy list of links, organized by chapter.

Don't miss a thing!
Sign up for the free Missing Manual email announcement list at missingmanuals.com. We'll let you know when we release new titles, make free sample chapters available, and update the features and articles on the Missing Manual website.